"Because I Said So!"

Other titles by John Rosemond

*John Rosemond's Six-Point Plan
for Raising Happy, Healthy Children*

*Parent Power! A Common Sense Approach
to Raising Your Children in the Nineties and Beyond*

Ending the Homework Hassle

Making the "Terrible Twos" Terrific!

To Spank or Not to Spank

A Family of Value

(Above titles published by Andrews and McMeel)

John Rosemond's Daily Guide to Parenting
(published by Thoughtful Books/STA-Kris,Inc.)

"Because I Said So!"

366 Insightful and Thought-Provoking Reflections on Parenting and Family Life

John Rosemond

ANDREWS AND MCMEEL

A Universal Press Syndicate Company

Kansas City

Library of Congress Cataloging-in-Publication Data
Rosemond, John K., 1947-
Because I said so! : 366 insightful and thought-provoking
reflections on parenting and family life / John Rosemond.
p.   cm.
ISBN: 0-8362-0499-9 (ppb)
1. Child-rearing—Miscellanea. 2. Parenting—Miscellanea.
3. Parent and child—Miscellanea. I. Title.
HQ769.R713 –1996
649' .1—dc20
96-14992

CIP

First Printing, August 1996
Fourth Printing, October 1997

Attention: Schools and Businesses

Andrews and McMeel books are available at
quantity discounts with bulk purchase for
educational, business, or sales promotional use.
For information, please write to
Special Sales Department,
Andrews and McMeel,
4520 Main Street,
Kansas City, Missouri 64111.

For Willie, Eric, Amy,
Nancy, and Jack Henry—
My "Family of Value"

Introduction

I began writing this book—my seventh in as many years for Andrews and McMeel—twenty years ago, in July 1976. It was in that year that I began writing a weekly newspaper column on child development and child rearing for my local newspaper, the *Gastonia Gazette*. At this writing, the column appears in some 100 newspapers around the country. I also write seven or eight articles a year for *Better Homes and Gardens* magazine, and yet another column appears monthly in *Signs of the Times*, a Seventh-Day Adventist magazine. My six-page Internet site is visited an average of 30,000 times per month, and in August 1996, the month this book was published, the premier issue of my newsletter, *Affirmative Parenting*, was mailed to five thousand subscribers. I am currently working on my eighth book—a much-requested opus on teenagers. The title will be something along the lines of *The Last Book You'll Ever Need to Read About Teenagers by the World's Only Legitimate Authority on the Subject*, or something equally understated. It will be released, assuming the muse remains with me, in the fall of 1997.

In addition to all this writing, I give around two hundred presentations and workshops a year for parents and professionals around the country. In case you haven't heard, I am generally regarded as the *World's Funniest Psychologist*, which doesn't say much, actually. For example, a significant number of mental health professionals—the more helplessly humor-challenged of the bunch—don't think I'm funny at all. In their view, I'm a downright dangerous guy, a disgrace to the mental health professions, a loose cannon, a maker of much mischief, an excitable boy. My evolution as a heretic/disgrace/loose cannon/etc. within my profession and my ongoing war with the mental health establishment is sufficiently detailed in my sixth book, *A Family of Value*, so I won't belabor it here. Suffice to say I threaten the establishment because I have the temerity to say that most—95 percent, perhaps—of the child-rearing advice so-called "helping professionals" (a dubious claim, if ever there was one) have dispensed over the last thirty or so years is pure hooey. That advice has contributed significantly to the problems currently besetting the American family and is the primary reason so many otherwise responsible parents cannot seem to secure a proper disciplinary "handle" on their kids.

In the short span of a generation, mental health professionals have erected a tower of parent-babble in America. They have managed to replace the realities of rearing children with the rhetoric of "parenting," complete with a cut-from-whole-cloth mythology about the traditional family and traditional child rearing that goes like this:

> All children born before the dawning of the Age of Parenting Enlightenment (circa 1965) were reared in dysfunctional families in which pathologically codependent parents infected their children with codependence and abused those same children psychologically, if not physically. If you remember the abuse, you were abused; if you do not remember the abuse, then you were most certainly abused.

This is one of the stupidest things I've ever heard, and it never fails to amaze me that mental health professionals have been able to successfully graft this myth onto our culture, but they have. The not-so-subtle message behind the myth: We baby-boomers must not, at all costs, rear our children the way we ourselves were reared. It is significant to note that since this nouveau parenting philosophy took hold in America, *every single indicator of positive mental health in our nation's children has been in precipitous decline.* As we approach another millennium, America's child rearing is offtrack, traditional family values have been similarly derailed, and the America I came to believe in as a child (which, contrary to yet another myth, actually existed!) is on the brink. Getting ourselves back on the right track requires that we reject professional lies concerning the traditional family as well as romantic, *nouveau* values and ideas concerning children and families, and begin once again *honoring our mothers and fathers.* Notwithstanding that a small minority of people have legitimate claim to having had lousy childhoods, the attitudes, methods, traditions, and values our forefathers and foremothers (imperfect beings, the lot of 'em!) brought to the rearing of children (imperfect beings, the lot of 'em!) were about as good as children anywhere, at any time in the history of the world, had ever enjoyed. This book is a celebration of those attitudes.

Contained herein are 366 excerpts from twenty years' worth of books, newspaper columns, and magazine articles, as well as some things that just occurred to me in the process of pasting it together. They cover child rearing from allowances to "zibling" rivalry. I titled it *"Because I Said So!"* because (a) I did, indeed, say all the things contained herein, (b) I am convinced that these ideas are self-evident, historically validated truths, as opposed to theories, (c) it's a great title and no one's ever used it, and (d) it's one small way I can honor my mother and father and stepfather and stepmother. They had no hesitation saying those four words to me, and I suffered not as a result. In effect, the entire book is in honor of our "mothers and fathers" because most of the ideas were inherent to the rearing of children for generations previous to our own. I am merely thawing them out of the state of deep freeze they've been in since the mid-'60s. After twenty-nine years of marriage, twenty-eight years of parenthood, twenty-four years of being a psychologist, and eighteen months (at this writing) of being a grandfather, I am absolutely convinced there is nothing—NOTHING!—new under the sun concerning children and their upbringing. Our ancestors understood it all. Most of all, they understood that just as it is a bad idea to make a big to-do over a child, it is an even worse idea to make a big to-do over child rearing. It's a big responsibility, but in the final analysis, it's nothing to get all worked up about. I hope that if you don't already agree, you will after reading this book.

Each entry (or *reflection*) is dated, which allows the reader to begin anywhere he or she would like—the day the book is received, perhaps—and read it "around the year," a "reflection" a day, from that point. The passages were organized with that in mind, but of course the reader may be inspired to consume it in some other fashion. Regardless, the idea was to give parents daily doses of food for thought concerning children, little tidbits that will hopefully help readers become slowly but surely more grounded in the rich soil of common sense concerning children and their upbringing.

As with every book ever published, this one was contributed to, wittingly or unwittingly, by a number of people, but mostly by my wife and partner for life, Willie, with whom all things are possible. Then come our children, Eric and Amy; our daughter-in-law/typist/proofreader/general-all-around-everything-person, Nancy; our grandson, John McHenry Rosemond (a.k.a. Jack Henry); my parents and stepparents, Jack, Emily, Julius, and Betsy; my parents-in-law, Nick and Wilma; and my editors, Donna Martin and Chris Schillig. I owe them all more than I can adequately express, so they'll just have to take my word for it.

In closing, I've decided to simply close. I need to get back to that book on teens. Meanwhile, enjoy!

(Editor's Note: For information on how to contact John at the Center for Affirmative Parenting as well as information on his newsletter and Internet site, see "About the Author" at the end of this book.)

Author's Note

For the reader who might want to do additional reading on some of the subjects covered herein, I've included a code at the end of each "reflection," indicating its source.

(FV)	*A Family of Value* (1995)
(SPNK)	*To Spank or Not to Spank* (1994)
(TT)	*Making the "Terrible" Twos Terrific!* (1993)
(PP)	*Parent Power!* (1991)
(EHH)	*Ending the Homework Hassle* (1990)
(6PP)	*John Rosemond's Six-Point Plan for Raising Happy, Healthy Children* (1989)
(NP)	Syndicated newspaper column
(BHG)	*Better Homes and Gardens*
(DGP)	*John Rosemond's Daily Guide to Parenting*
(TOH)	*Off the top of my head*

"Because I Said So!"

Once upon a time, people got married, had children, and reared them. It wasn't something they spent a lot of time fussing and fretting over. It was just something they did, along with planting seeds in the spring and harvesting them in the fall. If they came up against a child-rearing problem, they sought advice from grandparents and great-aunts and older brothers and sisters who'd already started their families. These were the experts of not so long ago, and they gave practical advice based on real-life experiences.

Along came a war and then a baby boom. Young parents took their children and went looking for the promised land. From the ashes of the extended family rose an entirely different class of child-rearing experts, ones with degrees, nameplates on their doors, and large, mahogany desks.

It wasn't long before rhetoric replaced reality as the primary shaper of our child-rearing practices. Nonsense replaced common sense. American families became child-centered, and American parents became permissive and democratic. And not surprisingly, American children became self-centered, self-indulgent, spoiled, sassy, and out of control. (6PP)

Marriage, the traditional family, and traditional, old-fashioned child-rearing constitute what I call "A Family of Value." I coined the term to refer to a family that is of optimal value to our culture, of optimal and enduring value to its members, and that succeeds at endowing children with the values that comprise good citizenship. Once upon a time not so long ago, the typical American family fit that description, which is not to say that the typical family was faultless, because *it is impossible for human beings to do anything that is without fault.* As Judeo-Christian scripture tells us, every human being is fraught with fault; therefore, everything human beings do is faulted. Our marriages are faulted, our families are faulted, our child rearing is faulted. For the most part, however, this is not dysfunction; it's simply reality. And furthermore, the notion that enough therapy with the right therapist will "resolve" the fault in a family is absurd. There has never been, and there will never be, a perfect family. Every human starts life with one strike against him. In the course of being raised in an imperfect family, by imperfect parents, he acquires another strike. Those first two strikes can't be avoided. A child has no choice where they are concerned. The challenge that lies before each and every one of us, once we reach adulthood, is to *not* acquire a third strike, the strike of choice. (FV)

A short forty years ago, a good father was a male who was first, a good husband, and second, a good provider. The amount of time he actually spent with his children was largely irrelevant to the consideration. Contrary to the myth, he wasn't remote, just busy.

He was involved with his work and involved with his wife, and together, they were involved with their friends and activities.

When his children needed him, he was there; not immediately, perhaps, but nonetheless in reasonable time. In short, a father's effectiveness as a role model was accorded more importance than the amount of attention given his children. Thus, the maxim: "The greatest thing a father can do for his children is love their mother with all his heart."

Gradually, all that changed. Today, the "good father" is a matter of how much "quality" time he spends with his children, how involved he becomes in their after-school and weekend activities, and the like.

As the masculinity pendulum swings from macho toward sensitivity and caring, being a buddy to one's children has become the mark of a sensitive, caring dad. One result of this renewed focus on fatherhood is that marriages become that much further displaced in America's families.

It's bad enough that parenting professionals have for thirty years encouraged women to believe that their primary role is that of mother; now we have the media and professionals telling men that father and fathering is where it's at. The fatherer, the better, or something like that.

In the first place, children should not have adults of either gender overly involved in their lives. Adults should interact primarily with other adults, children primarily with other children.

There is a time and a place for the twain to meet, but God did not intend the twain to be every evening and through the weekends. That's why marriage vows read, "Till death do us part" and not "Till children do us part."   (NP)

Prior to World War II, young parents who met with difficulty in the course of rearing their children didn't take themselves or their kids to therapists of one sort or another. Instead, they sought out older, wiser members of their extended families. I will refer to these genuine experts as "Grandma."

Grandma gave advice to young parents that was based on *a life she had led.* As such, it was firmly rooted in the soil of *common* (as in commonly held and commonly regarded as indisputable) sense. It was down-to-earth, practical, and easy to understand. You didn't need a college degree or a dictionary to figure out what Grandma was talking about. Perhaps more important than anything else, her advice was reassuring. And so these young parents left Grandma's possessed of not only a clear sense of direction, but also a renewed sense of confidence in themselves.

Grandma's advice reflected a body of traditional understandings that had been implicit to the rearing of American children since before the signing of the Declaration of Independence. These understandings constituted America's child-rearing model, or *paradigm.* According to that paradigm, a parent's primary responsibility was that of seeing to it that his or her children were endowed with those traits of character that constituted good citizenship: specifically, *respect* for persons in positions of legitimate authority; a willingness to accept *responsibility* for one's own social behavior as well as in terms of assignment from authority figures; and *resourcefulness*, a hang in there, tough it out, try and try again attitude toward the many challenges of life. Respect, Responsibility, Resourcefulness: I refer to these timeless values as the "Three Rs" of child rearing.   (FV)

The teaching of the "Three R's" begins at home. Respect is developed first toward one's parents, whose responsibility it is to command (not *demand*) it by being authoritative models and directors of proper moral behavior. Having been successfully "rooted," respect extends outward to include other authority figures—teachers, police, lawmakers, employers—then further still to include every honest, law-abiding person regardless of background or station in life. Having completed its "social circuit," respect comes full circle back to the child, now perhaps in his or her late adolescence, as a relatively matured sense of *self-respect*. It is, after all, a scriptural truth that in order to achieve respect for self, one must first give respect away, not selectively, but universally. To "love thy self" you must first "love thy neighbor" and "love thy God." In the final analysis, then, self-respect is something *earned*, not something that can be either learned or given. (FV)

A child develops a sense of responsibility in two ways:

1. Doing chores in and around the home. By age four at the latest, every child of sound mind and body should be participating in housework on a daily basis. From the very beginning, these acts should be selfless; in other words, they should not be compensated with money or material things. A child should do chores because, and only because, he is a member of the family. As such, he shares in the family's responsibilities as well as its bounty.

2. Being held accountable for his own behavior. Scripture tells us that parents should not suffer the "iniquities" of their children. When a child misbehaves, therefore, the *child* should feel bad about it, *not* his parents. The child should suffer the "iniquity" of his wrongdoing in the form of undesirable consequences that enforce a state of *penance* upon the child. Penance motivates atonement, both actively and proactively.

In these ways, a child becomes a responsible citizen of his family. Pray tell, if good citizenship does not begin at home, then from whence will it spring? (TOH)

Resourcefulness—the ability to do a lot with relatively little—is neither earned nor learned, but rather brought forth. It is, after all, every child's nature to be resourceful. It is *not* human nature to be respectful or responsible, but resourcefulness is a different matter. To bring forth the resourcefulness of a child, parents should provide their children with everything they *need* along with a small—very small, in most cases—amount of what they *want*. In short, parents should say "no" more often—*much* more often—than they say "yes." Thus "creatively deprived," the child must learn to solve problems on his own. He must do his own homework, occupy himself, solve his own social conflicts, and so on. He is forced to *invent* solutions to problems in these areas because his parents, for the most part, will not solve those problems for him. His parents want him to learn to "stand on his own two feet"; therefore, they are quite conservative when it comes to letting him stand on theirs.   (FV)

Two year-olds are consumed with the desire to figure everything out. As a consequence of this gluttony for information, they are highly active and "get into everything." They have yet to develop a tolerance for frustration. Therefore, when things do not go their way—when people do not successfully read their minds, when they don't get what they want when they want it—they suffer instantaneous cerebral meltdowns accompanied by much wailing and thrashing about. Twos have every reason to believe that their parents exist to pay attention to them; therefore, they pay infuriatingly little attention to their parents.

Two-year-olds ask lots of questions, but they don't really listen to the answers. They talk to themselves a lot, and when they talk to other people, they're often in their own little world. What results is a monologue that makes little sense. If you are the audience to one of these soliloquies, don't worry about understanding what's being said (because you won't) or making any sense yourself. Just nod your head, look interested, and say whatever comes to mind (as in a word association exercise). These "conversations" have no rules and can be fun.

Twos tend to want everything on their terms. When you want to pick them up and give them a cuddle, they push away. When both of your hands are busy with something else, they demand to be picked up and cuddled. Their egocentricity knows no bounds; therefore, they think you should be able to read their minds. They want milk. You bring milk. They scream and knock the milk off the table. You fool! They said milk, but meant orange juice. You apologize and bring orange juice. They knock it off the table. Wrong cup! You bring orange juice in the right cup, meanwhile, they've decided milk doesn't sound so bad after all, so . . . and on and on it goes. The good news is they tend to sleep anywhere from twelve to fourteen hours a day. The bad news is some of them hardly sleep at all. In short, this is the best of times, but it can also be the worst of times.   (TT)

The way a child is disciplined will do much to shape his or her attitudes toward and perceptions of men and women. As much as is possible, then, discipline should be handled such that children do not wind up viewing their fathers as "heavies" and their mothers as "pushovers" or vice versa. When Mom is on the front lines, she should handle the discipline. The same goes for Dad. And their discipline should be relatively consistent, not only from situation to situation, but also from parent to parent. That prevents either parent from coming across as stronger/more competent than the other.

But these are *general* rules, and they can be violated when circumstances demand. There are times when it's completely appropriate to say, "I'm going to wait until your mother/father gets home. We're going to handle this problem together. Meanwhile, you're going to stay in your room." That's the way to handle the Big Stuff, the stuff that doesn't happen every day; stuff like talking back to a teacher or throwing a rock at a passing car.

This application of "wait until your father (or mother) gets home" sends the child a strong message: "We stand together. This is not a one-person show." And the more a child "hears" that message, the better. (6PP)

Is there anything wrong with a parent admitting to a child that he or she has made a mistake? Answer: The only parent who cannot admit to having made a mistake is a parent lacking in self-confidence. There's a critical difference, however, between apologizing from a position of self-confidence and apologizing from a position of guilt.

Secure parents have no problem saying "I'm sorry," but tend to make no big deal of it when they do. They accept their own imperfections as no big deal. Their children come to see them not as ideal, but real; faulted, but blameless. As a consequence, their children come to better grips with the realities of life. And that, my friends, is what raising children is all about.   (FV)

It's almost inevitable that at my speaking engagements someone will ask if I *believe* in spanking. I've always felt this was a peculiar way of asking the question, as if spanking was a doctrine or principle of child rearing rather than a selective disciplinary act. Using the word *believe* in conjunction with spanking also suggests that a parent's entire attitude toward and approach to the rearing of children can be summed up in terms of whether or not the parent spanks. In any case, to say that I *believe* in spanking children implies that spankings are in some way essential to their proper upbringing. I do *not* hold that opinion; therefore, I do not *believe* in spanking. On the other hand, I spanked both of our children on occasion and while this decision did not always produce the desired outcome, I have no regrets about doing so.

It was never in my plans to spank. I simply did it when I was so moved. In general, I spanked when one of them was blatantly disrespectful, flagrantly disobedient, outspokenly defiant, extremely rude or insensitive, or in the early throes of a tantrum. But I did not spank on all such occasions. Only sometimes. Selectively. When I felt like it. When I spanked, it was spontaneous, like the proverbial bolt out of the blue. But don't get me wrong. My spankings were definitely not impulsive, emotionally driven acts. I was in control, always, *using* my temper rather than *losing* it. I spanked not because I had become upended by the child's behavior, but to demonstrate that I was *not* upended; not frustrated, but definitely disapproving.   (SPNK)

Some twenty years ago, mental health professionals, who had by then appointed themselves guardians of the rights of children, successfully sold public schools on the notion that their primary obligation was that of promoting self-esteem. A child with good self-esteem, the professionals said, would *want* to learn, and from that desire all good things would flow.

Making children "feel good about themselves" thus became the foremost goal of American public education. Teachers were sent to self-esteem workshops in which they learned to "facilitate" rather than instruct. They were taught that reward and praise fostered self-esteem, while punishment and criticism destroyed it. Bad grades were punishing; therefore, teachers were directed to avoid giving any grade lower than a C. The misbehaving child was not to be scolded or punished, but rather ignored (when he did wrong) and rewarded (when he did right). Instead of "failing" students (destructive to self-esteem) when they did not measure up to grade-level standards, the curriculum was to be adjusted by means of "special education."

The sum of these ideas extended to children what amounts to "educational entitlement"—the vain attempt to extend to all children not just a guarantee of educational opportunity, but also a guarantee of successful outcome or the illusion thereof. One result of this is that teachers can no longer tell children the truth. Why? Because the truth about oneself often hurts. The truth, therefore, is incompatible with the promotion of self-esteem.   (TOH)

If you want your child to become a winner, then I have three radical suggestions:

• First, say "no" to his requests more often than you say "yes."

"No" is the most character-building two-letter word in the English language. Children who hear "no" sufficiently often learn to tolerate frustration. This tolerance enables them to persevere in the face of obstacles and adversity, and perseverance, need I remind you, is the essential ingredient in any success story. Whether the pursuit be vocational or avocational, social or spiritual, perseverance makes the difference between those who consistently reach their goals and those who don't. It may sound strange to say, but if you want to help your child develop a successful attitude toward the challenges of life, you must not be afraid to frustrate him.

• Second, buy your child very few toys.

Parents tell me that today's children complain of being bored more than they complain of anything else. This is new. Boredom was something I didn't know as a child, and I wasn't alone. I've asked countless numbers of people who raised children in the '40s and '50s, "Did your children frequently complain of being bored?"

"No," is their answer. Always.

Why not? Because when the people of my generation were children we didn't have a lot of toys. We had to learn, therefore, how to do a lot with relatively little. And *that's* what resourcefulness is all about.

• Third, don't let your children watch much television, especially during their preschool years. The developmental skills that comprise and support the act of reading are acquired during the preschool years in the course of the most natural of childhood activities, play. Television-watching is neither a natural nor playful activity. In fact, it is not an activity at all, but a passivity. Evidence that television has taken its toll on the competency and literacy of America's children can be found in the fact that since 1955, when television became a fixture in nearly every American home, academic achievement at all grade levels has declined and learning disabilities have become epidemic.   (EHH)

Introducing the large, uneconomically sized version of the "Terrible Two": He pouts, he stomps his size-9 feet, he bellows at the top of his lungs. . . . Ladies and gentlemen! A big Bronx cheer for that second most terrible of all terribles: The Tweenager! (Author's note: The insertion of a "w" between the "t" and "e" in "teenage" is not a misprint. The term "tweenager" refers to an eleven-, twelve-, or thirteen-year-old person. I coined the phrase in 1978 to distinguish this three-year period in a youngster's life, which is completely unlike the years immediately before and after. Most eleven-, twelve-, and thirteen-year-olds are no longer children, but they are not quite adolescents. They are betwixt and between definition; therefore, the term "tweenager.")

Like the two-year-old, the tweenager is a rebel in search of a cause. His defiance of parental (and most other) authority is blindly reflexive. However, the tremendous growth of language during the intervening decade has replaced the monosyllabic "no!" with a peculiar form of self-centered ranting that makes no sense to anyone but the speaker.

Like his predecessor, the tween is an emotional basket case, careening wildly from one passionate extreme to another—a bull in the china shop of feelings.

The two-year-old is also father to the tween in his maddening self-centeredness. The tweenager is willing to inconvenience anyone to get what he wants. And excuuuuuuse *you* for leaving your foot where his royal tween-ness would step on it.

Just like the two-year-old, the tween is making a leap in his ability to flush out the mysteries of the universe. His mind, after ten years of grappling with the logic of concrete, measurable relationships, is beginning to grasp the abstract, the hypothetical, the stuff of no-stuff-at-all. Not surprisingly, the tween is as hopelessly drunk on this process and its attendant revelations as the two was in his time. He thinks, therefore, he knows everything! (PP)

While I'm by no means suggesting that you should become your child's primary playmate, it's important that you make time for relaxed, playful interactions with your toddler. Play is, after all, the most important thing young children do. Play promotes the growth of imagination and creativity. Games of "let's pretend," which children begin showing interest in shortly after their second birthdays, help them understand and prepare for adult roles. More sophisticated games, which come later, promote social problem-solving skills and help children develop healthy attitudes toward competition. Play also provides children a safe way of expressing socially unacceptable thoughts and feelings. The list goes on: Play exercises gross and fine motor skills, strengthens language development, and stretches attention span. In addition, play bolsters initiative and resourcefulness. Because it is self-rewarding, play fosters good self-esteem. Last, but by no means least, because it is fun, play helps children develop a good sense of humor. Playing with a toddler is as simple as providing a few things to play with (a ball, some blocks, a few toy cars) and letting the child take the lead. Just let yourself be a kid again! Roll the ball back and forth, build a block tower and knock it down, crash your cars together! Laugh! Laugh a lot! (TT)

Allowances are fine as long as they are not connected to the child's responsibilities around the home. In other words, an allowance should not be used as either a reward for doing chores or a punishment for failing to do them. Properly given, an allowance can help a child learn to manage money. In that regard, I recommend that an allowance describe certain fiscal responsibilities. When our children became teens, we established checking accounts for each of them. On the first of every month, we deposited their allowances into their accounts. They were responsible for purchasing their own nonessential clothing and any recreation that did not involve other family members. We continued to buy winter jackets, for example, but would not pay for team-logo sweatshirts. If one of the kids needed new jeans, we would provide only the cost of a basic pair. The difference between the basic pair and the "designer" look would come out of the child's allowance. Likewise, if the family went to the movies, we paid everyone's admission. If the kids went to the movies with friends, they paid their own admission. As a result, the children began learning the fundamentals of conservative money management—a big step toward a responsible adulthood.   (PP)

The successful rearing of a child is a matter of three simple rules, or understandings. These rules, as will become readily apparent, cannot be communicated to infants or young toddlers. Properly timed, the communication begins when a child is around eighteen months of age, give or take a few months. The introduction of these rules into a child's life almost invariably causes great consternation, to the point sometimes of rage. The reason for this is quite simple: There have been no rules at all to speak of before this time. Well, that's not exactly accurate. For eighteen months, the child has been led to believe that *he* rules. These three rules are not just new, however, but contradict the child's understanding of how the world works. They upset the child's applecart, so to speak, because the child had every reason to believe *he* ran the show, and would do so forever.

So, the child screams in protest of the rules, denies that his parents are capable of enforcing them, and does many destructive things to demonstrate his defiance. This upheaval goes by the popular term "The Terrible Twos." If parents "stay the course" through this much-maligned stage, then by his or her third birthday, the child will have accepted that the rules are fixed, as in permanent.

The First Rule (from parent to child): "From this point on in our relationship, child of mine, you will pay much more attention to me than I will ever again, as a general rule, give to you.

The Second Rule: "You will do as I say."

The Third Rule: "You will do what I say not because of bribe, brutality, threat, or persuasive explanation. You will do as I say because I say so. Period.

These three rules are indispensable to the parent-child relationship. They are the foundation of the child's "disciple-ship" and, therefore, his or her later success in every dimension of life.   (FV)

In the aftermath of World War II, extended family clusters, which had once been the demographic norm, began breaking up into nuclear family units that dispersed across the American landscape. As extended family supports became less and less readily available, young parents began turning to various professionals—psychologists, family counselors, clinical social workers, and other members of the so-called "helping" professions—for child-rearing support.

The problem—it was a problem from the outset, and it continues to be a problem today—is that professionals have not, by and large, dispensed advice based on lives they have led. Rather, their advice has been based *on books they have read.* Their perspective has been shaped less by real-life experience and more by an academic one. As a consequence, their "take" on child rearing has been intellectual rather than commonsensical; more "in-the-clouds" than down-to-earth. "Helping" professionals have created a child-rearing jargon that is full of abstractions and speculative theories. It is difficult to understand, imprecise, confusing, and for all of these reasons, it has not been reassuring. It is an undeniable fact that since professional advice achieved dominance in the "parenting marketplace," American parents—and especially those who, like yourself, dear reader, consume this advice—have become the most insecure, anxious, indecisive, guilt-ridden bunch of parents ever to inhabit any culture on earth at any time in history. (FV)

A child needs to become convinced at an early age that there are virtually no limits to his parents' abilities. The young child's sense of security rests upon the belief that his parents are capable of protecting him, providing for him, and preserving him under any and all circumstances. This requires that parents convey to their children an unquestionable sense of personal power—of *Parent Power!* to borrow the title of my first book. Developmental psychologists have long recognized that young children believe, or want to believe, in their parents' infallibility. This belief is called the "Omnipotency Myth."

An infant's view of the world is egocentric, or self-centered. He believes that all things exist for him and because of him. For the first eighteen months or so of a baby's life, parents cooperate with this upside-down conception of how the world works. Sometime during a child's second year of life, however, parents begin establishing limits and saying "no!" to certain demands. This turnabout contradicts the child's self-centered concept of how the world should work. His sense of security thus threatened, he struggles to keep things the way they were during his first eighteen months, and the struggle can be a fierce one. This is the essence of the so-called "Terrible Twos."

The paradox is this: In order for a toddler to develop an enduring, stable sense of security, his parents must first make him temporarily insecure. They do this by firmly, but gently, dismantling his egocentric point of view and building, in its place, one based on the premise that *they* run the show. If they are successful in replacing egocentricity with *parent-centricity,* the child develops a respect for them that goes beyond what they are truly capable of. In his eyes, they become *omnipotent.* This perception reflects the child's need to see his parents as all-knowing, all-capable people.

It follows that parents have a responsibility to present themselves to their children in precisely that light. The idea is not to make them subservient, but to create for them a nonthreatening authority upon which they can permanently rely.   (6PP)

In the real world, there is no possibility of a truly democratic relationship between parents and children. Not, at least, as long as the children in question live at home and rely on parents for emotional, social, and economic protections. Until a child leaves home, there can only be *exercises* in democracy, and these exercises must be carefully orchestrated by the child's parents, lest they get out of hand.

If we're going to draw analogies between families and political systems, then the most ideal form of family government—the one that works best for both parents and children—is a "benevolent dictatorship." The word *dictatorship*, I realize, has a negative flavor to it, but keep in mind that it is preceded by the word *benevolent*, meaning that the parents in question are lovingly authoritative as well as authoritatively loving. Besides, the root word of *dictatorship* is *dictate*, which means "to instruct with authority." In other words, a tyrant is to a bona fide dictator what an apple is to a kumquat. (6PP)

Nothing will kill a discipline plan quicker than weighing it down with dozens of unnecessary "if/then" considerations. Example: "If you clean your room, you get a star. If you don't, you get a check. At the end of the week, we subtract checks from stars, and that determines your allowance. If there are more checks that stars, however, you owe *us* money, which we take off the top of the next week's allowance. If there are *no* checks, you get a bonus. If, however, you owe us more than the bonus, the bonus is applied to the debt." See what I mean? Einstein couldn't have kept that straight.

Another sure way of dooming discipline to failure is to bite off more than you can chew. Let's take, for example, a child who is destructive, disobedient, irresponsible, unmotivated, aggressive, disrespectful, bossy, and loud. Instead of tackling all the problems at once, which would be like wrestling with an octopus, his parents would do better to concentrate their energies on just one of them. Solving one problem puts them in a good position to solve another, and then another, and so on.

In summary, one of the most effective keys to successful discipline is simply *organization*. Invariably, the best disciplinarians are those parents who are well-organized.   (6PP)

Here's a tip for parents of toddlers when the youngster picks up something fragile, like a piece of valuable crystal: The child is almost certain to drop and break the item if an adult puts on a horrified express, says, "Give me that!" and moves rapidly toward the child with arms outstretched, hands open like claws. Panic breeds panic. Instead, control your fears, stay in one spot, squat down so you're at eye-level with the child, put a smile on your face, extend your hand palm-up, and say, "Ooooh, how pretty! Will you put it in my hand so I can see it?"

If you've done a good acting job, the child will smile in return and place the item gently in your palm. Let the child know this wasn't a trick by sitting him or her on your lap and examining the object together for a minute or so before getting up and saying, "I'm going to put this up here so we can both look at it. Isn't it pretty?" This little technique satisfies the child's curiosity, saves money, and helps build a cooperative, rather than antagonistic, parent-child relationship. (6PP)

Spanking: A swat (or perhaps two) swiftly applied to a child's rear end by means of a parent's open hand. The purpose is *not* to cause pain, but to (a) secure the child's immediate, undivided attention, (b) quickly terminate an undesirable behavior, (c) secure control of a situation that threatens to quickly deteriorate, (d) provide a forceful reminder to the child of your authority, or (e) all of the above. In other words, a spanking is nothing more than an occasionally effective form of nonverbal communication.

Especially in cases where a child is rapidly losing control or has just been flagrantly disrespectful toward a parent, a spanking should be like a lightning strike. In the midst of a sudden storm of misbehavior, *ka-boom!* The element of surprise all but insures that the misbehavior in question will be brought to an abrupt halt and that the child will be focused intently, expectantly, upon you, at which point you can deliver your "Now hear this!" message and, if warranted, a truly effective consequence.

Can you properly discipline a child without ever spanking? Yes, but both my professional and personal experience tells me there are times with certain children when a spanking is the most effective disciplinary option. Some children, when their behavior gets off track, can be moved back on track relatively easily. Others, however, often require a more forceful means, as in spankings, to accomplish the same end. No pun intended, but as they say, different strokes for different folks.   (SPNK)

Some thirty years ago, a revolution only slightly less transforming than the Civil War took place in America. The end result of this upheaval—initiated by mental health professionals eager to prove themselves better at giving child-rearing advice than was Grandma—was that the emphasis in child rearing shifted 180 degrees, turning the American family upside-down. In previous times, that emphasis had been on *character development,* as reflected by the child's social behavior. At the urging of well-intentioned professionals, the issue of greatest import (supposedly) became children's *psychological development.* With this shift, children's *feelings* assumed paramount importance, and good parenting became defined not in terms of how well one disciplined, but how well one understood and communicated with one's child(ren).

When issues of character and social behavior were at the crux of child rearing, it was a fairly clear-cut proposition. Parents knew when things were going well and when they weren't; when to discipline and when not to; when their discipline had worked and when it had not. The shift to issues of psychology and feelings, however, because it involved a shift from concerns and issues that were self-evident to ones that were beyond the grasp of the benighted, caused parents to lose confidence in themselves and their actions. Supposedly, the only people who knew for sure whether a given child was or was not okay, whether parents were or were not acting properly, were psychologists and other mental health professionals. Because nothing in child rearing (now "parenting") was any longer self-evident, parents became anxious and insecure concerning the consequences of their actions; therefore, they began to hesitate taking any action at all. Whereas parents of previous generations had not been easily intimidated by either their children's behavior or demonstrations of affect, many modern parents are intimidated by both and generally scared to death that anything even slightly out of the ordinary not only *means* something, but *means something bad.*   (NP)

There are no quick fixes in child rearing. You can get a meal in a minute at McDonald's, but there's no such thing as McParenting. I have often had the feeling, during conversations with parents who are seeking solutions to problems they're having with their children, that they think psychologists can perform feats of time-defying magic.

A typical encounter: The parents describe the problem, I propose a means of solving it, and the parents counter with, "Oh, we tried that already, and it didn't work." It is almost inevitable that upon further investigation I discover that "it" didn't work simply because the parents didn't work at it. They believe in McParenting.   (DGP)

Permissive and authoritarian parents are far more alike than dissimilar. Neither, for example, can think straight when it comes to children. The former's ability to do so is hampered by worry and guilt; the latter's by anger. (DGP)

Since the '50s, the American family has shifted from being adult-centered to being child-centered. Whereas it once was implicitly understood that—except for infants and toddlers—children were to pay more attention to adults than adults paid to children, good parenting today is defined largely in terms of the amount of attention parents pay to their kids. As a consequence, large numbers of children are not learning to pay attention to adults, and they bring that deficiency with them to school.

At the other end of the spectrum are those parents who don't pay *enough* attention to their children. The end result, however, is the same: children who haven't learned to pay sufficient attention to adults.

In the '50s, nearly every child in America was expected to perform chores on a daily basis. Today's child, by contrast, is assigned chores haphazardly, if at all. The upshot of this is that large numbers of children come to school not having learned to accept assignment from adults. We can reasonably predict that in school these kids often will be "off task."

Then there's the matter of television, which increasing numbers of researchers finally are realizing has the potential to seriously compromise a child's attention span. Note that the average American child has watched close to five thousand hours of TV before he or she enters kindergarten. In 1955, the number was less than one thousand.

Put those three sea changes together and you've got the makings of a short-attention-span epidemic. (NP)

Like sugar, praise can be habit-forming. Children who are praised excessively often develop a dependence on outside approval. A child so hooked is like a tire with a slow leak: Every so often, he must be pumped up or he'll go flat.

Sometimes, adults praise things that shouldn't be praised, like using the toilet properly. We need not, should not, praise children for simply growing up. A simple acknowledgment will suffice. After all, growing up is its own reward. The adult who praises for an act of self-sufficiency is, in effect, appropriating the inherent pleasure of the event—stealing the child's thunder, so to speak.

Praise can also backfire, particularly in the case of a child with a negative self-image. Praise is inconsistent with this child's perception of himself. The mismatch between message and self-image generates anxiety (psychologists use the term *cognitive dissonance*), which the child then attempts to reduce by misbehaving, thus setting the record straight.

In other words, praise is not something to be tossed out carelessly. Be conservative and thoughtful about it. Above all else, with praise as with punishment, take aim at the act, *not* the child.   (6PP)

Personally, I think parents who expect siblings to really and truly love one another—while they are both still children, that is—are expecting too much. Think about it: Husbands and wives choose one another; friends choose one another; ah, but siblings *don't* choose one another.

Someone might say, "But, John, children and parents don't choose one another, either, yet it isn't unreasonable to expect children and parents to love one another."

True, but we're talking apples and anchovies, believe me. Indeed, parents and children don't choose one another, but (1) children naturally develop a sense of obligation to their parents, and (2) parents naturally feel very protective of and responsible toward their children. Neither is the case with siblings. Some siblings get along, some even wind up loving one another, but some don't get along and don't love one another. More often than not, this has nothing to do with parents. It's chemistry. Parents who expect siblings to fall madly in love with one another set themselves up for disappointment and nearly always blame themselves if their expectations don't pan out. So, expect the worst, I say. That way, you can only be pleasantly surprised. (FV)

In the '60s and '70s, *nouveau* child-rearing "experts" led parents to believe that obedient children were robots whose personalities and self-esteem had been squelched by parental heavy-handedness. That simply isn't so. While it's true that some parents do bring about obedience through fear, their children are likely to look for opportunities to disobey whenever they think they stand a good chance of not getting caught. Fear does *not* teach obedience; rather, it teaches a child to be cunning. Truly obedient children—that is, children who have invested great amounts of security and, therefore, respect in their parents' authority—are also the world's happiest, most outgoing, and creative kids. These same "experts" also made a big deal of the need for parents to respect children, pointing out that respect is a two-way street. With that, I wholeheartedly agree. But be not deceived! Children show respect for parents by obeying them. Parents show respect for children by expecting them to obey.   (6PP)

Nothing is more important to a teenager than freedom—the freedom to go to parties and hang out at the mall and date and stay out past midnight and sleep late the next morning. Freedom is the currency of adolescence, and teens crave it like adults crave prestige and influence. The more freedom teenagers have, the more in control of their own lives they feel.

To the question, "How much freedom should parents give?" there is no simple answer. No one would argue that teens should enjoy more freedom than younger children, but this age child is generally guilty of wanting more freedom than he or she can responsibly handle. On the other hand, many parents are equally guilty of dispensing freedom far too slowly.

Somewhere between the teenage urge to be a free bird and the parental urge to keep teens in check there lies a happy medium. Finding that middle ground is the secret of negotiating this potentially tumultuous period in your relationship with your child. The consequence of giving too much freedom may be a teen out of control, intoxicated on an overdose of independence. The result of giving too little may be a teen who, out of frustration, rebels.

That fine line is easier to walk when parents focus on teaching that freedom, in whatever amount, always has its price. Making the vital connection between the acceptance of responsibility and the enjoyment of privilege—that is the task confronting parents of teens.

(PP)

Q: *What should we do with a seven-year-old who won't share his toys with other children? He's fine as long as he's at someone else's house, but he has a great deal of difficulty letting go of his possessions when a playmate is in his territory.*

A: Before a playmate arrives, help your son pick out three to five "prized" possessions he doesn't want the other child to play with. Put them away with the understanding that if he decides he wants one, he must share. In any case, he must share the rest of his things. Giving him this option beforehand will greatly reduce the threat he feels when someone else is handling his things. If, while the playmate is there, he still refuses to share something, put him in a "penalty box" (e.g., a chair in the dining room) until he's willing. By the way, this problem is not all that unusual and isn't something to worry about. Some children are more territorial than others, that's all, and need more structure and adult guidance when it comes to learning to share. (NP)

When a youngster says "I hate you!" to a parent, it's a sure bet the child means exactly that. No, the child hasn't thought it through, but he means it nonetheless. In this regard, it's important for parents to understand several things.

First, children don't generally experience emotions in moderation. If a parent makes a decision a child doesn't like, the child isn't going to say he's "annoyed" or "disappointed." He's likely to act as if the world is coming to an end. He'll wail piteously, as if he's been mortally wounded, or he'll stomp his feet and scream he "hates" you, or both. In the case of the latter, he really means it, for the moment at least.

Second, these episodes of really and truly hating one's parents don't last long, because within hours—a couple of days at most—the child in question must come back to the parents and ask them for something else. And in order to elevate the likelihood that they will look favorably upon his request, he must pretend to like them again. Such is the roller-coaster ride that is parenthood.

Third, anytime a child screams that you've been "unfair" or he "hates" you, it means you've just done the right thing and should keep doing it. You're mean? To a child, a parent is "mean" when the child discovers the parent truly means what she says.

Lastly, none of this is to be taken seriously. "I hate you!" in all of its manifestations is nothing more than an example of the foolishness inherent in children, as spoken of in Proverbs 22:15. Such outbursts don't merit anxiety, guilt, or anger.

The most appropriate, honest, respectful, accepting, authoritative, and loving response you can give a child when the child tells you he hates you is, "I understand. If I were you, I'd hate me right now, too."   (TOH)

Meeting your baby's needs involves meeting your own as well. Stated differently, you can't take good care of someone else unless you also take equally good care of yourself. New parents who feel they must devote themselves exclusively to their babies and forget about themselves eventually begin feeling frustrated and resentful. If there's one thing a child doesn't need, it's parents who feel that parenthood is drudgery.

Somewhere between wearing your baby like a sweater and a state of totally selfish neglect, there's a point of balance where it's possible for you to meet both your needs and your child's. There's no getting around the fact that fussy, high-need infants require more attention and physical closeness than is typical. And, for the most part, it's good practice to respond to an infant's cries shortly after they begin. However, even if he cries when you do so, there's no harm in putting your baby down for a few minutes to take care of something you can't do if you're holding him.

In other words, if it's practical for you to "wear him like a sweater," do so. If it's not, put him down and do what you must. If you leave the room, keep talking to him or at least call to him every ten seconds or so. The sound of your voice may not stop him from crying, but at least he'll know you're still there, somewhere. Besides, there's only one way he's going to learn that you aren't going to abandon him, and that's if you occasionally put him down, do what you have to do, and then come back. (6PP)

Unresolved disciplinary issues impede communication and expressions of affections between parent and child. Resolving those issues removes the impediments. It's impossible for parent and child to have truly good communication—and, therefore, be optimally affectionate—with one another until the child completely trusts and feels he can rely upon the parent's authority. As they say, the horse must always precede the cart. In this case, the horse is your authority as a parent; the cart is an open, loving parent-child relationship.

The same is true of teachers and their students. A good classroom teacher recognizes that she can teach only as effectively as she governs. So, on the first day of school, before doing anything else, a good teacher puts the horse in front of the cart by going over the rules. Realizing that some children are going to want her to prove herself, she also explains exactly what's going to happen when a child breaks a rule. Then, when rules are broken, she follows through as promised. In so doing, she demonstrates her reliability to her students. They don't resent her for this. Quite the contrary, they trust her and respect her *because* of it.

In the long run, obedient children are the happiest of children, and the happiest of parents are those who succeed at enforcing obedience. Just remember, one can't exist without the other.   (6PP)

Indecisive parents are usually afraid of making mistakes. They think bad decisions scar children for life, so they end up making no firm decisions at all, which is one of the biggest mistakes a parent can *ever* make. The fact is, it's better for a parent to make a mistake every day than to be generally indecisive. Bad decisions can either be shrugged off with an "Oh, well" or, if absolutely necessary, corrected. In either case, the "deal" is not a big one. A faulty decision-making style, however, can spell long-term trouble.

A child's sense of security is founded upon parental love and authority. Parents demonstrate the latter by being decisive. Parental indecisiveness causes children to feel insecure. That insecurity is likely to be expressed in the form of behavior problems. So you see? The more you try to avoid making mistakes that could cause problems, the more problems you cause. (6PP)

February 6

This generation of American children interrupts conversations epidemically because they've been included in too many adult activities (and because adults, conversely, have included themselves in too many of their children's activities); because their parents can't bring themselves to say, "Since you can't listen while we're talking, you may leave the room" for fear of stifling their "energy"; because their parents give themselves little permission to do anything without the children except go to work and the bathroom. Maybe.

Almost every day, I see more evidence of the general lack of respect on the part of children for adults. This is tragic, because a child who doesn't respect adults won't pay attention to them. And a child who isn't paying attention is a child who isn't learning. That's why, when parents ask me for ways of improving a child's IQ, I answer, "Forget improving IQ. If you want a child to be the best student he can possibly be, improve his respect for adults, beginning with yourselves."

(FV)

Toddlers are uncivilized; therefore, they're likely to do bizarre things, like bang their heads on hard objects (such as the floor), when they become upset. No problem. This isn't a symptom of bad parenting, childhood schizophrenia, or brain damage (nor is it likely to cause any). Furthermore, it's fairly easily solved, if parents will just keep their cool.

First, find a section of blank wall in some relatively out-of-the-way, yet accessible, part of the house. Using a washable crayon, draw a two-foot diameter circle on the wall, positioning the center at the height of the child's forehead. Make sure that any wall studs are off to the side of the circle, rather than dead center. Show the little savage the circle and tell him that this is his very own head-banging place. Whenever he wants to bang his head, he should come here and bang because this is the best place in the whole world for that kind of thing.

If the child is also a foot-stomper, draw a circle on the floor, directly beneath the head-banging circle, and tell him it's his very own special foot-stomping place. Now he can bang his head and stomp his foot at the same time, which is bound to help his coordination, if nothing else. Demonstrate how convenient it will be for him to bang his head in the special place by getting down on your knees and banging your own head a few times. Tell him how good it felt and encourage him to give it a try.

Yes, I know this sounds strange, but it's kind of like fighting fire with fire. Your miniature maniac will look at you like you've lost your marbles, and the next time he gets mad he will start banging his head in just any old place. When that happens, pick him up, take him to the special circle. Say, "Bang here in your special place!" and walk away.

If you do this every time he bangs his head, head-banging should begin to taper off in a week or so. There's no future in banging your head unless your parents get upset over it. Within a month, it should be a thing of the past. Then he'll probably start biting himself, in which case you draw a circle on his forearm and . . .   (TT)

Someone once told me that if Jesus had been a parent, he would not have spanked his children. That may be true, but so what? Jesus didn't sign contracts, either. Nor did he require his disciples to be at work at eight in the morning. Because Jesus *didn't* do something doesn't make it improper.

The rod, in ancient days, was a symbol of authority, when associated with a king, and guidance, when associated with a shepherd. In this regard, I prefer to think that we are under divine instruction to discipline our children properly and guide them with loving authority. And no, I can't imagine Jesus taking a child over his knee and delivering a spanking, but then again, the Bible tells us that God has used methods a whole lot more devastating than spankings to terminate humankind's misbehavior, communicate his disapproval, and get us back on track. He's destroyed cities, He's flooded the whole world, He's caused people to drop dead in their tracks, He's turned people into pillars of salt.

Given the historical consequences of his wrath, I can't imagine God has any problem at all with a well-administered spanking.

(TOH)

In one often-cited study purporting to "prove" that being retained (held back) damaged children's "self-esteem," children who had been retained were solicited as to their feelings about it. Guess what they said! They said things like "It was embarrassing" and "I don't like to talk about it" and "I didn't like it." Conclusion: Their "self-esteem" had been damaged; therefore, concluded the authors of the study, children should not be retained. Similar perversions of "logic" and "science" were used to justify eliminating grades and to implement such educational fads as "cooperative learning," wherein children are not graded according to individual achievement; rather, they work on problems in groups and the group, as a whole, receives the "grade." Huh? So how, one might ask, do teachers know who are the better students? The theory, at least, is that they won't. That's the point, you see. No one is better than anyone else; therefore, no one's "self-esteem" suffers because of unfavorable comparisons. And one might also ask, does not this "cooperative" arrangement result in the brightest, most motivated child in any given group doing most, if not all, of the work? The answer to that is obvious: One child ends up pulling the load for four others. But no one's "self-esteem" suffers, and that's the most important thing (ha!). In this and numerous other ways, public (the operative word) schools were transformed from places of learning to places of coddling, and their primary mission, once to educate, became that of doing therapy. It can accurately be said that in today's public school, seeing to it that children acquire "good self-esteem" is the primary objective, not seeing to it that children learn basic skills. (FV)

Yes, it is necessary for adults to demonstrate respect for children, but the adult-child relationship cannot be democratic. Therefore, showing respect for children is not a matter of treating them like equals. Rather, it's a matter of accepting children for what they are; patiently nurturing them toward what they are capable of becoming; expecting a lot of them.

Accepting children for what they are means accepting their misbehavior—not approving of it, mind you, but accepting it. It takes most of eighteen years to civilize a child, and the process is one of trial and error, with an emphasis on error. As the errors occur, adults must be ready to correct them. To effectively correct, one must communicate well, and to communicate well, one must be reasonably composed (albeit disapproving). One cannot remain composed in the face of a child's errors unless one accepts (respects) that the child is a child.

To patiently nurture means not only to give adequate love and affection, but also to deliver proper discipline. These are the two sides of the coin of good parenting. Love without discipline in equal measure is indulgent, and discipline without an equal measure of love is punitive. Walking this balance beam, with grace, is the task set before parents.

Expecting a lot of children means setting high standards. It is, of course, possible to set unreasonably high standards. But the more common mistake is to set standards too low. In the real world, mediocrity is not rewarded. To accept mediocrity of any sort from a child is disrespectful. Parents should expect children to do well in school, display excellent manners, treat other children fairly, and perform chores (for no pay) around the home.

Within reason, the higher parents set standards, the more they elevate their children. And that, in the final analysis, is what respecting children is all about. (FV)

The marriage is the bedrock upon which a family is built and upon which everyone in the family depends. The marriage is "where it's at" and always will be. The marriage *precedes* the children and was meant to *succeed* them. If you put your children first, if you plan your life around them, the fabric of your relationship may not be able to endure the wear and tear of the parenting years. The marriage is the nucleus of the family. It creates, defines, and sustains the family. It transcends the identities of the two people who created it, and yet a healthy marriage not only preserves those identities but also brings them to full flower.

A child's needs are met if, and only if, the needs of his parents' marriage are successfully met. Children who experience their parents' relationship as an ever-present source of stability at the center of the family will feel as secure as they can possibly feel. From their parents' example, they learn how to share, how to disagree in ways that don't compromise anyone's dignity, and they learn the human art of caring. They learn that their parents' relationship does not include them—and yet they eventually realize that they are more complete because of it. Children discover who they are by first having it defined for them who their parents are, and who *they* are *not*. They discover their own place by first being told where it *cannot* be. It is this clear sense of "separateness" that encourages the growth of autonomy and pushes a child toward the fulfillment of his or her own promise.

(PP)

Parents who function responsibly during a child's first eighteen or so months of life ingrain in the child the belief that he or she is the One for whom the world has been waiting. The next eighteen years are spend undoing what it took those first eighteen months to do. The child, meanwhile, clings with all the tenacity he can muster to the infantile belief that the world should bend to his will. He stubbornly maintains it is his "right" to have things his way, and that his parents and teachers are being "unfair" when they deny him this right.

A child's socialization can proceed only as quickly as does the divestiture of his self-centeredness. In fact, self-centeredness prevents not only proper socialization, but spiritual growth as well. In order for an individual, at some point in his or her life, to accept that the Center of the Universe is occupied by God the All-Mighty, Creator of all things including himself, he must shift his focus, his "centeredness," first from self to other (the first "others" being his parents), then from other to God. Under optimal circumstances, this journey begins during the second year of life and is properly oriented (but by no means complete) by the end of the third.

The first step in this process of emotional/social/spiritual growth finds the child stepping down from the false throne of "I Am" and elevating his parents to the position of "You Are."

The requirement that the child pay more attention to his or her parents than they pay to him is not, therefore, for his parents' benefit. The purpose behind this rule is *not* to elevate them, but to provide for the ultimate elevation—emotionally, socially, and spiritually—of the child. The child has no way of understanding that he must elevate his parents in order to eventually be elevated himself and will, in any case, cling to self-centeredness if allowed to do so. Therefore, parents cannot afford to be passive concerning this process. They must get actively behind it and exercise whatever force is needed to move it along and keep it on track. The child, being foolish and short-sighted, will not do so on his own.　　　　(FV)

In a young child, the initial desire to become involved in a sport or activity is nothing more than an expression of curiosity. For this reason, a child should not feel obligated to participate, or continue participating, in a sport or activity because of parental pressure and should, generally speaking, be as free to quit as he is to join. He shouldn't be required to have any better excuse for quitting than "I want to."

A child who is not free to quit may well become increasingly reluctant to join for fear of becoming locked into something that might seem attractive at first, but ultimately is not. On the other hand, a child who's free to leave an activity he entered into of his own initiative is in no danger of developing a "quitter's attitude" toward life. Quite the contrary. The stuff of success—initiative, achievement, motivation, and persistence—grows only when it is allowed to take root and flower within the child.

There is occasional value to be had from contracting with a child for specified periods of commitment regarding certain activities, especially those that involve significant monetary investment. For example, parents might require that a child agree to two years of lessons before buying a musical instrument the child has expressed interest in learning to play. In these sorts of cases, the child learns something about obligation and responsibility. (6PP)

The truth is, *any child is capable of just about any misbehavior.* Yes, your child, too. The good news is, most of your child's foolishness isn't your fault. But it is your responsibility to correct it when it occurs. Taking disciplinary responsibility for your child's misbehavior isn't the same as taking the blame. The blame, if there is any to go around, belongs to the child. Taking your proper responsibility simply means doing something that makes the child a bit less foolish than he was before.

You can begin taking this responsibility, dear parent, by never, ever denying that your child is capable of foolish mistakes. When someone informs you of a foolish mistake your child made, just say, "Thanks! I'll take care of it, believe me!" and go do your job.

In short, don't be as foolish as your child.   (DGP)

Between birthdays two and six, the typical American preschool child watches some five thousand hours of television. Based on a fourteen-hour day, this means that preschool children spend roughly one-fourth of their discretionary time sitting in front of a television set.

In order to fully appreciate what these numbers mean, you must understand that those years between the second and sixth birthdays are among the most important years of the child's life. They comprise that period during which the young child is discovering, developing, and strengthening the skills he/she will need to become a creative, competent person.

Nearly every human being is born already programmed for giftedness of nearly every conceivable form—intellectual, artistic, musical, athletic, interpersonal, spiritual, and so on. During the formative years, these programs are activated by exposing the young child to environments and experiences that "push the right genetic buttons," so to speak.

Regardless of the program being watched, television watching fails to exercise initiative, curiosity, resourcefulness, creativity, motivation, imagination, reasoning and problem-solving abilities, communication skills, social skills, fine and gross motor skills, eye-hand coordination, and visual-tracking abilities. Because television's constant "flicker" means the child isn't looking at any one thing for longer than a few seconds, television watching interferes significantly with the development of a long attention span. Last, but by no means least, because the action on a television set shifts constantly and capriciously backward, forward, and laterally in time, television fails to promote logical, sequential thinking, which is essential to an understanding of cause-and-effect relationships. In short, a child watching television isn't doing anything competent at all. Every hour, therefore, that a preschool child spends watching television is an hour of that child's precious potential being wasted.   (6PP)

Parents who are interested in what their teenage children are doing and maintain proper supervision concerning their comings and goings will usually be able to sense when something is amiss. They may not know the details, but they will *know* nonetheless. The test for trouble: Ask yourself, "How often do I have a feeling of discomfort concerning what my child is doing or says he's doing with his time?" If your answer is once a month or more, then you'd better take a closer look. Some of the more definite danger signals include (1) dramatic changes in behavior, friends, or attitude toward school, (2) secretiveness concerning whereabouts, (3) outright lying, often concerning unimportant things, (4) refusing to participate in family activities, and (5) prolonged periods of self-imposed isolation when at home.

If you suspect a problem, you should first share—not accuse, mind you, *share*—your observations and feelings with your child and try to engage him in a discussion of the problem. As a general rule, the more defensive a teen becomes when parents share concerns, the more on target his parents probably are. (BHG)

Q: *My seven-year-old daughter has always been extremely shy. Even as an infant, she seemed extremely sensitive to new situations and new people. Her teacher recently expressed concern about her shyness and said it might be the result of low self-esteem. She then ventured that Sandra possibly didn't feel as loved or wanted as our other children and that my husband and I had unrealistically high expectations of her. It's true that we insist upon appropriate behavior from our children, but the suggestion that we've damaged her psychologically was very upsetting.*

A: I'm sure Sandra's teacher is very well intentioned; however, she is equally misinformed. The latest, and best, body of evidence strongly suggests that shyness is an inborn temperamental trait. Researchers at Harvard University have found that children who are timid during infancy and toddlerhood tend also to be socially inhibited at age seven. They estimate that 15 percent of children—significantly more girls than boys—are shy. Those researchers also discovered that over time, however, many children seem to "outgrow" their shyness.

The best "medicine" for shyness is parents who are gently encouraging, supportive, and who themselves are not inhibited. It goes without saying that criticism of an inhibited child is more likely to make matters worse, as will a lot of parental anxiety concerning the child's social reticence.

My best advice to you is to encourage her to try new things, but don't push too hard. In the final analysis, she's going to emerge from her "shell" when she's ready and not before. In addition, Sandra's teacher needs to stop being so concerned about her mental health and focus instead on positive ways of coaxing her out of hiding.

(NP)

It is every parent's job to teach his or her children a fundamental, untransmutable law of reality: *You cannot get your bread buttered on both sides. In fact, there will be times when you cannot get it buttered on either side, and there will even be times when you won't have a piece of bread.*

This applies regardless of one's standard of living. Whether you earn $4,000,000 a year or $40,000, it is your bounden duty to your children (and our culture) to teach them they cannot get their bread buttered on both sides, etc. In other words, the "richer" you are, the more important it becomes that you not completely share your standard of living with your children. Instead of sharing your success with your children in material terms, share with them the skills and values they will need to eventually achieve success on their own. I call this the Principle of Benign Deprivation. Deprive your child now, and he/she will be better equipped later to strive and thrive!   (TOH)

The overly involved parent *hovers* over his/her (it's usually, sad to say, *her*) child, obsessively preoccupied with the possibility that the child may make a mistake, and determined to anticipate and prevent that unthinkable possibility. In the act of hovering, the parent *assumes responsibility,* however unwittingly, for the child's academic (or social or recreational or extracurricular) decisions and/or performance. He overdirects, overmanages, and overcontrols. This is overprotection in its purest form—trying to protect the child from failure and one's self from the implication that the child's failure is a reflection of one's own *failures.* In the act of hovering, the parent encourages continuing *dependence,* weakens the child's tolerance for frustration, and thwarts the growth of initiative and resourcefulness. What a terrible price for a child to pay because a parent "only wants to help"! (EHH)

At a speaking engagement, I will ask the audience, "How many of you have argumentative children?" In an audience of 500, at least 350 will raise a hand.

At this point, I say, "I have good news, or bad news, depending on how you look at it: *None of you has an argumentative child.* In fact, there is no such thing, and none of you will ever get a grip on the arguing that takes place between you and your supposedly argumentative child as long as you persist in the belief that these arguments originate in the child.

"To put an end to the arguing requires somewhat the same first step required of people in twelve-step programs. You must say to yourself, 'I am completely responsible for these arguments. My child has nothing to do with them whatsoever. He is only taking advantage of an opportunity which I continue extending in his direction.' That may sound discouraging, but it actually means that since you are in complete control of whether an argument takes place or not, *you can stop them, and permanently so, whenever you decide to do so.*"

At this point, I always hear some people making noises of disbelief, so I prove that what I'm proposing is within their grasp. "How many of you," I ask, "grew up with parents who absolutely, completely refused to argue with you, ever?"

Close to half the people in the audience raise their hands. "See?" I say, "Your parents knew that they were in total control of whether you argued or not. And they would not allow it! And you can do the same, whenever you'd like! You can stop giving your child opportunity to argue. The next time your child disagrees with a decision you've made, or an explanation you've offered for a decision he didn't like, just look at him and say, 'Yes, well, I'd feel the same way if I was your age. No problem.' And at that critical point—the point of 'nuff said,' turn around with a shrug of the shoulders and walk away!

"Pull the plug on the power struggle! This will not guarantee compliance, but it increases its likelihood threefold. Now, I challenge you to prove me right!"   (NP)

Psychologists have been promoting "time-out" as the be-all, end-all of discipline for going on twenty-five years. And they persist in the face of mounting anecdotal evidence that time-out works with children who are fairly well behaved to begin with, but does not work nearly as well with children whose behavior problems are pronounced and/or chronic.

One aspect of this problem is that time-out can't be employed consistently. It is difficult, if not impossible, to use if a behavior problem occurs away from the home or when parents are rushing out of the house to make an appointment. And children who are inclined toward misbehavior figure out these things quickly.

Furthermore, time-out doesn't speak loudly enough when the problem is outrageous. An otherwise well-behaved five-year-old ignores a parental instruction? Sure, put him in time-out for five minutes. But let's say that same child hits a family member. In that event, a more *memorable* response is called for, one that "nips" the offense "in the bud," as my parents would have put it. There's something absurd about making a child sit in a chair for a few minutes after he's attacked a family member.

Many psychologists hold to the "party line," which is that the disciplinary methods employed by previous generations of parents were excessive, if not abusive. I, on the other hand, hold to the heretical position that children of previous generations were more well behaved than today's children because their parents used more effective means of discipline, as in sending children to their rooms for entire days and (gasp!) spanking. (TOH)

In my estimation and the estimation of many educators, *Sesame Street* cannot rightly be called "educational." In the first place, there is no good evidence that programs of this sort contribute positively to the later academic achievement levels of their young viewers. One very objective study found that children who as preschoolers watched a lot of *Sesame Street* tended to do *less well* in school than children who watched little, if any.

Second, a classroom is to *Sesame Street* like an apple is to a potato. Children who watch programs of this sort are likely to come to school expecting teachers to be as entertaining as Big Bird. The fact is, in order for an education to be meaningful, it must involve hard work. So-called "educational" children's programs may be charming, but are one reason why teachers tell me that today's child comes to school expecting to be entertained and then complains of being "bored" when teachers don't make three-ring circuses of their classrooms.

If you need further convincing, just ask yourself: First, did you learn to read in first or second grade, and do you currently enjoy reading? The fact you're reading this book says the answer is an unqualified "yes." Second, did you watch *Sesame Street* as a child? If you're old enough to have children, then the answer is probably "no."

Conclusion: You don't need to watch *Sesame Street* to learn to read and enjoy reading. Convinced? (NP)

Teachers have no business assigning work that children can't do, for the most part, on their own. Those who do need to be gently reminded that the primary purpose of education is to help outfit children for self-sufficiency. When I was in school, it was clear that parents were *not* to help with projects. If it was obvious that a child had received parental help, his grade was docked. Today, it's taken for granted that parents are *supposed* to help, and teachers will reward with better grades those children whose parents got involved, and the more involved the parent got, the better the "child's" grade (ha!) is likely to be. This upside-down practice means, in effect, that children who do their projects on their own are punished for exercising initiative and independence and resourcefulness.

Look, I hate the word, but just this one time, I feel compelled to invoke it: That's not *fair*! (EHH)

It's a simple fact: The more parents do for and pay attention to children, the more children whine. Likewise, when children are expected to do for themselves and be responsible members of their families, they aren't likely to be whiners. The fact that whining is *not* a normal child behavior is attested to by parents from other countries, who never cease to be amazed, they tell me, at how "whiny" American children are. I spend nearly all of my vacations on a small island in the Bahamas, population sixty-five. I've never heard any of the children on the island whine. I've never heard any of them complain to adults about one another. I've never heard any of them throw a tantrum. If they aren't in school, they are playing and they require no adult direction to keep themselves occupied. I've never seen them play with what American children would consider a "toy." They fashion their playthings with the alchemy of imagination, transforming sticks into horses, leaves into plates, stones into food. That, folks, is *normal* childhood behavior. But then people who are old enough to remember tell me American children were once that normal. (FV)

Q: *Our fifteen-year-old daughter, who has always been a fairly good student, says she wants to get a part-time job. We're not sure it's a good idea. What advice can you give us?*

A: I think you should let her begin earning her own money. Your daughter's initiative and willingness to take on obligations outside of home and school—especially one that will allow her less time with peers—should definitely be encouraged. At the very least, she'll find out she really isn't ready for a job. Either way, it will be a tremendously valuable learning experience, one she shouldn't be denied.

If your daughter was not already a motivated student, I would advise telling her she could get a job when and if her grades come up. With improvement in her grades, you would allow her to work a certain number of hours per week. As she showed further improvement, you would allow her to increase her hours to a certain maximum. In that case, I would point out that her desire to work presents you with a "strategic opportunity"—a chance to turn her motivation for doing one thing (getting a job) into motivation for something else (better grades). In the long run, seizing upon a strategic opportunity of this sort benefits the child more than the parent. It may take the child a while to figure that out, however. (BHG)

When my daughter Amy turned three, she decided to turn bedtime into a game of "Let's See How Crazy You Can Make Your Parents." Five minutes after we tucked her in bed, she'd be downstairs asking "When's my birfday?" or something equally cute. We'd answer her question, lead her back to bed, tuck her in, go downstairs, and wait. Sure enough, five minutes or so later Amy would be standing in front of us, looking as innocent as a kitten, yet another question on the tip of her tongue.

After several months of this, realizing that persuasion, threat, and fear were not going to work to keep her in bed, we thought of a way to outsmart her (no small feat, since children this age are much, much smarter than their parents). One night, while tucking Amy in, I leaned over and whispered, "When we leave your room, Amos, you can fool us by quietly closing your door, turning on the light, and playing with your toys. If you're berry, berry quiet, we won't hear you! Mommy and Daddy will think you're asleep, and we won't get mad, and you can play until you fall asleep!"

Her eyes got big and she giggled. "But if you make a noise, or open your door," I went on to say, "then we will have to put you back to bed and turn out your light. So let's see if you can fool us tonight, Amos. Let's see how quiet you can be."

Magic! From that night forward, Amy delighted in "fooling" us. Every evening, as we would tuck her in, we'd remind her of our gullibility. We'd share a conspiratorial giggle with "the Amos," as she is known, go downstairs, and revel in freedom from parenthood. (TT)

Every time I write something favorable about spankings, I draw a lot of virulent criticism, mostly from other professionals. It disturbs my critics that I don't share their very psychologically correct point of view, which has it that children who are spanked (a) hate themselves for being such rotten kids, (b) learn to solve problems by hitting people, (c) will someday abuse their own children, (d) will grow up to become violent criminals, or (e) all of the above. I have good news. Those things are the result of constant, cruel *beatings*, not occasional, lovingly-administered spankings. I have more good news. It is possible to spank a child well, to do it right, and to make it work. The problem with spankings is simply that a lot of parents make a sorry mess of them. (PP)

I am reminded of Miss Grimsley, my tenth-grade composition teacher, and her proclivity for truth in education. One day, Miss Grimsley, who had been grading papers while we students were writing themes, suddenly looked up and called me to her desk. When I stood before her, she fixed me with the most victimizing of looks and launched into a veritable tirade concerning my most recent submission.

"This is the worst paper you have ever turned in to me, Mr. Rosemond," she began, in a volume that surely carried out the door and down the hall, "and, to come straight to the point, I will not accept it. Not only will you do it over, but instead of three pages, you will write five, and as you do, keep in mind that the very best grade you will receive will be a C, so you had best put your best foot—or shall we say hand—forward on the rewrite, do you understand (?), and do not ever, and I mean ever (!) . . . "

At this point, all I could hear was mass snickering building behind me. I felt my face burst to crimson and butterflies launch themselves into a frenzy in my stomach. When Miss Grimsley was mercifully done, I wobbled back to my seat knowing that all eyes were upon me, mocking my humiliation. It is supreme understatement to say I felt bad about myself. Real bad.

I never tried to hoodoo Miss Grimsley again. In fact, I worked much harder in her class to make up for that futile attempt to slide. In my adulthood, it dawned on me that I'd insulted her intelligence, and she had not let me get away with it. What a lady!

I am indebted to Miss Grimsley for telling me the awful truth on that fateful day and, in so doing, making me feel bad about myself. She, along with most other teachers of her era, understood that the best truth is often a truth that carries a bit of a sting. But then, they hadn't yet heard about self-esteem, had they? (NP)

When giving instructions to children, parents should be commanding, concise, and concrete. These are the "Three C's of Good Communication."

Be Commanding: Speak directly to the child and preface instruction with authoritative statements, such as "I want you to . . ." or "It's time for you to . . ." or "You need to . . ." In other words, don't beat around the bush. If you want a child to do something, you must tell him in *no uncertain terms*. The more uncertain your terms, the more uncertain the outcome.

Be Concise: Don't use fifty words when five will do, as in, "Don't ever do that again." Almost all of us were lectured as children, and we all remember hating it. We know from that experience that as soon as the lecturer gets going, a fuse blows somewhere between the child's ears and brain.

Be Concrete: Speak in terms that are down to earth, rather than abstract. Use language that refers to the specific behaviors you expect, as opposed to the attitude. "I want you to be good in church this morning" is vague, abstract. "While we're in church, I want you to sit quietly next to me" is clear and concrete.

C+C+C = Compliance. (6PP)

When I was a teenager, I did my homework to the strains of Elvis, Buddy Holly, Dion and the Belmonts, and later, the Beatles and the Rolling Stones. My parents thought the music was a distraction. I always thought they objected more to my *selection* than to the idea of music in the background. Mozart would have been fine. After all, *he* was a genius. But they were convinced that Elvis's brains were in his pelvis and feared that too much exposure to his music would render me intellectually impotent. Little did they know how hard I wished that I, too, could be afflicted with Elvis's learning disability.

Actually, I think my grades were *better* because of rock 'n' roll. My English themes had rhythm, a backbeat. Math seemed to resonate with harmony. The music kicked me in the right side of the brain, unleashing imagination, a sense of possibility, the power to see through the concrete to the abstract. A bop-shu-bop-a-bop-bop-shu-bop yeah! Remember that a kid's brain isn't as cluttered as an adult's. It's no sweat for a teenager to listen to rock 'n' roll with one part of the brain, do homework with another part, and still chew gum!

(EHH)

In any healthy relationship, one in which the two people involved retain autonomy while maintaining commitment, a certain amount of disagreement is inevitable. Because of differences in background and biology, each of you sees and responds to things differently. It's inevitable, therefore, that your parenting styles will at times be on slightly different wavelengths.

There are several advantages to disagreement. First, different people bring more than one point of view to a situation. Your differences create options. This has the potential of imparting more flexibility and adaptability to the manner in which you raise your children. Second, your differences create a more exciting dynamic within your relationship and increase your potential for growth—both as individuals and as a couple. Third, assuming you find creative ways of resolving your differences, your children not only learn a lot about conflict resolution but also see there is more than one way to do it.

Disagreement can quickly become a barrier to, rather than a vehicle for, growth and change if you focus too much energy on it. The more attention you pay to disagreement, the further apart you'll seem and the worse your disagreements will be. Under these circumstances, you can quickly lose sight of the fact that you actually agree about more than you disagree.

For example, although you might differ on how to get the children in bed at night, you may agree on such things as the time you want them in bed, that it's important for the two of you to have time together in the evening without children, that you're not going to let the children get in bed with you, that you're not going to get in bed with them, and so on. Finding your common ground makes it easier to find mutually acceptable solutions.

Discussing your differences within earshot of, or even in front of, the children is okay as long as the discussion is low-key and creative. Children need to see that conflict and hostility are not the same.

(NP)

One natural consequence of having secured your child's attention is that your child will respect your wisdom and seek your guidance. This all but eliminates communication problems. Yet another natural consequence of having secured your child's attention is that your child will place great value on your approval. Your child will *want* to behave in ways that are pleasing to you (honor you!), do as well as possible in school, and accept ever-increasing amounts of responsibility for his/her life.

There is a distinct difference between a child making a mistake (Fact: All children make mistakes) and a child *choosing* to misbehave when he knows better. A child who is paying attention to his parents and who values their approval will realize when he's made a mistake (be penitent) and seek to correct it (atone). If the child isn't aware of the mistake, pointing it out and making it clear that repeat performances will not be looked upon favorably will usually suffice.

Too often, parents punish when correction could, and should, have been accomplished with far less drama—a look, a word, a brief expression of disappointment. There are times, for sure, in the rearing of every child when drama is necessary in order to create a permanent memory in the child's mind, but if you lay the cornerstones properly, those times will not predominate.   (FV)

In the same sense that adults *should* be intimidated by God, children *should* be intimidated by adults. One of the major problems in today's society, as educators, juvenile judges, police, shopkeepers, and retirees will affirm, is that too many children are *not* intimidated by adults. Intimidation, in this context, is nothing more than an immature form of respect. In fact, children are not capable of truly respecting someone. They are too self-centered. As they mature, self-centeredness is replaced with respect for authority. Meanwhile, authority figures—parents, teachers, coaches—must intimidate in order to effectively teach children the social and academic skills they must have in order to someday function as responsible adults. The child who is not intimidated by adults has no reason to pay attention and do as he/she is told. Intimidation, therefore, serves a positive purpose, and adults capitalize upon it *for the child's own benefit.*

And, yes, there is a difference between fear and intimidation. Some adults rule by causing their children to fear them personally. These are adults who do not know how to command. As a consequence, they must constantly *demand* obedience from their children. Those demands always involve threat, whether explicit or implicit. Parents who succeed at commanding do not have to invest their instructions to their children with threat. They *command* by means of the matter-of-fact exercise of legitimate natural authority. Their children have no reason to fear them personally; yet, their children are indeed *intimidated* by them.   (FV)

Many children begin sucking their thumbs before they're born. A rather ingenious way of passing the time, wouldn't you agree? They continue doing so simply because it reminds them of the peace and security of the womb. Since there's nothing wrong with thumb sucking, I don't advise that parents try to stop it. In fact, attempts in that direction are likely to create problems where none existed before. Some parents have been successful, however, at gently and patiently persuading infants and toddlers to substitute pacifiers for thumbs. This makes it somewhat easier to later limit or even stop the habit altogether. In most cases, children stop on their own during the early elementary years. Keep in mind, however, that some very well-adjusted children have sucked their thumbs—privately, of course—until well into their teen years. In short, it's not worth worrying about. By the way, orthodontists will tell you that whether a child sucks his or her thumb has little to do with a later need for braces.   (TOH)

The problems crippling America's schools are not going to be solved until every man and woman in this country realizes that "lack of discipline" is the crux of the matter and further realizes that the problem doesn't rest with administrators, teachers, or school boards, but with parents.

Yes, you-who-prefer-to-keep-the-wool-pulled-over-your-own-eyes, the discipline problems in America's schools come primarily from America's homes. They are a matter of parents who send children to school without the discipline it takes to dig in and *get* an education; parents who overindulge and undercorrect; parents who neither indulge nor correct; parents who let TV sets run day and night and rarely read anything more than the morning newspaper; parents who will not give total, 100 percent support to teachers' disciplinary efforts; parents who expect schools to do what they themselves have been too busy or too lazy to do—namely, teach their children the three R's of respect, responsibility, and resourcefulness.

Nor will the problems in America's schools be solved until everyone realizes that more money has nothing to do with these problems. America's public schools are wasteful. They do a worse job with more money than either private or parochial schools. When America's public schools impose strict fiscal discipline upon themselves (or have it imposed upon them), and America's parents impose strict behavioral discipline upon their children, America's public schools will again thrive. (NP)

Although it's certainly possible to teach a three-year-old basic academic skills, there is no reason to believe that such instruction will have lasting benefits. In fact, study after study confirms that the early gains achieved by such programs have disappeared by the third grade. Other research suggests that premature reading instruction can contribute to later learning disabilities as well as a lack of interest in reading. Most children are ready to begin learning to read by first grade. Until then, I recommend that parents seek out preschool and day-care programs that give children ample opportunity to strengthen social, motor, and creative skills. In the final analysis, the best preschool reading program consists of parents who spend a significant amount of time reading to both their preschoolers and themselves.   (TOH)

March 8

It's perfectly all right for parents to require a teenager to participate in a certain activity, such as a church youth group, as long as the mandate is the exception rather than the rule. It's generally better, however, to encourage participation in an activity rather than insist upon it. Nonetheless, parents can, and should, provide direction when they feel direction is needed. Oftentimes, a teen's reluctance to get involved in something is based on inadequate information or the fear of not "fitting in." If parents see a gap that's begging to be filled, they have every right to take steps to fill it. If, however, the push comes from parents, the teen may dig his or her heels in that much more. To circumvent that possibility, I recommend that parents discreetly ask another teen who's already involved in the activity to extend the invitation. (BHG)

Beginning some forty years ago, so-called "helping" professionals began encouraging parents to approach the rearing of children as if it were an intellectual challenge, rather than a relatively simple matter of common sense. Let me point out simply that if intellect was key to successful child rearing, the smartest people would be the best parents. That is hardly consistent with my observations.

An intellectual approach to child rearing is likely to result in the perception that child rearing is difficult, as in "the hardest thing I've ever done," a complaint I hear from many parents. Consider this: Ours is the first generation of American parents to make this complaint. Consider this: Only American parents are making this complaint. Conclusion: There is nothing about the rearing of children that is inherently difficult, but there must be something in our American approach (post-war) to child rearing that creates the illusion of difficulty. That something, I submit, is an overload of intellect and a corresponding paucity of common sense.

If you bring too much intellect to the child-rearing process, you will analyze your own behavior and the behavior of your child to neurotic excess, you will question yourself and your decisions constantly, and you will waffle and waver and consume yourself with anxiety. In so doing, you will fail to communicate to your child that you know where you stand and know where you want him/her to stand. Your child will be forced to test compulsively. The level of stress in the relationship will rise, and the constant rocking of your household's "ship of state" will threaten your child's security and, therefore, self-esteem.

A commonsensical approach to child rearing is not, by any means, unthinking. It is simply unintellectual. Common sense comes from the heart and the gut, not from the head. When a parent thinks too much, the heart becomes confused. When the heart rules, the head thinks clearly. (TT)

My wife, Willie, and I resolved, along with thousands of parents of our generation, to "break the chain" of generations of autocratic suppression by creating a democratic family. In short order, Eric was running our lives. We did nothing without either consulting him or anticipating how he would react. If we did something "wrong," he let us know by throwing a tantrum. He would flop backward onto the floor and begin screaming at the top of his little lungs, arms flailing, eyes rolled back in his head. Linda Blair, she of *The Exorcist,* had nothing on Eric.

We interpreted Eric's screams to mean we had made yet another mistake, which we immediately corrected, thus making him "happy" again. All day long Willie and I did what I refer to as the "tantrum dance." Eric screamed, we danced, and Eric stopped screaming—until the next time, that is. Naturally, the more we danced, the more he screamed, and the more we danced, and . . . you get the picture, I'm sure. It was parenting hell. One day, Willie and I came to our senses. We realized that the chaos in our family was a result not of two inherently bad parents, but of the inherently bad advice we were trying to follow. We promptly began breaking all of the *nouveau* "parenting" rules, and just as promptly, Eric turned into a relatively civilized human being (understanding that with children, a state of civility is always relative). Other parents, unfortunately, were not so bold. Traveling as I do, speaking to parents all over the country, I have the distinct impression that the majority of today's parents, as was the case with Willie and myself some twenty-six years ago, are *trying to keep their children from screaming.* They are not just intimidated by their children's tantrums, they are downright *afraid* of them. They will do just about anything to prevent tantrums, and if one occurs, they will do just about anything to make it stop. All of which, of course, makes tantrums inevitable. (FV)

Enrolling the slightly immature child in kindergarten when the law allows is, in my mind, a "nothing ventured, nothing gained" proposition. A child who begins the year at a slight developmental disadvantage stands a fairly good chance of catching up by the end of the year. If that hoped-for progress doesn't occur, then a second year in kindergarten may be appropriate. Many parents who choose delayed enrollment are motivated by a desire to enhance their children's chances of "going to the head of the class." That stands a good chance of backfiring, particularly for a child who was ready to start school at age five, and who, that following year, is bored stiff in a kindergarten setting. Furthermore, if delayed enrollment for "summer children" becomes the norm, then a new group of late-birthday kids is created (those, in other words, with birthdays after March 1) who, relative to the rest of their kindergarten classmates, are "immature." If we carry this to its absurd extreme, then in another ten years or so children might not be entering kindergarten until age seven. The most practical solution, or so it seems to me, is to first, stop pushing significant chunks of a traditional first-grade curriculum down into kindergarten; second, enroll all children except those with significant developmental delays in kindergarten when the law says they can be enrolled; third, exercise the option of having certain children repeat kindergarten when that seems appropriate. I should note that many schools are now offering transitional K-1 programs for children who need an additional readiness year before first grade. A tip of the hat to those innovative systems!   (EHH)

Each and every one of us is a flawed, imperfect being. When two imperfect people join together in an inevitably imperfect union, their imperfections begin colliding with one another and, like atomic particles, begin spinning off new imperfections.

This is why, sometimes during the first year of marriage, nearly every spouse quite accurately accuses the other of not being the person he or she married: "You've changed!" (and never for the better). These ever-more-imperfect beings bring other imperfect beings into their imperfect union, creating more collisions, producing more imperfections, more flaws.

This, folks, is not dysfunction; rather, it is reality. It is the very struggle of life, and it is nothing short of disingenuous to refer to it otherwise. (TOH)

From day one parent or parents and child are engaged in an almost constant exchange of sound and movement. The poetry of this "dance" forms an emotional attachment that secures the child's trust in the environment, and enables the child to begin moving away from his or her parents and into the world. As he explores the environment, the child exercises and thereby strengthens competency skills. I would argue that in all but the most extreme cases there is no one more in tune with the child, and therefore more capable of properly responding to this process, than the child's parents. The good intentions of the most well-trained day-care workers simply do not compare. To this I would add that the only people who can properly help the child make the critical transition from self-centeredness to parent-centeredness during the second eighteen months of life are, as well, the child's parents.

For the last twenty years or more, the professional community has been engaged in a cover-up concerning these issues. Not wishing to offend anyone, much less appear out of step with the times, developmental psychologists, early-childhood educators, and the like have acted as if home-care and day-care were fundamentally equivalent; that if parents know what to look for in a day-care center, a young child will be as well off in the care of strangers for forty-plus hours a week, fifty weeks a year, as in the care of a parent. That's a myth.

Here's the truth, the whole truth, and nothing but the truth: Being cared for during one's tender years in one's own home by a responsible, committed parent is distinctly different, both qualitatively and quantitatively, from being cared for in even the best of day-care centers. If these are two distinctly different situations, then the outcomes must also be distinctly different. Having proposed what I believe is not debatable, I am simply convinced that a child's needs are better served in the former situation. And anyone who's upset by what I just said, I submit, *needs* to be upset.   (TT)

Most parents accustom their children to a material standard that is completely out of kilter with what they can ever hope to achieve as adults. Consider also that many, if not most of these children, attain this level of childhood affluence not by working, sacrificing, or doing their best, but by whining, demanding, and manipulating. In the process of overinflating their children's materialistic expectations, overindulgent parents teach their children that something can be had for nothing. Not only is that a falsehood, it's one of the most self-destructive attitudes a person can ever acquire.

Children who grow up believing in the something-for-nothing fairy tale may never realize that the really important things in life come from within, rather than without. As adults, they are likely to be emotionally stunted, immature people, fixated at a grasping, self-centered stage of development. At the very least, they will tend to confuse the giving and getting of *things* with a deeper and more meaningful level of sharing and trust in relationships. When they themselves become parents, they're likely to confuse their children's value systems in a like manner—by overdoing them with things. In this sense, materialism is an inherited disease, an addiction passed from one generation to another. But materialism is not so much an addiction to things as it is an addiction to *acquiring* things. This explains why a materialist is never content. No sooner than he's acquired one thing, he wants another. This also explains why children who get too much of what they want rarely take care of anything they have. Why should they? After all, history tells them that more is on the way. (6PP)

Manners and respect are inseparable. Children begin developing respect for others by first developing it for their parents. Therefore, children should be taught to behave in mannerly ways toward their parents. That means children should not be allowed to call their parents (or any adult for that matter) by their first names, interrupt adult conversations unless in crisis, or—beyond age three—throw tantrums when they don't get their way. I'll even go so far as to recommend that children be taught to respond to all adults, including their parents, with "Yes, Sir," "Yes, Ma'am," and the like. When adults speak, children should pay attention; and when adults give instructions, children should carry them out. It's as simple as that.

If today's parents taught children the same things *they* were taught as children, the world would be a better place. Unfortunately, that doesn't seem to be happening. Veteran teachers tell me today's child is, in general, much less respectful and much less mannerly than the typical child of a generation ago. The tragedy of this is that unless children learn respect for others— beginning with parents and expanding outward from there—they can never develop true respect for themselves. Respect for others is the horse that pulls the cart of self-respect. Without respect for others, one never advances beyond the stage of self-absorption. So, in the final analysis, this isn't a matter of exalting adults, but a matter of helping children feel good about themselves. (FV)

Any and all attempts to "reason" with young children are fruit-less. *A child cannot understand an adult point of view* (please read that again, out loud). *A child will understand an adult point of view when the child is an adult* (again, read out loud). Therefore, your child does what you say not because you are persuasive, but because you say so.

Does this mean you should never tell a child the reason or reasons behind your decisions? No. It simply means you make no attempt to *reason*; no attempt, in other words, to persuade the child that your reasons are right, good, in his best interests, holy, pure, or whatever. You give your reasons knowing fully that the child will not agree with them. You give your reasons in order to provide the child with a reference point. Later, when the child is an adult, this reference point will be indispensable. In the meantime, understanding that, like fine wine, no *mind* matures before its time, you do not expect agreement from a child concerning your adult point of view; therefore, you are not disappointed when the child does not agree. Because you are not disappointed, you are not upset when the child demonstrates his or her disagreement. You stay calm, and as such, are able to communicate to the child that you know where you stand, and furthermore, you know where you want him to stand. He may not, at the moment, like it. In the long run, however (and believe me on this), he will come to appreciate it and love and respect you all the more for it. (TT)

Children need parents who know where they stand and who stand firm. When parents stand in one place one minute and in another place the next and yet another the next, it becomes impossible for their children to become convinced of their parents' ability to protect and provide for them. These parents are unreliable, and unreliable parents make for insecure children. Their insecurity drives what is called "testing behavior," which is nothing more than an anxiety-ridden search for where their parents stand. The child who constantly tests is really asking, "Please stop moving around, Mom and Dad, because every time you change position, every time you are inconsistent, every time you say one thing and do another, every time I'm able to wear you down by whining and pleading, every time you give in to one of my tantrums, I am forced to test that much more."

Parents who are inconsistent engage their children in a perpetual game of hide-and-seek, and the fact that their children have no choice but to play consumes enormous amounts of their developmental energies—energies that would otherwise be available for creative pursuits, for self-expansion, for activities that bring success. Testing *never* brings success. It is not possible, therefore, to test and feel good about yourself at the same time. (EHH)

Kitchen timers, the portable kind, should be standard issue to all parents. A kitchen timer can be used to organize activities. It can help young children understand the concept of time. It will, upon demand, establish routines and define limits. It supplements parental authority and helps everyone detour around power struggles. Last, but not least, it is a virtually infallible way of communicating when "time's up." In other words, a timer can help with all those tasks parents try to accomplish using words alone—the "in-one-ear-and-out-the-other" method—which has never proven reliable, especially not with preschoolers. Here are seven suggested "parenting" uses for kitchen timers:

1. Use a timer to signal "when." For instance, when the child can go outside. Take the timer on trips to serve as an audio-visual answer to, "When are we gonna be there?" Instead of repeating "in just a little while," set the timer and let the ringer do the talking.

2. Timers are an excellent way of defining how much time you will spend playing with your child before going back to your chores.

3. Is there a struggle in your house every morning to get your child dressed and out of the house on time? Play "Beat the Bell!" Make a game of getting dressed before the bell rings.

4. The timer will answer the question, "Can I come out of my room now?" which the child usually begins asking within thirty seconds of being sent there. Set the timer when he goes in and tell him that he may come out when the bell rings.

5. Use the timer as a prompt for getting chores done.

6. The timer can answer how-much-longer questions, such as, "How much longer can I (stay in tub, play outside, bounce on my bed, play in the toilet, drive you crazy)?"

7. The best use of all is when Mom or Dad (or both) want a little time to be alone (together?). This is known as Parent's Time-Out and is easily set aside with the help of a timer.

Remember, "A watched (timed) tot never spoils."   (PP)

"**M**y children come first" is a one-way ticket to a place where parents worry about children who whine and fuss and won't do what they're told to do by parents who finally lose their patience and scream and then plunge headlong into that dark hole called guilt. It's a place where husbands come home to wives who complain because being a mother—whether "working" or not— takes so much energy they have none left to be wives. It's a place where people hurt, but hide the hurt behind "my children come first." In the last forty years, American parents have been encouraged by the "experts" to create positions of preeminence for their children within their families. The child has been placed on a pedestal and the American parent has adopted a self-sacrificing reverence toward his "potential" and his "self-esteem." We have accepted into our vocabulary the phrases "child-centered family" and "democratic family," seeming not to realize that when a child is regarded as being central, or equal, to his parents' relationship, their relationship is in jeopardy. There is but one proper place for children within a family—the backseat. The driver's seat is reserved for parents, and parents only. Unfortunately, too many of today's parents are not found there.   (PP)

When you make a contribution of time, money, or any other personal resource to a political, religious, educational, or charitable organization, you acknowledge two things: First, that you share values with that organization; second, that you want to do something tangible to help support and maintain those values in our society. The same applies to a child's contribution of time and energy to the family. Children who are enabled to contribute to their families on a regular basis come to a clearer understanding of their parents' values. Furthermore, they are much more likely to use those same values in their own adult lives to create success and happiness for themselves and their children. (6PP)

Do I recommend spankings? No, I recommend that if you choose to spank, do it properly, with the following points in mind:

- The more a parent spanks, the less effective it will be. A child will "immunize" to frequent spankings.

- Spankings are generally more "useful" with children who are excitable and active. There are times when nothing short of forceful drama will reach these children.

- Spank with your hand only, and only to the child's rear. Your hand can be used more spontaneously, is more personal, and helps prevent you from going overboard.

- One or two swats is sufficient. Remember, you're not trying to scourge the child of "badness" or beat some lesson into him.

- Spank as a *first* resort. The more you let your frustration build, the more likely you will go too far.

- Spank in "anger." Ah, but if you spank as a first resort, then it's unlikely you'll be in a rage.

- Always follow a spanking with a stern message and a consequence. Remember, folks, *that's* the discipline, and discipline is the purpose, *not* pain.

(NP)

Teachers tell me the average child needs help two out of ten times he asks for it. My figure—one out of four—gives the child the benefit of the doubt. The other three requests are symptomatic of frustration.

When someone—a parent or a teacher—takes it upon himself or herself to help a child every time he asks for it (or even a majority of those times), that very well-intentioned, helpful person—an enabler, actually—is doing the child no favors at all. By rescuing the child from frustration, the "helper" is diminishing the child's ability to accept that frustration is part of nearly every problem-solving process, and to learn to persevere in the face of it. The "helper" is also validating the child's kneejerk "I can't!" reaction, thus devaluing the child's self-concept. That good-intentioned "helping" is unraveling, if not the child's moral fiber, then certainly his ability to stand on his own two feet; his ability to stand up to the challenges of life and say, "I can! I know I can!"

No, I'm not giving parents permission to be lazy. I'm advocating that they stop letting their sentiments and their good intentions drive their behavior. I'm suggesting that they be a bit more hardheaded and practical when it comes to the rearing of children. I'm saying that the most helpful thing one can say to a child who's saying "I can't!" is "Oh, yes you can, and to help you prove that to yourself, I'm not going to give you any help at all.

"Because I love you." (NP)

In the late '60s, parenting professionals coined the term *child-centered family* and proclaimed it the ideal. Self-esteem could not flourish, said the professionals, unless the child's needs came first. Nearly everything, by the way, that made children happy was defined as a "need." Understandably, parents understood all this to mean they were to keep their children happy. What other conclusion was there to draw?

In 1776, Thomas Jefferson told Americans that it was impossible to make someone happy. He wrote, in the Declaration of Independence, that all men, created equal, were entitled to three inalienable rights: life, liberty, and the *pursuit* of happiness. Jefferson was a very wise man. He understood that people could be guaranteed the right to *pursue* happiness, but could not, under any circumstances, be guaranteed its attainment. In fact, reading between Jefferson's lines, it follows that if someone tries to *make* someone else happy, they unwittingly disable that person's ability to engage successfully in the pursuit.

Jefferson was right. You cannot "make" self-esteem in a child's life. You can only create opportunity for its discovery. Growth in self-esteem takes place as the child realizes that despite initial anxieties, frustrations, fears, even failures, he is capable of standing on his own two feet and dealing squarely with the challenges of living. The road to that discovery is paved not by parents running ahead of the child, making sure he encounters nothing but positive experiences along the way, or by parents running behind the child, picking up after him, but by parents who have the courage and good common sense to "make" a good amount of reality in his life; most importantly, the realities that (1) you can't always get what you want, (2) you always learn the most valuable lessons of life the "hard way," and (3) you pick up after yourself.   (TT)

Parents who possess self-confidence project this attitude in four typical ways:

1. *They communicate their expectations in no uncertain terms.* When it comes to communicating expectations, many, if not most, parents either beat around the bush or beat on it. They plead, bribe, cajole, and "reason." When none of this accomplishes anything, they begin screaming threats of bodily harm. Self-confident parents, on the other hand, come straight to the point. Such a parent, for example, would *not* ask, "How about doing Mommy a favor by picking up these toys?" She would say, "It's time for you to pick up these toys."

2. *When the need for enforcement arises, they do so without brutality or bribery.* Self-confident parents accept that even the "best" child will misbehave; therefore, their children's misbehaviors don't pull the proverbial rug out from under them. Keeping one's "balance" in the face of misbehavior enables an even-handed, and therefore, truly powerful, response.

3. *They don't argue with their children.* A self-confident parent knows that a child cannot, even with the best of explanations, understand an adult point of view. Instead of trying to persuade the child that the adult point of view is more valid, he says something like, "If I was your age, I wouldn't like it either, but I've made the decision, and it stands" and walks away. That's nothing more, by the way, than an eighteen-word version of "Because I said so."

4. *When their children misbehave, self-confident parents make sure* those same children *get upset.* They, on the other hand, remain calm. They realize that only the penitent atone. They also understand that penance is not an inherent part of man's makeup; rather, it must be taught; first instilled, then evoked. Penance, furthermore, cannot be *talked* into a child. It must be *forced* in (albeit there's no reason for this force to be hurtful) using enough pressure to insure that it will take root. With some children, the force can usually be slight, but it is nonetheless *force*. With other children, only the force of the "boom" will do. (FV)

A completely, 100 percent obedient child never has existed, doesn't exist, and never will. Parents should expect a certain amount of disobedience from even the "best" of children, but wanton disobedience is a horse of a different color. Wanton disobedience is completely unnecessary. Occasional disobedience is normal; wanton disobedience is abnormal. Furthermore, whether parents are willing to admit it or not, wanton disobedience has little, if anything, to do with the child in question. I know, because my son, Eric, was at one time what I would describe as wantonly disobedient. For several years, I deluded myself into thinking there was something "wrong" with Eric. When I finally realized that Eric's problems were largely due to failures on my part (definitely more mine than Willie's, by the way) and saw that I was going to have to set myself straight before there was any hope of setting him straight, things began to turn around. One of my most glaring failures was a "failure to communicate." I was wishing he'd obey, I was constantly surprising him with instructions that came out of the proverbial blue, and worst of all, I expected him to disobey. Every time I gave him an instruction, I expected a negative reaction, and negative reactions were just about all I ever got.

There's no magic to this, folks. If you begin expecting a disobedient child to obey—communicating clearly, straightforwardly, matter-of-factly, in calm "no uncertain" terms—the child is not going to suddenly become little Mister or Miss "How Can I Help You, Dad?" This is going to take some time, but not long, really.   (FV)

There's a time for being a parent and a time—a much later time—for being a friend. You can't put the cart before the horse, nor can you put it alongside the horse. In this case, the horse is your authority and the cart is the potential for friendship contained within the relationship.

In trying to be both friend and parent, you will fail at both. When the exercise of authority causes your child to become unhappy with you, as it often will, you will worry that you are destroying the friendship. As a consequence, you will be unable to take and maintain a firm stance on any issue. As your child learns to take advantage of your attempts to be a friend, your frustration will drive behavior that is decidedly unfriendly. This will not only introduce conflict and confusion into the relationship, but will also saddle you with an almost constant burden of guilt. Under the circumstances, your child is likely to grow up either resenting you or manipulating you, neither of which forms the basis for an eventual friendship.

In short, the better a true parent you are during the first eighteen years or so of your child's life, the better friends you will later be. Put first things first. (TT)

For years the politically correct crowd has been claiming, without a shred of evidence, that toy guns somehow implant in the minds of the little boys who play with them that killing people in war is the highest of manly achievements, and that guns themselves are legitimate devices with which to solve all manner of conflicts. Parents actually believe this, and sales of toy guns are down considerably from what they were twenty-five years ago. No matter. Boys now fashion their pretend weapons of war out of tree branches and PVC pipe.

Several years past, feminists launched a campaign to have Barbie submit to breast-reduction surgery, claiming that her absurdly disproportionate figure causes little girls to internalize unrealistic ideas concerning the female form, thus leading to low self-esteem and eating disorders. Again, there is no evidence to support such claims, yet certain people believe they must be true. After all, almost every woman with poor self-esteem and/or an eating disorder played with Barbie when she was young. Proof! (NP)

By the mid-1970s, *nouveau* ideas concerning the politics of the parent-child relationship had become the "party line" within psychology and related professions. "Low self-esteem" became the standard explanation for nearly all problems of childhood. The implication behind this pseudo-diagnosis was that a problem child's parents were unenlightened throwbacks, needing parent "education." As this mythology became ever more widely accepted by lay and professional alike, so did the notion that traditional—call them old-fashioned—forms of discipline, even if they did not result in bruises, were harmful and therefore *de facto* forms of abuse. With the help of the media, the professional community succeeded in convincing significant numbers of Americans that whole previous generations of parents had controlled their children by means of psychologically destructive disciplinary techniques. At a wholesale level, parents of previous generations were made out to be villains who created "dysfunctional families" and rained abuse upon their children. That fiction was essential to the successful marketing of professional child-rearing advice. After all, if the child-rearing advice dispensed by "helping" professionals wasn't better than "Grandma's," why buy into it? So, psychologists and other mental health professionals created a *nouveau* philosophy of child rearing out of whole cloth, then used their credentials to discredit the philosophy that had successfully guided American parents for generations. How thoroughly dishonest! (SPNK)

The primary function of being a parent is that of distinguishing between what children truly need and what they simply want. This is akin to separating wheat from chaff, the necessary from the unnecessary. In this regard, it is interesting to note that the Hebrew word for "rod" as used in Proverbs 13:24 ("He who spares his rod, hates his son,/but he who loves him, disciplines him diligently") is also used in Isaiah 28:27 to suggest a relatively flimsy instrument used to thresh caraway, thus separating the useful part of the grain from that part which is of no use, while insuring—now, pay attention, folks—*that the useful part will not be damaged in the process.*

Children cannot "thresh" themselves. On their own, they cannot make the distinction between need and want. To a child, a state of need and a state of want feel exactly the same. In fact, children often express *want* more urgently than they express *need.* Take, for example, the child who acts as if obtaining the latest video-game cartridge is a matter of life and death, but must be constantly reminded to drink sufficient water on a scorchingly hot day. Because need and want are virtually synonymous—and therefore indistinguishable—to children, adults must make this vital distinction for them. Adults—parents primarily—must "draw the line" between need and want in every single area of a child's life.   (FV)

The foremost *obligation* of parenthood is that of giving children *all* they truly need along with a *small* amount of what they want. In other words, parents should take great care with the wheat while being relatively careless concerning the chaff.

I have often observed that today's parents seem to have no appreciation for the point of diminishing returns. They do not understand that simply because a child may indeed need a certain something, more of the same is not necessarily better. Children need food, for example, but it is not true that the more food children consume, the better off they are. In fact, too much food—as is the case with too much of any good thing—is harmful. Likewise, children need a certain amount of one-on-one attention from their parents, but too much parental attention prevents children from learning how to solve problems on their own, tolerate frustration, persevere in the face of adversity, and—in general terms—stand on their own two feet.

The fulfillment of this obligation gives a child a gift he can obtain in no other way, that being the gift of opportunity to figure certain things out for himself—how he's going to organize his time, occupy himself, solve academic and social problems, and so on. In the process of figuring things out for himself, the child learns to persevere and be resourceful, the two keys to success in any endeavor. When parents give excessively to a child, in whatever area, he not only doesn't have to figure anything out for himself, but is eventually rendered incapable of doing so. His parents, bless their big hearts, are figuring too much out for him. (FV)

The ultimate *purpose* of rearing a child is to help the child out of your life and into a life of his or her own. You read that right, but you better read it again, slowly, or you may make the same mistake a fellow in Lincoln, Nebraska, made several years ago.

After talking to several hundred parents in that midwestern city, I was approached by a man who said, "I liked that one about getting the child out of your life and into a life of his own."

"I didn't say that," I told him.

"You sure did!" he insisted.

"Nope. I said the ultimate purpose of rearing children is to *help* them out of our lives, not *get* them out."

"What's the difference?" he asked.

"The difference is everything," I answered. "It is every child's mission to get out of his parents' lives and into a life of his own. This mission begins asserting itself in the first year of life. After all, when a child first begins to crawl, he crawls *away from*, not toward, his parents. Later, when he learns to walk, then run, he runs *away from*, not toward, his parents. And so it goes. I'm simply saying it's our job to support this mission, to affirm its legitimacy and empower the child's ability to carry it out."

The "mission" is called emancipation, and emancipation is a process, not an event that spontaneously occurs in the late teens or early twenties. It's a parent's job to get behind the process and gently urge it along. Too many of today's parents, by contrast, are out in front of their children, sweeping the path clear of obstacle and adversity, frustration and failure. Bless their big hearts, they're only trying to make childhood a happy time for their kids.   (FV)

A behavior problem is not necessarily indicative of an emotional problem. All children, at one point in time or another, exhibit behavior problems. On the other hand, very few children have full-blown emotional problems. Another way of looking at this is to say that all children, because they are human—and humans are gifted/cursed (depending on your point of view) with emotions that are always a struggle to tame—have "emotional problems." But very few of these problems, or the behaviors that accompany them, are out of the ordinary. Most of them are just part of the struggle.

If you keep this in mind, you'll be more able to laugh at things other parents take all too seriously, like kids pooping in their pants, or telling you they hate you, or threatening to run away, or throwing up at the dinner table because you've served them broccoli, or letting the air out of your tires for an April Fool's joke. Ha, ha.   (PP)

Yesterday's parents saw to it that by age four, children had been inducted into full, contributory participation in their families. They accomplished this by assigning their children *routines* of chores that consumed blocks of time each and every day.

This work was expected of the child for immediate, practical reasons, yes, but the most important reasons behind it were far-reaching.

• First, participation in the work of the family *confirmed the child as a valued member of the family*. The more responsibility a child accepted, the more status he had in his parents' and siblings' eyes.

• Second, *the child learned the principle of reciprocity* (or, simply stated, give-and-take), which is the centerpiece of every workable social contract. This constituted the child's first experience with *social accountability*.

• Third, *chores enhanced the value of the family to the child*. They were a means, in fact, of bonding the child to the values that defined and enriched the family. The proof of this is in the proverbial pudding. Family values and traditions have been passed on most reliably from generation to generation in rural, farming areas of America. And the one thing, besides the smell of manure, that most distinguishes the upbringing of a farm-reared child from that of a child reared in a city or suburb is chores. Expecting children to do a meaningful amount of housework on a daily basis is essential, therefore, to creating, maintaining, and immortalizing *A Family of Value.* (FV)

April 3

Today's parents have been told that the more attention they pay their children, the more they do for them, the more "involved" they become in their lives, the better parents they are. That's not true.

Knowing that shock is the present state of many a reader, I'm going to share several facts. That's right, *facts*. Psychologists usually talk strictly in terms of theories that are supported by this or that study, blah, blah, blah, but not me! I'm going to give you the facts. And you will be convinced, I guar-an-tee it!

Fact: In the parent-child relationship, the *parent* is the teacher, primarily responsible for the child's social and spiritual education. If you don't think that's a fact, you are a hopeless case. Put this book down and go join a New Age cult. Don't even pass "Go."

Fact: A teacher cannot effectively teach unless the student is giving the teacher his or her undivided attention. If you have any doubts as to whether this is a fact, just ask a teacher.

Fact: A child will not pay sufficient attention to a parent who is acting as if it is his or her most pressing obligation to pay as much attention to and do as much for the child as possible. Please read that again, slowly and out loud. I'll wait.   (FV)

Actually, whether they're willing to admit it or not, all parents are dictators. The root word of *dictator* is *dictate*, which my dictionary (*The American Heritage Dictionary of the English Language, Third Edition*) defines thusly: "to prescribe with authority . . . to control or command." Isn't that what parents do? Furthermore, isn't that what parents are *supposed* to do? After all, if parents don't prescribe with authority, their prescriptions are going to be ignored. And if they don't stand ready to control when children are in danger of losing control and command when children need commanding, then children will surely run amok. Unfortunately, because it is no longer "psychologically correct" to be a dictator with one's children, a significant number of today's children *are* indeed running amok, in desperate need of parent-dictators who will rein them in.

It's true that dictators often abuse their power, but dictatorships are not necessarily evil. History is replete with examples of dictatorships that have been essential to the stability of certain cultures at certain points in time. A dictatorship is nothing more than a system of government where one person is in control and is responsible for making decisions for a group of people who count on him in order to make good ones. And that's what parents do, isn't it? Indeed, parents must be willing to give their children greater freedom and more choices as they grow older—even the freedom at times to make mistakes. But parents must always retain control of the decision to give those freedoms. Parents must never, as long as children are in their dependency, hand complete control of their lives over to them. Increasing degrees of independence must be given as a child matures, but given from a secure position of authority. It is the parents' right to give the child privilege and, likewise, their right to take it away. Within that framework, children learn the value of independence, not as something to be taken for granted, but as something to be worked for—and therefore something worth taking care of. You are the boss. For your children's sake. (PP)

A leading proponent of *nouveau* parenting, with whom I was sharing a podium in Detroit, said, "Children do not like being told what to do! We must give them choices so they learn to make good decisions!"

In the first place, no one *likes* being told what to do. It is, however, a sign of maturity that one *accepts* being told what to do by legitimate authority. The first authority children encounter is that of their parents. If they do not learn to accept their parents' authority, then when and how, I ask, do we expect them to ever fully accept any authority whatsoever?

Second, the fact that a child does not *like* something an adult does is no indication that the decision or action in question was wrong. Children will react with great distress to decisions that are clearly in their best interests, and with great glee to ones that just as clearly are not. The implication that parents must be *pleasing* to their children is subversive. The fact is, children should want to *please their parents*.

Third, children will, when the time comes, make good decisions if good decisions are made for them before that time. Children respect parents who take the bull by the horns. That respect enables them to slowly but surely internalize their parents' values, and it is a heritage of solid values—not a childhood full of "choices"—that makes for good decision-making as an adult.

Fourth, the job of parent is that of shepherding children into adulthood. This requires that within the workshop of childhood, parents help children assemble the values, understandings, and skills they will need to lead successful adult lives. In that regard, I am not aware of any workplace where employees are given a choice concerning when assignments are to be carried out. Nor am I aware of any law that allows U.S. citizens the option of obeying it later if one is not inclined to obey it now. If a child chooses between a jacket or a sweater in the morning, fine. But to let "choice" prevail in the child's life is irresponsible and morally reprehensible.   (FV)

There are four keys to parental success during early adolescence:
The first is understanding. Parents must realize that the needs of a child are changing radically during the early teen years. Socially, the peer group is becoming more important, both as a source of approval and a source of values. For better or worse, the young teen begins pulling away from family and identifying more with his own generation.

The second key is a combination of tolerance and accommodation. Tolerance because early adolescence is rarely permanent. Accommodation because the radical changes taking place during this critical developmental period necessitate equally radical changes in how parents respond to their children. Oftentimes, the child's accelerating need for freedom catches parents off guard, and they react by hanging vainly onto a style of child rearing that no longer works.

The third is communication. Parents must be willing to listen to this age child, even when he makes no sense; to listen to his fears, expressions of insecurity, hopes, ideas, and opinions; to listen to his many complaints—about friends who don't do right, clothes that don't look right, hair that won't lay right, and parents who are never right—and to reflect the majority of their moanings and groanings back to them in an accepting, nonjudgmental way.

The fourth is interest. There is no better antidote to the potential pitfalls of peer pressure than parents who are interested. Take the time to ask questions, to listen, to participate. It's one of the best investments you can make in your child's future.   (PP)

How can it be that today's children, for whom parents provide so much in the way of things and activities, are so constantly bored? Actually, the question answers itself. Today's children are bored precisely because parents provide them with so many things and activities.

Too many toys overwhelm a child's ability to make creative decisions. He can't decide what to do next because the clutter presents too many options. So he retreats from the chaos, saying, "I've got nuthin' to do."

The child's boredom also has a lot to do with the kinds of toys his parents buy. In most cases, today's toys are one-dimensional—a truck, a boat, a this, or a that. The singular nature of most mass-produced playthings limits a child's ability to express imagination and creativity, making boredom that much more likely.

What it boils down to is that, with the best of intentions, we've successfully prevented today's children from getting in touch with the "magical make-do" of childhood. For the most part, today's children don't know how to make-do. Why? Because they've never had to. Too much has been done for them, too much given to them. Through the magic of making-do, children exercise imagination, initiative, creativity, intelligence, resourcefulness, and self-reliance. In the process, they practice discovery and invention, which are the basics of science. Making-do is not only the essence of truly creative play, which is, in turn, the essence of childhood, it's also the story of the advancement of the human race. Throughout the parade of history, the art of making-do has been significant to nearly every important invention and nearly every famous discovery. Making-do, therefore, is at the heart of being human. (6PP)

April 8

One of my pet peeves is parents *who complain about their children's grades.* Look, folks, it's a fact that today's grades are already inflated. In other words, the likelihood is that your child has indeed received plenty of grades he didn't deserve. Most of these, however, were grades *better* that what he deserved. You don't go to the school and ask for those to be lowered, do you? No? Then don't ever again whine about a low grade not being "fair." If fairness was the issue, you'd be at that school nearly every week, demanding the teacher grade more strictly, pointing out that the disproportionate number of good grades she's handing out are giving your child unrealistic notions of how the real world works. (NP)

April 9

Some people think spankings of any sort constitute child abuse. I don't. Some parents *do* spank abusively, but then *any* form of discipline, even talking to a child, can be delivered destructively.

Other people think spankings are the most effective form of discipline there is. I don't agree with that either. In and of themselves, spankings do not motivate appropriate behavior. A spanking accompanied by a period of restriction or a short, sharp reprimand (or both) will have a much greater positive effect than a spanking alone.

A spanking serves as a reminder of parental authority and a demonstration of disapproval. But it's no substitute for more effective forms of discipline, verbal or otherwise. (6PP)

Children must be attended to and money must be made. Nonetheless, wives can, and should, remain wives first and foremost, even after they become mothers. Likewise, husbands can, and should, remain husbands first and foremost, regardless of the demands of their careers. Mother, father, breadwinner—these are all secondary roles. Husband and wife are the primary adult roles in the family. If all of this is somewhat difficult to accept, it's only because the mother/breadwinner programs are demanding and insistent, so powerful and persuasive, that we succumb to them without thinking through the consequences.

The bad news is that many American families are in trouble because husbands and wives have lost touch with their primary commitments. The good news is that this problem is easier to fix than it is to live with. You can begin by giving your marriage some quality time. More, in fact, than you give your kids. Really!   (6PP)

Parents need to understand that sibling *conflict* and sibling *rivalry* are horses of entirely different colors. Sibling conflict is as inevitable as marital conflict. Like marital conflict, sibling conflict involves two people. Sibling rivalry, however, involves a third: a parent who believes it is his or her responsibility to "referee" the children's squabbles, thus helping them learn to be fair and get along with one another. But despite the parent's best intentions, all this "helping" has the ultimate effect of causing the children to compete for what I call the "Victim Award." The child who "wins" is always the child the parent designates as the victim—the child who was treated unjustly by the other sibling. As a consequence, the children learn that the way to get the parent's sympathies is to act like a victim. For every victim, there must be a villain. In this case, the child who is designated as such is angered at what he or she perceives as an injustice. The only way to discharge this anger is to retaliate—against the supposed victim. A vicious circle thus develops that drives a wedge into the sibling relationship and creates untold stress within the family. In most instances, therefore, I recommend a policy of nonintervention when it comes to sibling conflict. When intervention is necessary to restore peace to the family, parents should do so in ways that hold *both children equally responsible* for the disturbance. Reprimand them both, take away the object of contention, send them to their respective rooms (or some other neutral corners) for a time; regardless, take care not to confer the "Victim Award." No victim, no villain, no escalating struggle to see who can come out on the bottom. (FV)

April 12

With our children, Willie and I applied the "Ask them no questions, they'll tell you no lies" rule. If, for instance, I was fairly certain that Number-One-Son had put a hole in the wall, I would say, "Eric, for putting a hole in the wall, we're going to behead you. Do you have any last wishes?"

In other words, instead of asking the foolish question, "Did you put this hole in the wall?" I would make an authoritative statement. More often than not, the statement would include a consequence. Statements are assertive. As such, they are highly effective at preventing games of cat-and-mouse.

"Did you do this?" questions, because they are passive in nature, invite denial. And once the chase is on, the child is squarely in control of how long the chase lasts. This introduces a second, highly reinforcing element into the scenario—namely, power.

Sure, if you ask no questions, you might be wrong, but in all likelihood, you'll be right. As a parent, I found that my first intuitions about who-done-it were correct at least 95 percent of the time. The way I figured it, my being wrong 5 percent of the time was less harmful to my children than giving them opportunity after opportunity to practice pulling the wool over people's eyes, beginning with mine.

(6PP)

In other cultures and in other times, children have slept with their parents *only when there are/were no other options.* For instance, it would have been impractical, perhaps even deadly, for our prehistoric ancestors to hold out for nothing less than a two-bedroom cave. Nor does it make sense for nomadic people to lug two-bedroom tents from site to site, or Eskimos to waste valuable time and energy building two-bedroom igloos. Whenever and wherever you find parents and children sleeping together, it's almost always out of necessity rather than choice. Furthermore, the fact that a certain child-rearing practice was or is common to more primitive cultures does not automatically qualify the practice as either more "natural" or more healthy. To give one example: In certain African tribes, young girls are disfigured in a certain way (sorry, but I'm not going to be specific) to insure that they will never experience pleasure from sexual intercourse. In many cases, these children also sleep in the same areas, if not the same beds, as their parents. Get my point?   (6PP)

April 14

A family is structured somewhat like a solar system, which is, in a sense, a galactic "cell." At the center of a solar system, there is a source of energy that nurtures and stabilizes the system. Around this central core revolves a number of planets in various stages of "maturity."

Likewise, a family needs a powerful, stabilizing, and nurturing source of energy at its center. The only people who are qualified to sit in that position of power and responsibility are parents. Their job is to define, organize, lead, nurture, and sustain the family.

Children are the "planets" in the system. When they are very young, they orbit close to the parent-sun because they need lots of nurturing and guidance. As they grow, their orbits increase steadily in diameter so that by their late teens or early twenties, they should be capable of escaping the pull of their parents' "gravity" and embarking upon lives of their own. Our children's ultimate task is to move away from us, and our task is to help them. Allowing a child to bask in the spotlight of attention, however, encumbers the child's ability to establish greater and greater degrees of independence. A child cannot be the center of attention in a family and move away from the center at the same time. It's either one or the other.   (6PP)

April 15

Her eight-year-old daughter, the mother told me with great concern, had recently thrown a tantrum over not getting her way about something, the child eventually getting so carried away she seemed unable to stop. The father favored a stern approach. He wanted to send the child to her room and take away a privilege or two in order to let her know that such behavior would not be tolerated. The mother favored an understanding approach. She wanted to hold her daughter on her lap and help her calm down. She had no intention of giving in, but felt confinement and punishment were unnecessary. The father thought this would "reward" the tantrum, but Mom prevailed.

"What should we have done?" she asked, worried that she had made a mistake.

Actually, as I told her, neither approach was more "correct" than the other. The problem was the parental conflict over discipline, which was apparently recurrent. The older I get, the more convinced I become that these conflicts reflect personality differences that are permanent. It is generally unrealistic, therefore, to expect that one of the participants is going to come over to "the other side." Furthermore, in most cases (and there are certainly exceptions to the following), either disciplinary approach will accomplish something the other will not. In other words, neither is perfect, but either is fine. The parental conflict needs to be quickly resolved from situation to situation, and can be by borrowing the "possession rule" from organized basketball: Simply decide in advance who's going to make the call the next time there's a difference of opinion concerning some disciplinary matter, and take turns making the call from that point on. In so doing, the child receives the benefits of both disciplinary styles. And two heads are always better than one.   (NP)

Some friends of mine, both of whom have careers, also have two school-age children. After school, the kids are transported to a day-care center, where they stay until shortly after five o'clock, when their father picks them up and takes them home.

Several years ago, my friends created a rather unusual rule: For thirty minutes after everyone gets home, the children are not allowed in the den, kitchen, or any other room where their parents happen to be. They can play in their rooms or, weather permitting, go outside. The parents take this time to unwind and talk as they prepare the evening meal.

Until they created the thirty-minute rule, my friends had felt obligated to devote themselves to their children through the entire evening. The more attention they gave the children, however, the more petulant and disobedient the children became. Eventually, and not a moment too soon, my friends realized that the kids had taken over the family. In pursuit of good parenting, they'd created a monster!

Realizing that their relationship with one another was more important that their relationship with their children, they moved their marriage back to center-stage in the family. The thirty-minute rule was one of many major policy changes.

Today, I would describe these children as independent, secure, outgoing, happy, mature, playful, obedient, polite . . . need I go on? Their parents cured them of their addiction to attention by putting the marriage first. In so doing, they defied a whole set of "shoulds" that operate in many, if not most, dual-career families.   (6PP)

April 17

It's almost inevitable that when I say traditional child rearing works as well today as it did years ago, someone will challenge me by saying that "times have changed." They mean, of course, that the world is not the same world it was for our parents and grandparents, etc.; therefore, it is naively unrealistic of me to propose that children can be reared as successfully using their attitudes and methods.

The fact is, times have always changed. Ours, however, is the first generation of parents to have introduced dramatic change into America's child-rearing practices. My grandparents were born in the late nineteenth century. Although the world changed more dramatically for them during the first thirty years of their lives than it did, relatively speaking, during the first thirty years of mine, they were reared traditionally, and they reared my parents traditionally. Likewise, change was more sweeping during the first thirty years of my parents' lives—one was born in 1919, the other in 1924—than during the first thirty years of mine. Nonetheless, they reared me pretty much the way they themselves had been reared. Up until the present generation, there was not only continuity from generation to generation concerning the rearing of children, but there was also consensus. Most everyone agreed as to the nature of the task and how to best perform it. There were minor controversies, but the operative word is minor. Today, both that continuity and that consensus have been broken, and there is no historical basis upon which to rest the argument that this has happened because "times have changed." It has happened because we became persuaded that traditional child rearing was bad and mental health professionals knew more about children than Grandma. With stars in our eyes, we veered off course, and everything suffers as a consequence. Restoring the values and traditions that once strengthened the American family and formed the foundation of our culture must become our national priority. Without that strong foundation, change quickly deteriorates into chaos.

(TOH)

By age three, a child has arrived at one of two intuitive conclusions concerning his or her parents:

Conclusion A: "My parents are here, primarily speaking, to be paid attention to *by me*."

Conclusion B: "My parents are here, quite obviously, to pay attention *to* me."

In the mind of a child, it is either the one or the other. It cannot be both. A child cannot hold Conclusion A one minute, and Conclusion B the next. And let me assure you, if the child arrives at Conclusion B, *discipline will be a major hassle.*

Discipline is the process by which parents make *disciples* of their children. A disciple is one who will follow the lead of the teacher, a source of legitimate authority. The fact is, you cannot expect your child to follow your lead if you have not first convinced your child that you, his parent or parents, are in his life to be paid attention to *by* him rather than the other way around.

Furthermore, *the conclusion the child arrives at has nothing whatsoever to do with the child.* In other words, whether or not your child pays adequate attention to you is 100 percent up to *you*.   (FV)

If children never lost control, they would hardly need parents. There are times when a child's loss of control can be ignored—as when the child becomes furious at a block tower that keeps falling over—and there are times when, even though the loss of control cannot be ignored, it can be dealt with patiently—as in sending a child to his room until a fit of hysterical laughing has subsided. But then there are misbehaviors that cannot be ignored, that unless "nipped in the bud" will only get worse. One cannot afford patience when it comes to disrespect, defiance, tantrums, and antisocial behavior. The child must know that these behaviors will not, under any circumstances, be tolerated, not because they are threatening to the parent, but because they threaten the child's ultimate *ability to succeed*. After all, whether the challenge is social, marital, professional, spiritual, political, or economic, true success comes to those who respect authority as well as their fellow man, know when and how to obey as well as when and how to lead, and are in control of themselves.

(SPNK)

There are those who, having been smitten by idealistic, romanticized notions concerning children and child rearing, naively believe that children will grow properly if left pretty much to their own devices. These parents fail to exercise sufficient force. They are lackadaisical, permissive, wishy-washy. Then there are those who exercise *too much* force, who push rather than guide. They are addicted to the ego-satisfaction of having "respectful," subservient children. When their children fail to satisfy their egos, they are likely to become enraged and threatening. Unfortunately, because they miss the point, their "rule" is nothing but superficial. Because these parents don't know how to *command* their children's attention, they wind up constantly *demanding* it. Their children comply subserviently in order to avoid punishment, but are never genuinely *obedient* in the sense of wanting, out of love, to please. This is nothing short of tragic, for a child who is not properly guided by his parents toward wanting to please them arrives at adulthood without precedent for wanting to please God. It's not that he will never be able to make that choice, but the decision, difficult to begin with, will be considerably more arduous. (FV)

April 21

Q: *My thirteen-year-old son ignores me, sasses me, refuses to do what he is told, and refuses to cooperate in any punishment I levy. I would have to literally fight him to get him to his room, and I'd have to hold the door to keep him there. My husband, whom Daniel obeys without question, travels through the week. I don't like a "wait till your father gets home" approach, because even though he doesn't seem to mind, I don't want to make my husband the heavy. What should I do?*

A: I'd recommend you go right ahead and make your husband the heavy. In the first place, you obviously need his support in order to solve this problem, and he obviously doesn't mind giving it. Furthermore, it will profit Daniel greatly to know his parents are in complete accord on the matter of his discipline. My experience as the father of a boy who was 9.5 on the strong-willed scale led me to conclude that the successful discipline of the average male child requires a strong male hand, especially during adolescence.

My plan is simple and my experience leads me to assure you that if you are consistent, you will solve this problem in no time at all. Whenever Daniel (a) addresses you disrespectfully, (b) ignores you, (c) defies an instruction, or (d) does anything to annoy you, tell him he has a choice: He can either go to his room for one hour, or he can refuse. In the latter case, or if he goes to his room but does not remain for one full hour, you will not make any attempt whatsoever to make him serve his punishment. Rather, you will simply tell his father when he returns from that week's trip, in which case his father will enforce much worse punishments on the weekend (i.e., complete restriction).

The success of this plan depends on your nonchalant consistency. In short, you must never threaten, warn, or otherwise waffle. This is known as being "mean," which children think their parents are when they discover their parents *mean* exactly what they say.   (BHG)

April 22

No question about it, the peer group exerts great influence on teenagers. From the way they dress to the way they carry their books, the stamp of peer pressure is upon them. If the influence is positive, parents can breathe easy. But what if the influence isn't so positive? What should parents do then?

Just knowing when to intervene in your child's social life is hard enough because many of the variables are intangible. There are the concrete facts, and then there are your intuitions, you biases, and your protectiveness, not to mention your ego. Sound confusing? It is!

These four rules of thumb will give you some direction:

First, be willing to let your teenager make mistakes. Don't forget children can't grow up unless parents let go.

Adolescence is a time of social experimentation. As such, we must accept that our children may not make the social choices we would make for them. In some cases, there may even be merit to letting a child make some social decisions you *know* aren't going to turn out well. There's a lot of truth to the idea that the most valuable lessons in life are those learned the hard way.

Second, hold your child responsible for his or her own behavior. Don't even entertain the idea that your child can do wrong only as a result of someone else's bad influence. Children won't accept responsibility for their behavior unless parents hold them responsible, regardless of who or what may have influenced them.

Third, don't ever force or manipulate a child toward choosing certain companions. This almost always ends in disaster (see Shakespeare, *Romeo and Juliet,* for a historical perspective on this issue). The greatest danger is that the youngster will rebel and take his friendships "underground."

Finally, don't pull rank unless you must in order to protect your child's safety and well-being. Given a little time, some potentially bad situations work *themselves* out. (BHG)

Let's say your second-grade son polls his classmates and discovers his bedtime—8:30—is the earliest in the class. He comes home and demands to know why he must go to bed so early. If you're like most parents, you will try at this point to *sell* your son on the idea that an 8:30 bedtime is to his benefit. As salespeople know, if you want to sell something to someone, you must describe the benefit to them of buying the something in question. In effect, you become a salesperson. You say, "Well, I know you think it's early, but when you stay up later than 8:30, it's hard to get you up and going in the morning, and you're generally too groggy to eat your breakfast, and you go to school without proper nourishment, and that's when I'm most likely to get a note from your teacher saying you didn't finish your work, or you weren't paying attention, or something. So, most precious light of my life, I put you to bed at 8:30 *for your own good.*"

Get real! You don't put your most precious to bed at 8:30 because *he* needs his sleep. You put him to bed at 8:30 because *you need for him to sleep.* You *desperately* need for him to sleep. You are over being a parent at 8:30. There is every reason to believe that if you changed his bedtime to 9:30, he would make the adjustment in less than a week, and his schoolwork, in the long run, would not suffer. So what?! You want him in bed at 8:30, so 8:30 it is. The truth, therefore, is your son's bedtime is for *your* benefit. It's because *you* say so! Period. (FV)

Several months ago, a mother approached me after a speaking engagement in Florida. She was worried, she said, because her eleven-year-old daughter was always happy. That's what she said! Nothing seemed to bother this little girl. She was a happy-go-lucky kid who let troubles and discord roll right off her back. That just didn't seem right to her mother. She was worried that her daughter might be "out of touch with her real feelings" and went on to express concern that her daughter (a) might have interpreted some unspecified something the parents had said or done to mean that negative feelings were a family taboo, (b) felt responsible for the happiness of the entire family, (c) was "in denial" about some thing or things that were truly bothering her, or (d) all of the above.

The reader may think this mother to be irrational or, at best, silly, but I don't think so. I think she merely reflects what "expert advice" has done to the typical parent—those, at least, who care enough to consume it. Her anxiety asks how a parent can retain a rational perspective concerning his or her child(ren) while operating from within a body of absurd, anxiety-arousing understandings concerning children, childhood, and child rearing that has babbled forth from the professional community over the last generation or so. Parent-babble has obfuscated rather than clarified the process of child rearing; it has replaced the realities of child rearing with a rhetoric of "parenting"; and it has demonized the traditional family unit and traditional family values. But worse of all, it has effectively deprived many a child of parents who are able to see the forest for the trees and act with compelling confidence in themselves. That apparently matters little to an eleven-year-old girl in Florida, but to the average child, it means everything. (NP)

Q: *What should teenagers be doing in their free time?*

A: There is no formula. "A variety of things" is probably the closest one can come to an answer. It's an almost sure sign of trouble when a teenager seems obsessed with doing only one thing, whether the thing is listening to rock music, hanging out at the mall, or doing homework. Well-adjusted teens spread their focus wide to encompass a variety of interests and activities. The well-rounded teen strikes a balance between activities that are adult-directed (clubs, scouts, church youth groups), those that involve only peers (going to movies, parties, ball games), and those that are solitary (hobbies, reading, listening to music).

Q: *Is it all right for parents to occasionally allow a teen to do "unproductive" things, like wander through the mall or just ride around in a car?*

A: These need not become major issues as long as they are but one or two of many ways a teen uses spare time. "Aimless" doesn't necessarily mean harmful, but these sorts of things should constitute but a minor part of the teen's total activity picture. When aimlessness is the rule, that probably spells boredom, and boredom during the teen years can lead quickly to all kinds of trouble, including drugs. Parents who see boredom developing in a teenager should take the initiative to guide the youngster into some productive extracurricular activities. (BHG)

Parents are sadly mistaken if they think television is a good way of keeping children occupied. The more a young child watches television, the more likely it is that the child will eventually come to depend upon it as a primary source of occupation and entertainment. Every dependency encumbers the growth of self-reliance. The young child who becomes dependent upon television will, when the television is off, seek to satisfy that dependency in other ways. Predictably, he will try to transfer it to the next most available and receptive object/person, and Mom is usually right up there at the top of the list.

A vicious cycle quickly develops. The more the child watches television, the more television pacifies his initiative, resourcefulness, imagination, and creativity. When the television is off, instead of finding something with which to entertain himself, he looks for Mom to take over where the television left off. He complains of being bored, he whines for Mom to find something for him to do, he demands that she become his playmate. Partly out of fear that the child will interpret a firm "no" as rejection, Mom initially cooperates with these complaints and demands. But when it becomes obvious that her child can't get enough of her, Mom begins looking for an excuse to let him watch television.

In short order, the child becomes addicted to watching television, and Mom becomes addicted to letting him watch. (6PP)

To illustrate the importance of consistency, consider the job of basketball referee: The referee's job is to simply enforce the rules, consistently and dispassionately. Imagine the chaos that would result if nearly every time a rule was broken, the referee complained, threatened, gave second chances, and vented his self-generated frustrations by launching into a red-faced emotional tirade.

This description, sad to say, typifies the disciplinary "tone" of many an American family. Children test rules, and parents threaten, berate, plead, and complain, all the while becoming increasingly frustrated. Finally, they melt down in spasms of exasperation. For a while, all's quiet. Then, slowly, the children come out of "hiding" and once again, the snowball begins its downhill descent.

Parents who truly expect obedience from children discipline consistently and dispassionately, like a good referee. Consequently, discipline never becomes a "Big Deal," something parents find themselves constantly stumbling over. A matter-of-fact attitude toward discipline creates a calm, relaxed atmosphere in which everyone's "place" is clear. This allows life within a family to be simple, as it should be. (6PP)

The reader might ask, "What is the secret to *commanding* a child's attention?"

Good question! The answer: Always *pretend* that you know exactly what you're doing.

That's right, *pretend*. After all, you cannot always know what you are doing. In fact, you can only know exactly what you are doing if you possess the ability to tell the future with unerring accuracy, which you don't. This same pose must be adopted by none other than the president of the United States—if he wants to effectively lead, that is. Being merely human, the president cannot know all there is to know about any given issue, nor can he predict the future. He must, therefore, hope that he is making, if not the best decision possible, then one that is good enough. Regardless, he must always *pretend* that he is making any given decision with complete, unwavering confidence in its outcome. If the president succeeds at so pretending, then the majority of American people will have confidence in his decisions and will, more often than not, follow his lead *even if they do not completely agree with him*.

All this is true of parents and their relationships with their children. Parents cannot always know exactly what they are doing, so they must *pretend* to know. Parenting, in short, is an act, and good parents are good actors. Those parents who succeed at being good actors inspire their children's confidence. Because they *command* their children's attention, their children follow their lead. We say about these children that they are "well disciplined." Like good disciples, they "look up" to their parents. Likewise, parents who vacillate, hedge, or are otherwise indecisive fail to *command*, and their children end up not following their lead. And so, dear reader, the bottom line is this: The misbehavior of a child has less to do with the child— much less!—than with the child's parents. (FV)

April 29

Parents who constantly bend over backward for their children eventually fall over backward. Parents who constantly go out of their way for their children eventually lose their way. Parents who always put their children first should not be surprised to eventually find that their children put them last. (DGP)

The facts are these:

• You cannot run constant interference for a child and then expect that as an adult, he will be able to successfully anticipate and deal with life's problems. (And isn't life full of them?)

• You cannot pursue happiness for a child for the entirety of his childhood and then expect that he will be able to successfully pursue it on his own as an adult. Child rearing may not be hard, but it does require a certain amount of hardheadedness.

Summing it up: The opportunity to figure things out, which accrues courtesy of parents who meet all of a child's needs and deny most of his wants, endows a child with incredible self-sufficiency, which is the true essence of self-esteem, which energizes the ability to succeed where others will fail for lack of resourcefulness and purpose. It can't be any simpler. (FV)

When my mother bought Dr. Benjamin Spock's *Pocket Book of Baby and Child Care,* it was one of two available child-rearing manuals. There are now thousands, with more soon to come. Is there any tangible evidence whatsoever that American parents—even if we consider only those who consume this verbiage—are rearing children better than did our parents and grandparents?

I don't think so. In fact, I've asked this same question of numerous audiences, and not one person has indicated that they think otherwise. When I ask, as a follow-up, "Is there hard evidence that psychological advice concerning the rearing of children has been counterproductive?" heads go up and down vigorously and there are shouts of "yes!" I can appreciate that many "helping" professionals want to believe, as I once did, that they are apostles sent out from academia to spread the miraculous gospel of *nouveau* parenting, but American parents are beginning to turn deaf ears. Hallelujah!

(TOH)

There are two entirely different ways of "going before" one's children. The first is to claim one's legitimate authority as a parent and *lead*. The consequence of this is that the children will follow. They become the parent's *disciples*, in the truest sense of the term, in which case discipline becomes a naturally exercised, inherent aspect of the parent-child relationship and will never be a big deal. The second way of going before is to run interference. The consequence of this is that one's children have no reason to follow. Rather, they have every reason to sit on their duffs and wait for the parent to solve their problems. They become demanding, whining, petulant little people who are generally irritating to be around, which is most "unfair," since they had no say whatsoever in the matter. (NP)

Once upon a time, not so long ago, the "Three R's" of Parenting—Respect, Responsibility, and Resourcefulness—were the standards of good child rearing. Parents were not measured by the grades their children earned in school. Everyone knew that a child possessed of the "Three R's" would do his or her best in school, and that was sufficient. Neither were parents measured in terms of how exhausted they made themselves in the course of driving their children from one after-school activity to another. In fact, parents were not supposed to do much of that sort of thing at all. For the most part, children were to come home from school, change their clothes, and find something to do. Their parents were not to find the something for them. Nor were parents measured in terms of how *involved* they became in such things as their children's homework. Children were to do their own homework, as they were to find their own after-school occupation, as they were to fight their own battles, as they were to stew in their own juices, as they were to lie in the beds they made, and so on. Parents of generations past were measured against the standard of the "Three R's." If, as a parent during those times, you had succeeded in the eyes of your peers at endowing your children with adequate amounts of each "R"—and whether you had succeeded or not was self-evident—your child-rearing skills would have been held in high esteem. Your friends and neighbors, therefore, would have said you "were doing a good job." Whether your child grew up to become a doctor or a janitor was secondary to the fact that your good child rearing had all but guaranteed that whatever path he chose to walk, he would be an asset to the community.   (FV)

Parents are obligated to rear children such that they slowly but surely learn to deal successfully with certain realities concerning frustration:

• *Reality Number One:* Frustration is part and parcel of every life. We experience frustration in response to not only our own limitations, but also the limitations other people and circumstances impose upon us.

• *Reality Number Two:* Through experience with frustration, one eventually develops a tolerance for it. People who learn to tolerate frustration are able to turn adversity into challenge and persevere in the face of it.

• *Reality Number Three:* Perseverance, that all-important, "if at first you don't succeed, try and try again" attitude toward life, is the primary quality in *every* success story.

Note that these three realities, which culminate in success, take place because of, not in spite of, frustration. Conclusion: If you want your children to become successful in their work, their play, their interpersonal relationships, and their feelings toward themselves, you are obligated to frustrate them. If you aren't doing so already, you can begin by giving your children frequent doses of "vitamin N," which is none other than the most character-building two-letter word in the English language. (6PP)

May 5

Conservatism in parenting has nothing to do with lots of rules, restrictions, and punishment.

A conservative parent has abiding faith in a child's ability to govern himself. Such a parent also realizes, nonetheless, that an "internship" of a certain length is required before such an ability is sufficiently mature. During this internship, the child is patiently taught the parents' expectations. Once they've been learned, the child is given an increasingly long rope, but always with the understanding that he'd better not ever yank on its end.

It is liberals, not conservatives, who believe in the perpetual power of regulation and social engineering. Conservatives deregulate. Along those same lines, a liberal parent is one who believes the more parenting—as measured by rules, discipline, attention, and involvement—the better. By contrast, truly conservative parents are minimalists when it comes to necessary regulation and dispense with it as quickly as possible.

In a business setting, this management style is known as "Management by Wandering Around." As it applies to children, I call it "Parenting by Wandering Around." In that regard, my wife and I used to say to our children, "Please don't make us be parents." This simply meant that if they conducted themselves responsibly at home, at school, and in the community, we would stay off their backs.

Our children enjoyed a lot of freedom. By age sixteen, in fact, they enjoyed more freedom than just about anyone in their peer groups. But along with that freedom came an equal amount of responsibility. By their mid-teens, for example, our kids set their own curfews. If one of them set it at one A.M., we expected him/her home no later than one A.M., and I cannot recall that either of them ever let us down. In this and numerous other ways, we made the transition (and relatively early on) from rules to commitments, from toeing the line to trust. (NP)

All too often, after a remarriage takes place, everyone continues to cling to old habits which, unfortunately, no longer work. The mother has difficulty moving out of a primary relationship with her children and into a primary relationship with her spouse. As a result, the stepfather begins to feel like a "third wheel."

Making matters worse is the fact that the stepfather's need to shift gears from "good buddy" to parent causes everyone anxiety, confusion, and even anger. He attempts to discipline, and the children run to their mother, complaining that he's being "mean." She, in turn, responds protectively, accusing him of overreacting and/or taking his "jealousy" out on the kids. And 'round and 'round they start to go and where and when they're gonna stop, heaven only knows. This, I think, is why second marriages, especially when there are children involved, have *less* of a chance of succeeding than first marriages.

All this can be avoided, or at least minimized, if people planning stepfamilies/blended families will, above all else, remember two things:

First, the marriage must be the most important relationship in the family. Stepfamilies are no different from other families in this respect.

Second, the stepparent must have authority equal to that of the natural parent. This means, of course, that the natural parent must be willing to share authority equally with his or her new spouse.

Lastly, remember that an ounce of prevention is always better than a pound of cure. Anticipate these problems and discuss just exactly what you're going to do to avoid them, as well as how you're going to handle them if and when they do come up.   (6PP)

Children do not require a lot of attention. Let me help you digest this bit of news by talking for a moment about children and food:

Children need food. But they don't need a lot of it. If you persist in giving a child more food than he or she needs, the child will become *dependent* upon continuing to receive excessive amounts of food. If you continue to feed that dependency, it will grow into an *obsession* that will function as a powerful, driving force in that child's life. The child's sense of well-being will lean increasingly on the idea that in order to feel secure, he must have ready access to food. Eventually, the child will become a food-aholic, and that addiction will hang like a stone around the child's neck, encumbering the growth of self-esteem.

Now go back and reread the previous paragraph, substituting the word "attention" wherever you see the word "food." Go ahead, I'll wait.

Done? Quite revealing, isn't it? You see, it is as absurd to say that children need a lot of attention as it is to say that children need a lot of food. Too much attention is every bit as damaging as too much food. No one would argue that it is part of our job as parents to set limits on how much food a child may consume. It follows, therefore, that it's also part of our job to set limits on how much attention a child is allowed to consume within a family. (6PP)

May 8

Allow me to address a patently ludicrous myth that originated some years back from within professional circles. I'm talking about the belief that confining a child to his room and/or sending him to bed early will cause him to develop "negative feelings" about his room and his bed, and that as a result he will start having nightmares and all sorts of low-self-esteem-related maladies. There is, let me assure, no support for this invention, which qualifies as late-twentieth-century folklore. It's an example of the highly nonscientific ideas "helping" professionals sometimes spin from whole cloth. It's also a testament to the power such professionals have attained in our culture that they can propose something that on its face is nothing but dumb but nonetheless persuade significant numbers of people to take it seriously. (FV)

May 9

Three-year-olds are able to participate in group activities and take turns with play materials, but spontaneous sharing is still rare. For some threes, especially young ones, even learning to take turns continues to be a real problem. Helping a three-year-old (or even an older two-year-old) over this hurdle requires no more than a kitchen timer and some firm, yet loving direction.

Take two children who are playing together but having difficulty with give-and-take over some particularly interesting toy. With kitchen timer in hand, the supervising adult should say, "We're going to use this timer to help you learn to take turns with that toy. I'm setting it for (three minutes initially, gradually increasing the time to five minutes). Billy, you can play with the toy until the bell rings, then I'll set the timer again, and Robbie can play with it until the bell rings."

This simple technique provides the structure these children need to take turns. In most cases, once the toy has alternated hands a few times, the timer will no longer be needed (until the next conflict arises, that is). (TT)

Let's say you begin misbehaving in your job—you start coming in late for work, you take too many breaks, and you're consistently behind schedule with the work you're supposed to do. Does your supervisor finally get fed up enough with you to say, "Okay, okay! I'll tell you what: If you'll do the job you're supposed to do this week, and do it well, I'll take you out and buy you a new car!" Not likely. He's probably going to take you into his office and say, "I can no longer tolerate your misbehavior. As a result, I'm writing you up. If you continue to misbehave, I'll have no choice but to terminate you." In other words, he *threatens your standard of living.* Everyone is motivated to protect and improve their standard of living. Once you become accustomed to a certain standard of living, you don't want to lose it. Children are the same as everyone else. They are also motivated to protect and improve their standards of living. Adults measure their standards of living in terms of purchasing power; Children measure *theirs* in terms of privilege—how often they can go outside, how far they can venture unsupervised, how often friends can come over, how much television they can watch, and how late they can stay up. Threatening a child's standard of living is central to the *Godfather Principle.* Borrowed from the late Sicilian philosopher Don Corleone, it states that in order to motivate someone to do what he or she is supposed to do, you must "make 'em an offer they can't refuse." For comic relief, I make it sound sinister, but it's really not. It's simply the way the real world works. And if it's the job of big people to equip children with the skills they will need to successfully negotiate the real world, then it's our job to describe that world to them in accurate terms.   (EHH)

Today's mother has been told she is a "good mother" to the degree she pays attention to her children, does things for them, and gets "involved" in the things they do. This is the *nouveau* standard to which mothers aspire, and over which they compete for the "Who's the Busiest, and Therefore Best, Mother on the Block Award." If Mrs. Jones is driving her kids to an after-school activity every day of the week and on Saturday mornings, and Mrs. Smith is only driving her kids to activities three afternoons a week, Mrs. Smith better get on the ball. Mrs. Jones is "out-mothering" her.

Today's mother doesn't think she has permission to sternly tell her children they're "underfoot" and need to "leave her alone." She believes she is there to serve. Unfortunately, children aren't skilled at give and take. In fact, if you let them, they will do nothing but take. So the more Mom serves, the more of her they want for reasons that are increasingly whimsical. Finally, at the end of her psychic tether, she begins ranting and raving. Then she feels guilty. And the only way to cleanse the guilt, of course, is to serve. Today's mother has been drained of the courage to inform her children that she's more than a mother. She's become a two-dimensional cardboard cutout with a sign around her neck that reads: *I'm Your Mother. How May I Serve You?* And she's so *involved!* That's the crux of the parent-game today. Get involved in your children's after-school activities, today's mother is told. Get involved in your children's schoolwork. Get involved in their friendships and the things they like to do. Get involved in an exercise program with your kids. Find a hobby you and your kids can share. The more involved you are, today's mother is told, the better a mother you are. Why, if you get involved enough, you qualify as a Miracle-Mom!　　　　　　　　　　　　　　(FV)

Every time a teacher reinforces the absolutely absurd notion that a high IQ is "where it's at," she shoots her entire profession in the proverbial foot.

In fact, teachers *do* know better. At one point in the workshops I do for teachers, I ask that anyone who *disagrees* with the following statement to raise a hand: "You would rather teach a child with IQ 95 who is respectful, responsible, and resourceful than a child with IQ 165 who is deficient in those character traits." We're talking about a seventy-point difference in IQ, folks, the difference between a kid whose general ability is slightly below-average and a so-called genius! I conduct about forty teacher workshops a year. Not one teacher has ever raised a hand in response to that statement.

The "Three R's" of Respect, Responsibility, and Resourcefulness are "where it's at," not IQ. Properly developed, they are the essence of true self-esteem and the elixir of success, whether academic, social, personal, spiritual, emotional, vocational, avocational, marital, or . . . have I left anything out?

The "Three R's" define the truly *educable* child. A child who has learned to respect his parents will transfer that respect to teachers. A responsible child, one who comes from a home environment in which he is held responsible not just for his own behavior but also for a daily routine of chores (contributed, not paid for), will come to school that much more willing to accept assignment from his teachers and do his best. A resourceful child, one who has learned to do a lot with but a little, will come to school prepared to try and try again until he succeeds, to persevere in the face of frustration. The "Three R's" add up to learning, folks. Without the "Three R's," a high IQ adds up to nothing.   (NP)

The problem of the child who is supposedly "bored" in school has two sides to it. On one hand, you've got the child who's never had to work for anything and whose parents have handed things to him on a silver platter, who comes to school completely unprepared to set goals and work toward them. He thinks the teacher should be an extension of his parents and do things for him. When she doesn't, he's bored, meaning, he doesn't know how to do for himself. On the other hand, you have parents who use the "my child is bored" excuse to absolve themselves and their kids of responsibility for poor school performance and classroom behavior problems.

Here's this child whose parents have given him everything he ever wanted, never set consistent limits for him at home, and never expected him to lift a finger around the house. All of his life, adults have done things for him. They've seen to his entertainment, they've put him at the center of attention in the family, they've always made sure he had something to do, they've been chauffeurs, and to top it off, they've solved every problem he's ever had. He comes to school, and he's not the center of attention, and suddenly he's bored.

And then his parents have the gall to come to school and complain that his teachers aren't challenging him enough. Ha! If they'd make him act responsibly at home and support the teachers' efforts to make him responsible at school, he'd stop being "bored" in no time at all.

In a nutshell, today's child comes to school expecting to be entertained, thinking an education is something given rather than something one gets through hard work. When his expectations aren't met, he begins to lose interest. So, what we're calling bored is what previous generations would have called spoiled.   (NP)

If, when your child forgets his lunch money, you run after the bus, your child has no reason to ever remember his lunch money. If, when your child does something "bad," *you* feel bad about it—as in, you feel guilty, anxious, and otherwise in a tizzy—your child has no reason to feel bad about it himself and no reason, therefore, to correct the problem. The fact is, a child will correct a problem (and mind you, there are very few academic or behavior problems a child is incapable of solving) if, and only if, the problem inconveniences *him* and *he* is made to feel bad about it. If, in the above example, the parent waves good-bye to the bus and shrugs her shoulders when the child complains of having to go without lunch that day, the child will start remembering his lunch money. His "forgetfulness" or Attention Deficit Disorder or whatever will suddenly go into remission.

(DGP)

All children can be counted on to throw tantrums of one sort or another. For one thing, they come into the world unequipped with any tolerance for frustration. For another, their original point of view is self-centered. Whatever they want, they believe they deserve. Part of our job as parents is to slowly but surely help our children dismantle that self-centeredness and replace it with a sense of social responsibility—a willingness to put personal concerns aside for the sake of family, friendship, and society. It could, in fact, be said that this is a parent's most important function. It is the essence of the socialization process, and that process involves a certain amount of discomfort for the person being socialized. A child's natural reaction to that discomfort, that disillusionment, is a tantrum. Looked at from this perspective, a tantrum is a child's way of coming to grips with reality and thereby growing into a more mature understanding of how the world works. For this reason, I say that a child throwing a tantrum is simply "wrestling with reality." Helping a child come to terms with reality requires that parents learn to say "no" and say it with conviction.

I chuckle inside whenever I hear a parent complain that a certain child "can't take 'no' for an answer." I'm amused because the comment always says more about the parent than it does the child. You see, a child who can't take "no" for an answer always has parents who can't say it and prove they mean it. It's not that the child can't accept "no," it's that he has no reason to believe it.   (6PP)

May 16

I once suggested to an audience that the typical sixteen-year-old can and should be trusted to set his or her own curfew. A fairly irate parent (it so happened her teenage son was in the auditorium) countered that if teens were allowed such freedom, they'd get into "nothing but trouble."

What an unfortunate, not to mention counterproductive, belief! The facts: First, only a small minority of teenagers ever get into serious trouble. Nearly all of them make mistakes, but very few make big mistakes, and of those, even fewer keep on making them. Second, it isn't early curfews that keep teens out of trouble; rather, it's proper respect for one's parents and family. In other words, the only parents who truly need to worry about what their teens are doing under the cover of darkness are those who haven't succeeded at commanding their children's respect. If you respect your parents, you will try not to disappoint them. It's as simple as that. Third, it's been my experience that teens who are allowed to set their own curfews actually set quite reasonable ones. If you treat someone as if he or she is responsible, you are likely to get responsible behavior in return. Again, it's as simple as that. (TOH)

What most parenting "experts" don't understand is that if adults treat children as if their opinions and feelings are equal in importance to the opinions and feelings of adults, children will have no basis upon which to build respect for adults. In order for children to respect adults, adults must act wiser than children. That shouldn't be difficult. After all, with relatively few exceptions, adults *are* wiser than children. Not superior to children. Not *better* than children. Wiser. Less foolish. Hopefully.

So, being wiser, parents make the decisions; and being foolish, children should obey their parents. As children grow, their parents should allow them to make more and more decisions on their own. But who, pray tell, decides what decisions a child can make on his or her own? Why, the child's parents, that's who! (FV)

Since the early 1950s, the divorce rate in the United States has climbed steadily. Interestingly enough, it was in the early '50s that television invaded the American home and began dominating the life of the American family, especially in the evening. In your average American family, the television is on six hours a day, or forty-two hours a week. In a recent poll, couples married for one year were asked to identify their most prized household possession. Not surprisingly, most of the people in the survey named their televisions. These couples were also asked what single aspect of their marriage needed the greatest amount of improvement. Ironically, and sadly, the majority answered "communication."

Another recent study found that the average American couple engages in less than thirty minutes of meaningful, one-to-one conversation in a week's time. Each of those two people, however, is likely to spend more than twenty hours a week staring at a television set.

The language of television watching conceals its reality. People talk about watching television "together," but the two things—watching television and togetherness—are mutually exclusive. You can't watch television and truly communicate or be intimate at the same time. It's either one or the other. Ask yourselves, what's more important? (6PP)

Sleeping in his or her own bed helps establish that a child is an independent, autonomous individual. This facilitates identity formation, which begins during early toddlerhood and is critical to the eventual success of the emancipation process. In addition, the fact that parents sleep together and separate from the child helps the child understand that the marriage is the cornerstone and focal point of the family. This enhances the child's respect for his parents and lays the foundations of respect for other adults. When parents and child sleep together, the child may well draw the intuitive conclusion that the marriage is a threesome. My professional experience leads me to conclude that the "blendedness" inherent to this arrangement promotes an extended dependency, encumbers the child's ability to separate comfortably from parents, creates numerous problems with peer relationships, and delays overall maturity. For all these reasons, I say, "Children to their own beds at a reasonably early hour!" I would, however, under certain circumstances, not be opposed to breaking this rule. I have no problem, for example, with letting children come into their parents' beds during illness or periods of stress and/or transition, such as might follow the death of a pet or a move from one house to another. (PP)

When parents ask, "How can we know a worthwhile toy from one that's a waste of money?" I answer, "If a toy was in production before 1955, it's probably fine." With few exceptions, every toy manufactured since then has been nothing more than an attempt to re-invent an already-existing wheel. Remember also that in most cases a toddler would rather play with the box a toy came in than the toy itself. When our son, Eric, was two, his toys consisted of some large cardboard bricks, a toy truck, a couple of stuffed animals, a ball, and a large appliance box I'd made into a playhouse. He could play for hours by himself, proving it's not important how many toys a child has, but what he's able to do with them. (TT)

School is a responsible environment. To the degree that children come to school primed with responsibility, they will accept the responsibilities expected of them by their teachers. *A teacher cannot instill a sense of responsibility in a child, she can only capitalize on what is already there.*

The most effective means of priming a child for responsibility is to assign him or her a regular, daily routine of chores around the home. Children should begin doing chores no later than age three. By the time a child is of kindergarten age, he or she should be practiced at sweeping, dusting, running a vacuum cleaner, taking out garbage, setting and clearing the table, helping with the washing and drying of dishes, and making his own bed. When it comes to answering the question, "What can parents reasonably expect of children at various ages, the general rule is: What the child is capable of doing, he/she should do. (EHH)

Rules protect. They insure a child's physical and emotional well-being. Rules are the mainstay of order in the family and in the world. They regulate and mediate a child's comings and goings in society. Children are helpless without them.

Paradoxically, a rule is both a constraint and a guarantee of freedom. A rule that is ill-defined, not enforced, or enforced only sporadically is not a rule at all. It is a fraud, a double-cross, and under this kind of "rule" a child is a victim, a prisoner of uncertainty. On the other hand, a child who tests a rule (as children always will) and finds that it is constant is then free (!) to function creatively and constructively within its boundaries. Children not only need rules, they *accept* them. What they cannot accept are rules that are here today, gone tomorrow. (PP)

The very language of the antispanking movement is disingenuous. Its spokespeople rarely use the word *spanking*. Instead, they talk in terms of "hitting" or "striking" or "beating." Parents who spank, they say, are "physically attacking" their children. Swatting a child's rear is referred to as an "act of violence" which supposedly teaches children that hitting is a justifiable response to someone who makes you upset. Spankings also *confuse* children, they claim. How, they ask, can children possibly be expected to understand that although their parents can hit them, they cannot turn around and hit their parents? With rhetoric of this sort, antispankers seek to create the impression that a beating and a spanking are one and the same; that swatting (a term they do not use, either) a child's rear end is no different, in the final analysis, from slapping a child in the face. They are both acts of child abuse, antispankers contend—equally violent, equally damaging to the child and society. One's just more likely to leave a visible mark, that's all.

This amounts to nothing more than misleading propaganda. The purpose is to create a climate of acceptance for the passage of legislation that will turn the majority of parents into criminals of the most heinous kind—those whose victims are defenseless children. The resulting body of law will play directly into the hands of ultraliberal social engineers as well as social activists within the professional community. (SPNK)

Beginning in the '60s, teachers were told by educational theorists (many of whom had never taught in either an elementary or high school) that a child with positive self-esteem would *want* to learn; therefore, it would be unnecessary to *make* him learn. In fact, applying any academic pressure at all, teachers were told, might cause learning to be frustrating. This, in turn, would cause the student to develop an aversive response to education.

Included among the things that caused kids to become frustrated and "turn off" to school were grades. Grades, the reasoning went, resulted in competition, which resulted in some children being rewarded more than others, whether or not they expended more effort than the lower achievers. This inequity caused children who weren't as "competitive" to feel defeated and lose self-esteem; therefore, grades had to go.

Here's a fact: *It is impossible for someone to improve his or her performance in a certain area without accurate feedback.* If, for example, every time an individual who's learning how to put together a small engine makes a mistake he's nonetheless told he's doing just fine, he'll never learn to put together small engines.

Here's another: *If a task is worth learning, the person trying to learn it will initially fail at it.* One of my graduate professors put it this way: If something's worth learning, it's worth failing at.

The obvious conclusion: *It is nothing short of immoral to not give children honest feedback on their performance in school.* If that means a child receives an F in a subject, so be it. To give the child a C when he deserves an F is to guarantee he will never truly succeed in that subject area. The educational theorists responsible for this crime against children ought to be ashamed of themselves, but they're not. They will defend what they did to the ends of the earth.   (FV)

Two-year-olds understand simple instructions, but not explanations. A two-year-old who's climbing on a table will understand a firm "Get down," but will not understand "Sweetie, you need to get down from the table because you could fall and hurt yourself and we might have to take you to the doctor and that would make Mommy sad because I don't like to see my little boy get hurt, okay?"

In this case, the child will only hear "Gibberish table, gibberish fall, more gibberish doctor, blah, blah, Mommy, goombah hurt." He'll translate: The table fell on the doctor and Mommy got hurt. So, do yourself and your child a favor and keep it to "Get down."   (TT)

To make a profit, a business must operate according to a plan. The same goes for parents who value effective discipline. I call this "Striking While the Iron is Cold," which simply means that the most effective time for dealing with misbehavior is *before* it occurs. In short, you *anticipate* behavior problems that *might* occur in any given situation, and decide how you're going to deal with them *if* they occur.

By striking while the iron is cold, you put yourself in the most effective position possible for striking when the iron gets hot. When the heat is on, implement your strategy, following through as decided, and continue to follow through, as needed, until the problem is solved.

To illustrate, let's take Rodney, a four-year-old who persists in getting out of bed to ask unnecessary questions and make inappropriate requests. To make him stay in bed, Rodney's parents have threatened, bribed, spanked, and screamed—all examples of ineffective, knee-jerk (reactive) emotional responses.

Finally, Rodney's parents decide Rodney will be allowed out of bed one time, and one time only. When they tuck him in, they'll give him a "ticket"—a small rectangle of colored construction paper which Rodney can use to "purchase" the privilege of getting out of bed. When he gets out of bed, as he surely will, Rodney hands his parents the ticket. In return, they let him ask a question or tell them something. Then, they put him back to bed. If, for whatever reason (including "needing" to go to the bathroom), he gets up again, his parents keep him indoors the next day and put him to bed one hour early (with a ticket).

Does Rodney get out of bed? Of course! Does he get out of bed more than once? Of course! You see, Rodney must test the rule in order to find out if it really exists. At last, Rodney stops testing. And Rodney sleeps easier, knowing his parents mean what they say.

(6PP)

Children may not always be happy with the decisions their parents make, but they will always feel more secure with parents who are firm and resolute when it comes to making decisions. And secure children are happier children, yes?

The moment a parent steps into a power struggle with a child, however, the parent loses all power. The child wins. Period. Even if the parent is ultimately successful at getting the child to do what he wants, the child has won by virtue of the fact that he succeeded at pulling the parent down to his level, however temporarily.   (FV)

The consequences of child-centeredness do not begin and end with children. One of the more insidious upshots of this inside-outness involves its impact on women. In the 1950s, a woman with children who worked outside of her home was called a "working wife." As the term implies, her employment was primarily a *marital* issue. As silly as it may seem today, a wife's employment outside the home was generally taken as evidence that her husband was not a sufficient provider. The fragility of male egos aside, the point to be made is that this was, first and foremost, a husband-wife matter.

Today, by contrast, a woman with children who works outside of her home is called a "working mother." The change in terminology reflects a change in our collective thinking concerning such things. Where once a woman's employment was a marital issue, today it is a child-rearing issue. Where once such things were negotiated between husbands and wives, today they are negotiated between mothers and their children. Most important, "working mother" indicates that where once a woman with a family was primarily a wife, today she is considered primarily a mother. Her most immediate relationship, and therefore her first obligation, is with and to her children. This puts a whole new spin on *everything* that happens in American families.

In bygone times, a woman with children who took care of hearth and home was called a "housewife." Today, she is called (and calls herself) a "stay-at-home *mom*." Again, the change in terminology reflects a sea change in our perceptions of a woman's role within her family. Once wife, now mother. Where once she spent the evening with her husband while the children did their homework, she now spends the evening with her children, helping them with their homework.

(FV)

Women of my mother's generation consistently tell me that not only were they content with their "lot in life," but they also pursued interests of their own outside of housework, husband, and children. Despite political and professional barriers, these were women who thought of themselves as fully whole. These supposedly unliberated women were our mothers only when we needed mothers. They were not at our beck and call, nor did they think the measure of a woman was how much she did for her children. They expected us to be independent, fight our own battles, occupy our own time, stand on our own two feet. They called themselves not "stay-at-home moms," but "housewives," referring thusly to themselves as women whose primary relationships were with other adults, not children.

Women of that generation either bristle or laugh when I ask if, in retrospect, they think of themselves as victims. They were, they insist, committed. They viewed their work as essential to the conservation of both family and culture. And in the way they lived their lives, they demonstrated that it's possible to be quite liberated and *not* work outside the home. The disingenuous attempt to discredit these women as role models is part of a larger attempt on the part of the self-appointed avant-garde to replace traditional values with *nouveau* values; ones that are endurable with ones spun from the whole cloth of rhetoric. If it succeeds, the sound we will hear will be that of our foremothers turning over in their graves.   (TT)

Any good teacher knows you cannot effectively teach a child unless you command the child's attention. Parents are teachers, too. Likewise, parents can effectively teach only if they successfully command their children's attention. Oh, and by the way, the difference between *commanding* a child's attention and *demanding* it is night and day. In the first place, the former succeeds while the latter does not. Second, you *command* by projecting self-confidence, as in you know where you stand, and you know where you want the child to stand. Adults who constantly *demand* the attention of children are simply demonstrating their failure to command; to wit, their lack of self-confidence. (TT)

"But, John," a parent might say, "I'm not always sure I'm making the right decision."

As any CEO of any large company will tell you, it is *impossible* for leaders, however effective, to always, in every situation, make the best decision possible. Furthermore, it's not necessary. What *is* necessary, however, is that a CEO—whether the president of the United States or the president of Ford Motor Company—always be *decisive,* that he or she always act as if there is but one decision, in any given situation, that makes any sense. The president of a major corporation will not last long if every time he makes a decision, he says, "Well, uh, I'm not so sure this is the best course to take, but I think maybe it is. That is, I hope it is. If anyone has a better idea, please let me know." That's not a leader talking. That's a vacillator. That's a wimp. His company's stockholders aren't expecting his decisions to be impeccable; they are, however, expecting his *leadership* to be impeccable. In short, how one makes and communicates decisions in a business environment is often more important than the "rightness" of the decisions themselves.

Again, the same is true of being a parent. As a parent, you cannot always be absolutely certain of the decisions you must make. But understand this: *Parents will almost always make better decisions for their children than their children would make for themselves* (and the exceptions to that rule are so few as to be insignificant). That is not to say that children shouldn't be allowed to make decisions, even bad ones, and learn from their successes as well as their mistakes. Indeed, they should. But when you, the parent, decide that you are the person better qualified to make a certain important decision, then make it! And once you've taken your stand, don't waver! Carry it off!   (FV)

June 1

The media and Madison Avenue glorify youth. And the more we adults fall for the myth that eternal youth is somehow attainable, the less respect the young have for us, and deservedly so. Children will respect adults only if adults *distinguish* ourselves; meaning that for the most part adults should dress differently, hold different opinions, and enjoy different recreation. This is not to imply that a bit of overlap in the above categories is bad, but the operative word here is "bit." The older generation should be gratified if the young think we're uncool. Likewise, we should be worried if our children think we're hip.

(NP)

June 2

I can still remember listening to one of my college professors—he was teaching a course in marriage and family relations—lecture on the difference between "democratic" and "autocratic" families. In the democratic family, he said, everyone was regarded as an equal. Therefore, obedience (from the children) was not mandatory, and disagreements were resolved through discussion, negotiation, and compromise. Cooperation and harmony were the hallmarks of a democratic family. "How marvelous!" I thought. In contrast, the autocratic family was a hierarchy, with parents at the top. Children were punished if they disobeyed and were not allowed to make decisions for themselves. Compromise between parent and child was possible only on the parent's terms. Obedience, rather than joyous cooperation, was the bill of fare for children of autocratic parents. "How awful!" I said to myself. I vowed I'd never, ever be a nasty old autocrat, and I tried my best, really I did. For the first three or four years after Eric was born, I regarded him as my equal. If he didn't like decisions I made, he rolled on the floor screaming and I reconsidered. I thought it unfair to make him obey, so he didn't. The result of this exercise in democracy, however, was not harmony. The result was anarchy. One night in a dream a wise-looking elderly gentleman appeared, calling himself the "Spirit of Rosemond's Future." In his hands he held a clear crystal orb, and while I gazed within, there appeared a vision of a slightly older Rosemond family, all of us trussed up nicely in stainless steel straitjackets. I woke up screaming, bathed in sweat, and life with father was never again the same.   (PP)

Willie and I eventually (and none too late!) created a nasty old autocratic family within which we were dictators—"Benevolent Dictators," to be exact. Benevolent Dictators are gentle authorities who understand that their firm, solid, reliable *power* is the cornerstone of their children's sense of safety and security. Benevolent Dictators rule by virtue of natural authority. They know what's best for their children. They don't derive any pleasure out of bossing children around. They govern because they must. They prepare their children for the time when they must govern themselves and their children. Benevolent Dictators do not need to instill fear in order to communicate their influence. They are authorities, but they are not authoritarian. They do not demand unquestioning obedience. They encourage questions, in fact, but make the final decisions. They restrict their children's freedom, but they are not tyrants. They restrict in order to protect and guide. They make rules that are fair and enforce them firmly. Life with a Benevolent Dictator is predictable and secure for children. That set of certainties guarantees more freedom, emotionally and otherwise, for a child than would be possible under any other circumstances.   (PP)

At thirteen, Phoebe looked every bit of seventeen. The boys at Hormone High, the local testosterone factory, were overjoyed. Her parents were not. Phoebe's father, who bore a striking resemblance to Al Capone, let it be known that under no circumstances would Phoebe be allowed to date until the day after her sixteenth birthday.

Several months after issuing this edict, Phoebe's dad showed up at my back door, looking decidedly out-of-joint. Under the pretense of working after school on a drama project, he complained, Phoebe had been sneaking off almost every afternoon with a sixteen-year-old boy.

"I can't think straight about this," he said, grinding his teeth together, fists clenched. "What do you think I should do?"

"Well," I ventured, getting ready to duck, "have you considered maybe lightening up a bit? You know, giving Phoebe a small measure of freedom along these lines so she doesn't have to sneak?"

"No way!" he bellowed. "I was sixteen once! I know what the boys are thinking when they look at her! Letting her date would be like sending her into the lion's den!"

Our "conversation" was over before it started. Over the next few years, things at Phoebe's house went from bad to worse. I came to expect regular visits from her father, looking for advice he wouldn't take. Once, he caught her at the shopping center with an older boy when she was supposedly spending the night with a girlfriend. On another occasion, he and his wife came home unexpectedly to discover a boy upstairs. This game of hide-and-seek continued until the day after Phoebe's sixteenth birthday, by which time she had proven her point to all but her father, who remained convinced he had successfully held the line. Meanwhile, the same old, same old had started with the younger daughter, who at age thirteen looked . . . yep, you guessed it. Some folks never learn.   (NP)

Contrast Phoebe's tale (see previous page) with one told me recently by the parents of one Alice, fourteen going on twenty in more ways than one. During a family vacation, Alice confessed to her mother that she'd met an older boy and, smitten, had smooched with him until their lips were sore. Mom promptly asked, "What do you think usually follows kissing, Alice?"

Alice thought for a moment, then answered, "Probably touching."

"And what do you think usually happens after touching?"

"Um, maybe lying down somewhere?"

Her mother followed each of Alice's answers with "and what do you think usually comes next?" until Alice reached the end of the line and said, "I guess that's when people have sex."

This very shrewd mother then asked, "At what point in this sequence do you want things to stop, Alice?"

"Um, I really don't want to do more than kiss right now, Mom."

"And if the boy doesn't want to stop at kissing, what are you going to do?"

Alice was stunned. It had not occurred to her that, fair or not, it was her responsibility to say "when." She and her mother talked at length about sexual responsibility, birth control, sexually transmitted diseases, date rape, and all the other realities appertaining thereto.

I had to applaud this mother (not to mention Alice's father, who agreed wholeheartedly with his wife's handling of the situation) for seizing the opportunity to educate rather than berate. In so doing, she had opened lines of communication and established a precedent of trust concerning this decidedly sensitive topic. Without dogma or condemnation, she had caused Alice to contemplate the downside of sexual activity. Lastly, she had gently forced Alice to confront a discomforting reality; namely, that boys don't generally stop unless girls are clear in saying "that's far enough." (NP)

In determining when to allow a female child to date, look more closely at the child than the calendar. From one point of view, neither Phoebe nor Alice (see two previous pages) were "ready" to date. From another, both can be prepared for responsible relationships with boys. Alice's parents, seeing the writing on the wall, correctly realized that management was a better strategy than restriction. Their response to her initial foray into sexuality was proactive. As such, it is likely to prevent disaster.

Parents are absolutely correct in perceiving that girls are considerably more vulnerable than boys when it comes to dating. Rules are definitely needed, but rules alone are likely to backfire. The most positive, productive, and preventive approach is one than educates the young girl to her responsibilities. Realistic rules tend to evolve naturally out of this context.

Most professionals agree that a warm relationship between father and daughter is the best deterrent to early sexual activity. A girl who feels approved of and respected by her father is not only less needy of approval from boys, but also better able to "just say no" and stick to her guns.

Last but not least, today's parents need to accept that times have indeed changed since they were teens. The biggest change involves the closing of the gender gap. In the world of the '90s teen, it's perfectly acceptable for a girl to call a boy, for the girl to drive on a date, for the girl to pay for her own meal and movie ticket. As a result, today's teenage girl feels herself to be more in control of her relationships with boys than did girls in bygone eras. Speaking both as a father and a one-time teenage boy, I think that's great!   (NP)

Q: *Once a child begins earning his or her own money, can parents rightfully place certain restrictions on how the child spends that money?*

A: Parents can, indeed, place restrictions on how children spend money they've earned themselves, but they'd better choose their battles carefully. It's reasonable to restrict purchases that put the child in danger (a motorcycle) or are in direct conflict with the values of the family (satanic paraphernalia). It's going to cause more problems than it solves, however, to try to enforce restrictions that are, in the final analysis, arbitrary and capricious. I'm thinking of such things as a youngster's tastes in music and clothing.

Attempts to restrict purchases of this sort are not only likely to fail, but also create problems in the parent-child relationship. Ask yourself, "Is forcing a confrontation over an article of clothing worth the conflict, communication problems, and even deceit that are likely to result?" Having lived with two teenagers, I would advise parents to save their strength for more important issues.   (BHG)

I have problems with most of what the major networks call "family sit-coms." The overt themes of these programs (*most* of them) are certainly not going to warp a child's morals. There's no sex, no violence, no sexism or racism. Underneath the innocence, however, I see a not-so-harmless consistency: First, children are given disproportionate significance in these sitcoms. Second, the manner in which adult-child relationships are portrayed is inappropriate. Children are accorded at least as much, if not more, "presence" in these programs as are adults. In and of itself, this is nothing new. After all, Timmy enjoyed second billing on *Lassie,* and Ricky Nelson was the only reason I watched *Ozzie and Harriet.* What's different is that Timmy and Ricky never talked back to their parents. They may have been stars, but they respected their elders. By contrast, sarcasm between parents and child is standard in today's "family" sit-coms. Maybe I'm losing my sense of humor along with my hair, but this bothers me. It further bothers me that every time child "scores" against parent, everyone's encouraged to guffaw right along with the laugh track. I wonder. Does this reinforce in the minds of children the idea that the parent-child relationship is one of equals, and that to verbally outwit one's parents is the pinnacle of achievement, not to mention humor? Do these programs lend to the already-insidious impression that the world revolves around children? Or is this just art imitating life? Come to think of it, the latter is what disturbs me most of all. (FV)

Concerning the term "learning disability," it's important that parents understand just exactly what the word *disability* means. It does *not*, as many people seem to think, imply an *inability* of any sort. Rather it refers to a *disruption* of ability. So, when someone says that a child has an auditory processing disability, this doesn't mean the child *cannot* learn by listening, just that the child has relative difficulty learning through strictly auditory channels.

The word *disability* also creates the impression that these problems are insurmountable, permanent; that we cannot reasonably expect the same level of academic performance from learning disabled (LD) children that we can from non-LD children; that LD children require esoteric teaching methods and materials, and so on. I haven't found this to be true. A learning-disabled child may have to put more time and effort into learning certain tasks, but he or she is capable of learning just as much and performing just as well as the next child of equivalent ability. The last thing an LD child needs is adults who, out of sympathy, help him avoid certain tasks just because those tasks are frustrating. The fact is that whatever the LD child's weakness or weaknesses, they can be strengthened, and therefore remediated, *only* by exposing the child to the very tasks that give him the greatest degree of difficulty. Unfortunately, most LD specialists teach predominantly to the child's strengths. Teaching strictly to the child's strengths may successfully conceal the consequences of the problem, but it also allows the child's weaknesses to get that much weaker.

(EHH)

June 10

If parents can be prohibited from spanking, what's next? The same justifications being used to advance antispanking laws—that spanking does psychological harm to children—can also be used to justify prohibiting other forms of punishment, including strong verbal reprimands, banishing children to their rooms, grounding teens for extended periods of time, and so on. If you think that a law against verbally reprimanding a child is beyond the pale of possibility, consider that just a generation ago, parents would have said that a law prohibiting a parent from swatting a child's rear end was not possible in America; that after all, *this* was a free country. Antispanking laws will be a foot in the door to grander schemes, believe me.

(SPNK)

Some thirty years ago, "helping professionals" (a term that awards the benefit of the doubt) snatched the child-rearing baton away from the older generation, took a sharp left turn, and led America's parents into a blind alley, where we are still piling up, unconscious of going nowhere.

My generation was persuaded that people with fancy degrees knew more about rearing children than did our parents and grandparents. We were told that it was not sufficient to simply supervise children, set a good example, and discipline them well; we had to pay them a lot of attention, praise them, and get involved with them, all in the cause of infusing them with ample amounts of "self-esteem." As this well-intentioned propaganda became embedded in the American family, the cart was put squarely out in front of the horse.

Every previous generation had understood the importance of *commanding* the attention and respect of the child. Children are inclined toward self-centeredness; therefore, command (along with consequences and consistency) was necessary to draw them out of self-absorption.

But tradition had no place in this *nouveau* child-centered ideology. The old-fashioned parent became a villain, intent on subjugating and exploiting the child-victim. The traditional family became a pathological structure, sustained by codependency and abuse.

Convinced of our own need for psychic surgery, fearing that if we followed our own instincts—much less the twisted tutelage of our elders—we would rain untold evil down upon our children, we allowed the professional community to lead us down the road never traveled, leading nowhere.

The American family has been playing without a clear set of rules for the better part of a generation. It's time we untangled ourselves, turned around, and found the drum major. And when we do, I propose but two words for helping professionals: "Fall in!"   (NP)

June 12

The never-ending "Why?" is typical of intelligent two-year-olds. It is, first, a request for information. As such, you should give information, but it isn't necessary that the information be scientifically correct. In fact, your answer can be total fiction as long as it relates in some way to the original question. For example, if a toddler asks "why?" the sun goes down, you can answer, "Because it's tired and needs to sleep," or "Because it's playing peek-a-boo with you." One answer is really as good as the next. It's even all right to give a different answer every time the child asks the same question! If you think that what I'm suggesting is tantamount to "lying," take a look at the books published for this age child. In them are fantastic creatures and trees that talk and all manner of impossible things. The point is, it's not necessary that you describe the world to young children in correct terms; only that you describe it in terms they can relate to and comprehend. If it was vital that young children always hear correct answers and descriptions, we'd read to them from the encyclopedia instead of storybooks.   (TT)

The standard explanations concerning Attention Deficit Disorder (ADD)—as in, the children in question have a neuro-genetic problem that renders them incapable of paying adequate attention to their parents and teachers—make no sense to me. I frequently speak to audiences of five hundred or more, and I generally talk for a minimum of ninety minutes at a stretch. Furthermore, *I accept full responsibility for whether my audience pays attention to me or not.* If they pay attention, I've done my job. If they don't, then I haven't done my job, in which case *they* don't have a problem—I do! Furthermore, I'd better find out what the problem is, and fast, or I won't be public speaker for long. I've heard speakers make excuses for why audiences didn't pay attention, e.g., the auditorium was hot or it was the end of the day and people were tired. They obviously don't "get it." They don't realize that whether or not a speaker *commands* the attention of his/her audience has absolutely nothing to do with the audience or the hall. It's the speaker, period! It seems to me that these pass-the-buck speakers are very much like the parents of children with these supposed attention deficits—parents who refuse to consider that the problem of their children's inattention may—in large part— rest with them. A pass-the-buck speaker will not get a grip on the problem of this audiences' inattention until he accepts responsibility for it. I likewise propose that parents of supposedly attention-deficit children will not get a grip on the problem until they accept responsibility for it—until, that is, they realize that they have failed to *command* and begin learning how to do so. (NP)

In the years since World War II, we have become increasingly, and neurotically, obsessed with the raising of children. Something that used to be a fairly commonsensical responsibility has taken on the trappings of science. Along the way, child rearing has become "parenting" with all of its high-pressure implications. In the process, we have elevated children to a position of prominence within families that they do not warrant, have certainly not earned, and from which they definitely do not benefit.

Within the child-centered family, which has become the American norm, the implicit understanding is that the children are the most important people in the family, and the parent-child relationship is the most important relationship. And the more child-centered the American family has become, the more demandingly self-centered American children have become. And the more demanding the task of raising them has become. One begets the other. (6PP)

Once upon a time not so long ago, nearly every American child spent Father's Day with both his father and his mother. Today, that state of affairs is exceptional. It is estimated that only 6 percent of black children and 30 percent of white children born in 1980 will live with both biological parents through age eighteen. The comparable figures for children born in 1950 were 52 percent and 81 percent, respectively. One in three households is headed by a single parent, and nine in ten single-parent families are fatherless. Thirty-six percent of all children are living apart from their biological fathers.

Today, the former sacrament of marriage is nothing more than a flimsy contract that any partner can walk away from at the slightest whim, with "I'm not happy" being the usual pretext. Indeed, people are more likely to divorce than to default on a home loan.

In recent years, it has become increasingly and painfully evident that children fare significantly better in every conceivable way—developmentally, emotionally, economically, socially, and academically—when they are reared by both biological (or adoptive) parents. Since the domino of no-fault divorce fell, every indicator of positive mental health and positive values in children has been in headlong decline. Compared with his or her 1960s counterpart, today's child is much more likely to: commit a violent crime (children are the fastest growing segment of America's criminal population); assault a parent or a teacher; abuse drugs and/or alcohol; become sexually promiscuous ("active" is the current euphemism) before age eighteen; have a child out of wedlock; become seriously depressed; develop a reading problem; and be a discipline problem and/or a chronic underachiever in school.

In the fiction of the ubiquitous dysfunctional family, the husband/father has been the villain, enforcing submission to his authority by abuse and manipulation of both his wife and children. In reality, women and children are safer when there's a man around the house and children are safer yet when the man is their father.

(NP)

June 16

A child who does not know where his parent stands must test, test, test, test, test, test, test, ad infinitum. The child has no other choice. Constant testing—also known as *disobedience*—is the attempt on the part of a child to pin a parent down. Here is an indisputable fact: *Testing raises the level of stress and tension in the parent/child relationship, thus obstructing the flow of affection and creative communication.* The way to minimize testing is to communicate to the child, "I know where I stand, and I know where I want you to stand." Under these circumstances, the child will test for only a short period of time, then stop. The resulting lack of stress between parent and child releases the full potential for affection in the relationship. So, you want a loving relationship with your child? Then you have no choice other than to communicate to him that, first, you are the center of attention in his life; second, he will do what you say; third, because you say so, and for no other reason (even if you give one).   (TT)

Technique is not the key to successful discipline.
Unfortunately, most parents think it is. They search "parenting" columns, magazines, and books for answers to an infinitude of "what should you do when?" questions: What should you do when your two-year-old bites the family dog? What should you do when your four-year-old throws a wild tantrum in a public place? (Answer: Hide!) Etc.

Today's parents collect the techniques recommended by "helping" professionals and store them for future reference in the "Discipline File," located in the upper portion of the left temporal lobe. When a discipline problem occurs, they retrieve the "proper" disciplinary technique and use it. In these parent's minds, that's what successful discipline is all about: *technique.* That's the impression, certainly, that "parenting experts" have created.

While certain techniques doubtless have more merit than others, the essence of successful discipline is not technique; rather, it is self-confidence. If, as a parent, you project self-confidence in your dealings with your children, then not only will discipline problems be "small potatoes" in your family, but when a problem arises, just about any disciplinary technique will work. If, on the other hand, you lack self-confidence, discipline is likely to be a major issue and no technique will work—not for long, anyway. At first, a new method may take a misbehaving child by surprise, resulting in temporary improvement. But sooner or later, the child will see through the "veil" of the technique and realize that *you* are no different at all. At that point, it's back to square one, because when all is said and done, it's *you* that makes the difference, not your methods.   (FV)

More often than not, today's child doesn't have to seek his parents out for help with homework. One of them (his mother, in all likelihood) is sitting right there at the kitchen table with him, pushing and prodding the homework to completion. This child gets good grades, but isn't learning to accept responsibility for himself, take initiative when it comes to life's little obstacles, set priorities, and manage his time properly, or use trial-and-error when it comes to solving problems. His helpful parent is making sure he makes no errors; therefore, he has nothing to learn from.

In the process of having unwittingly abused their trust, this child's parents—unfortunately typical of today's parents—have deprived him of one invaluable opportunity after another to learn "the hard way," which is to say, the most valuable learning of all. Then they scratch their heads in wonder at how a child blessed with such generous and caring parents can be so ungrateful, so often at a loss as to what to do with himself, so whiny, so dependent.   (FV)

June 19

I happen to be fairly old-fashioned when it comes to raising children. I believe the primary function of being a parent is that of acquainting children with reality and helping them toward self-sufficiency. It's a reality that, even in a democratic society, authority figures—teachers, lawmakers, employers—frequently make and impose arbitrary decisions. Somebody decides things are going to be done this way rather than that way, that the line is going to be drawn here rather than there, that the standard will be based on this measure as opposed to that one, and so on. And that's the way it is. Why? Because that particular somebody or body of somebodies said so. And having said so, the rest of us have to live with it, at least until some other authority comes along and arbitrarily decides something different.

Likewise, approximately four of every five parental decisions are founded on nothing more substantial than personal preference. When that's the case, "because I said so" (or a variation on that theme) is the most honest answer. Not snarled, mind you, but clearly and calmly stated. (EHH)

June 20

Several years ago, I talked with the mother of a toddler who screamed and clung to her for dear life every time Mom tried to hand the child over to the teacher at her morning preschool program. This mother was convinced her child's reluctance to separate from her was indication of some deep-seated insecurity (example of the mischief psychologists and other "helping professionals" have made in the world). I told her to simply encourage her daughter to scream, as loudly as possible, in fact.

So the next time they were on their way to the program, the mother began saying things like, "This is a fine morning for screaming. You know, when you scream at school, I know you love me, so please scream this morning, okay? And scream real, real loud, because then I know you love me a lot!" When they arrived at the center, the little girl announced that she could walk in by herself. She probably didn't want to be seen with a mother who'd obviously gone over the edge. In any case, there was no more screaming.   (TT)

Q: *Our friends tell us that teens are going to drink, no matter what, and that we're being unrealistic to tell our sixteen-year-old daughter that she may not, under any circumstances, consume alcoholic beverages until she is of legal age. Are we?*

A: Here's what's inevitable: Parents who think drinking—or drug use, or sexual activity—are "inevitable" at this age are going to have children who drink, or use drugs, or become sexually active. Although significant numbers of teens do, indeed, indulge in such things, significant numbers do not. The major difference between the first group and the second are parents who take a firm, but not punitive, stand concerning such issues. (BHG)

Q: *My second-grade daughter Amanda has become somewhat of a behavior problem in school. Nothing serious, but I'd like to nip it in the bud. Any suggestions?*

A: Using index cards, make up a batch of "daily report cards" for Amanda to take to school. Each card simply reads: "Today, Amanda's behavior was excellent/good/fair." At the end of every school day, Amanda takes a daily report card to the teacher, who circles the appropriate description and signs the card, putting any comments on the reverse. Amanda is then required to bring the card home. At home, her after-school privileges depend on the teacher's rating. *Excellent* means she enjoys all of her privileges; *good* means she loses one important privilege; *fair* means she loses all of her privileges. If she fails to bring the card home, no excuses are accepted. In that event, she loses all of her privileges and must go to bed one hour early. The daily report card builds a bridge of communication and consequences between school and home. Now what Amanda does in school affects what she wants to do after school. If the teacher's ratings are accurate, and if you follow through consistently at home, Amanda should solve her classroom behavior problem in short order.   (BHG)

June 23

Grandma's "secrets" of successful child rearing were expressed as terse, sometimes cryptic, "kernels" of child-rearing wisdom, which she had "inherited" from her parents, who had "inherited" them from theirs, and so on. The understandings represented by these sayings were the stuff of a *common* sense concerning children and their upbringing; common in that it was communal, shared, universally agreed-upon. It was not a matter of academic controversy. Yesterday's parents understood these nonintellectual declarations of the obvious and "did what they had to do, that's all." Grandma's "parenting proverbs" included:

- "Children should be seen, not heard."
- "You can't get something for nothing." (Also expressed as "If you eat, then you work," and "You're going to earn your *keep* around here."
- "I'm going to give you enough rope to hang yourself."
- "You're going to have to lie in the beds you make."
- "I'm going to let you stew in your own juices over this."
- "Children want their bread buttered on both sides." (Also expressed as "Children want to have their cake and eat it, too.")
- "You paddle your own canoe." (Or, "You fight your own battles.")
- "It's time I lowered the boom on you."
- "A watched pot never boils."

These "parenting proverbs" *informed* the way Grandma disciplined her kids, thus transforming wild things into responsible citizens.   (FV)

Midway through a radio talk show during which I was talking primarily about children's need for discipline, a gentleman called in and, after identifying himself as a family counselor, said that he disagreed completely with my point of view.

"Our primary job as parents is not to discipline," he opined. "Rather, it is *to facilitate the unfolding of our children's souls and help them discover who they are.*"

This is a perfect example of why American parents should listen with great skepticism to anything said by mental health professionals (and please keep in mind that I am one) concerning the rearing of children. What, pray tell, does it mean to "facilitate the unfolding of our children's souls" etc.? The answer, of course, is that this is completely meaningless tripe, rubbish of the highest caliber, nothing more and nothing less than psychobabble. Mental health professionals who engage in this sort of romantic rhetoric are hiding the fact that when it comes to the realities of children and their upbringing, they haven't the slightest clue.

The reality: Parents who discipline children well, with the goal in mind of teaching them the tenets of good citizenship, will turn out adult children who will be fully capable of spiritual and personal fulfillment. Before the cart must go the horse. Furthermore, the idea that children are capable of "discovering who they are" is nothing short of absurd. The fact is, one finds out "who one is" no sooner than one's middle years, if ever. Such a discovery requires the understanding that the most valuable things in life do not exist at the material level. This understanding, in turn, requires a significant divestment of self-centeredness. Children don't qualify on either count, and anyone who thinks otherwise has his head in the clouds and his feet off the ground. (NP)

If you want raising children to be difficult, you need only put your children first in your family, and it will be. By putting your children first in your family, you guarantee they will become manipulative, demanding, and unappreciative of anything and everything you do for them. You guarantee they will grow up believing they can do as they please, that it's unfair of you to expect them to lift a finger of responsibility around the home, and that it's your bounden duty to give them everything they want and serve them in every conceivable way. Putting children first in the family further guarantees that you will experience parenthood as one of the most frustrating and unrewarding things you've ever done. It further guarantees the ultimate unhappiness of your children, because happiness is achieved only by accepting responsibility for one's self, not by being led to believe that someone else is responsible for you.

It's a question of priorities. In a two-parent family, the marriage must come first. After all, the marriage created the family, and the marriage sustains it. The marriage preceded the children, and is meant to succeed them. If you don't put your marriage first, and keep it there, it's likely to become a mirage.   (6PP)

To a child, a parent who treats different children *differently* is playing favorites. If, for example, you allow your fifteen-year-old to stay out until 10:30 on weekend nights, but insist that your thirteen-year-old be in by nine o'clock, you will undoubtedly be accused of being "unfair." (Take heart, however, because any time you do something that causes one of your children to cry "Not fair!" you must be doing the right thing. Keep on doing it.) Likewise, if your fifteen-year-old notices that his younger sibling is not required—as was he at that age—to mow the lawn every Saturday morning, then you are again playing favorites. No matter that the thirteen-year-old is accident-prone or can't tell the difference between flower beds and grass. Number One Son will no doubt take this as a personal affront, and no explanation will convince him otherwise.

Given that children will think whatever they want to think about such things, the best thing to do when you stand accused of prejudice is simply agree. In the first case, tell your thirteen-year-old that he's right, his curfew is not only unfair, it's a clear violation of the Equity in Child-Rearing Act (ECRA). As such, he should consider hiring an attorney who specializes in such matters and suing you for everything you've got. (Then he could support you!) On the matter of mowing the lawn, simply tell your fifteen-year-old that scientists have discovered a connection between mowing the lawn and high intelligence. They speculate, tell him, that a substance released into the air by grass cuttings stimulates brain cell growth. You are simply making sure, therefore, that he has a lifetime advantage over his younger sibling. In other words, he must mow the lawn because he's your favorite! (FV)

Many parents mistakenly think that for any given child-rearing situation, there is but one correct course of action. That's like believing that of the forty or so items on a restaurant menu, there's just one perfectly suited to your taste. The fact is, the *way* in which parents make decisions is far more important than the content of the decisions themselves. The same applies to managing a business.

An effective manager is decisive. He doesn't waste time and energy obsessing over details. He trusts his intuition and common sense. More than anything else, a good manager realizes it's less important to always be "right" than to always inspire confidence and a sense of purpose in those he manages. He knows that wrong decisions are less harmful to an organization than a faulty decision-making style. To the degree that a manager is obsessive or indecisive, he promotes distrust, insecurity, and conflict in the workplace. Indecisive parents create similar problems in the home.

Do you see yourself in the following description?

- You dwell on decisions, rather than trusting your feelings and your common sense and just "snapping them off."

- You include your child in a lot of decision-making.

- If your child dislikes a decision you've made, you're almost certain to compromise, if not give in.

- You constantly explain yourself to your child.

If that shoe fits, you need to stop making your life—as well as your child's—so complicated. Start trusting your feelings. Stop worrying that you're going to traumatize your child for life if you make a bad decision. Bad decisions don't do long-term damage. Bad *people* do.

(6PP)

In order to successfully emancipate himself, a child must be secure in his or her parents' power, as represented by their loving authority. The more effectively they communicate that authority, the more secure the child feels, and the better able he is to move away from them toward a life of his own. During this lengthy process, whenever he feels threatened, he turns back toward the safety of his parents' love and authority. In other words, it is impossible for a child to successfully emancipate unless he knows exactly where his parents *stand*, both literally and figuratively. That requires, of course, that his parents know where they themselves stand. If *they* don't know where they stand—if, in other words, they are insecure in their authority—they cannot communicate security to their child, and he cannot move successfully away from them. Under the circumstances, he will become clinging, or disobedient, or both. (TT)

June 29

There is absolutely no excuse for not expecting children to perform a regular, as in daily, routine of chores in and around the home. Unfortunately, there are more children in this country who do *not* contribute to their families on a regular basis that there are children who do. Parents rationalize this failure in a number of ways:

• They say, "It's more of a hassle to get the kids to do something around the house and do it right than it is for us to do it ourselves." This is a cop-out of the first magnitude.

• They say, "What with all of the after-school activities they're involved in, there's no time for our children to do much work around the house." This is a cop-out of the second magnitude.

• They say, "We believe childhood should be a relaxed, carefree time, not filled with responsibilities. We feel that expecting them to do well in school is enough." This is a cop-out of the third magnitude.

In the first place, it is indeed worth the hassle, which will be short-lived if parents will simply take a stand on the subject of chores and stand firm.

In the second place, if a child is involved in so many after-school activities that he has no time to do chores, then he's involved in too many after-school activities. It's a simple matter of priorities—first things first.

In the third place, a child who is responsible around the home will be *more* responsible at school. He will be a better all-around student because he will bring to school a stronger desire for accomplishment.

Lastly, if you have a cleaning service, do your children a favor and save yourself some money by letting the cleaning service and the yard service go!

(EHH)

Discipline is the process by which parents make *disciples* of their children, a child-disciple being one who pays close attention to his parents and follows their lead. The ultimate goal of parental discipline is to produce an adult who requires minimal "management" of his or her behavior; an adult who is self-disciplining. The idea, then, is to discipline such that the child in question is enabled to eventually take the reins of his discipline into his own hands, and successfully so.

Discipline is not primarily a matter of punishment, although punishing inappropriate behavior is certainly part of the overall process. The goal is not to make the child passively subservient, but to make the child autonomous. The goal is not to "break" the child's will, but to "bend" it, to direct it toward rewarding ends. Discipline is not a matter of anger, although there are times when it is certainly appropriate for parents to demonstrate anger in the course of "disciplining" a child. Discipline is not a matter of spanking, although there are times when spankings are called for. Discipline has nothing to do with making children afraid of adults, although it is definitely in the long-term best interests of children that they be *intimidated* by adults. Discipline is not the sum total of a number of "disciplinary methods." It is an art, the "whole" of which is far greater than the sum of its parts.

Underlying all of the above is one basic fact: *Only self-disciplined adults can be successful at disciplining children.* (FV)

July 1

When you have a disagreement with your spouse, you don't call it "marital rivalry," do you? That's because there's no third party trying to make you get along, and if there was, you'd never learn how to. The problem, you see, isn't that siblings have conflict. That's to be expected. It's that instead of holding both children equally responsible for disturbing the peace of the family, parents usually blame one child for "starting it" or being "unfair." As a consequence, the conflict between the siblings escalates as each tries, ever more desperately, to get the parents to blame the other, and every time Child No. 1 "scores" on Child No. 2, the latter becomes focused on payback. Holding both children equally responsible—regardless of what may have happened!—will keep sibling conflict to a manageable minimum, but there are only two ways of avoiding it altogether: First, have no more than one child; second, if you have more than one, space them at least eighteen years apart.   (DGP)

During a break in a seminar I was conducting in Sacramento, California, a woman asked what I'd recommend she do concerning her eight-year-old daughter, who had recently taken to talking back in a provocative tone of voice.

"It's getting worse," she said. "Twice during the past week, my daughter's actually cursed at me. You know, used 'swear' words. I just don't know what's making her so angry or what to do about it."

Being the intuitively brilliant psychologist that I am, I told this mother I was certain I knew why her daughter was angry: to wit, she wasn't getting her way. I suggested to my petitioner that she continue making her daughter angry at least three times daily.

"But what should I do about the cursing?" she asked.

"What would your mother have done if you cursed her?" I answered.

"Ha!" she replied. "My mother wouldn't have put up with that for a moment. She'd have spanked me on the spot, then she'd have taken me to the bathroom and washed my mouth out with soap, then she'd have banished me to my room for the rest of the day. And then, when my dad got home, I'd probably have been spanked again."

"And would you have ever cursed your mother again?"

"Obviously not," she answered.

"And did you love and respect your parents, and do you think they did a good job of rearing you?"

"Yes to both," she replied.

"And are you an emotional basket case today because of how they disciplined you?"

"Oh, heavens no!" she emphatically responded.

"Then the next time your daughter curses you, why don't you consider doing *exactly* what your mother would have done?"

She looked taken aback. "But, but," she stammered, "I didn't think we were *supposed* to do that kind of thing anymore."

"Yes, I know," I said, "and that's the problem." (NP)

To say that young children who try to hit their parents have anger "built up" inside them suggests their parents are doing something to cause these children psychological problems. Maybe some children *do* have anger built up inside them. I really don't know, and neither does anyone else, for that matter. Some professionals pretend to be able to see inside the psyches of young children and explain their behavior. These pseudo-profound explanations amount to nothing more than psychobabble. They can be neither proven nor disproven. Unfortunately, these psychobabblistic explanations tend to intimidate parents and prevent them from disciplining with confidence.

The fact is, young children are easily frustrated. They don't tolerate "no" well. The fact is, it's not all that unusual for young children to hit, or attempt to hit, their parents when they don't get their way. The fact is, some children are predisposed to aggressive behavior, while others are not. The fact is, being predisposed to aggressive behavior has nothing whatsoever to do with bad parenting.

When a child loses control to this degree, parents need to act quickly and authoritatively, which they aren't able to do if they're fretting over the "why?" of the child's loss of control. I've said it many times: Thinking too much is the bane of good discipline.

(NP)

July 4

Paradoxically, learning to be obedient advances a child's ability to function *independently* of his or her parents. Obedient children have parents who effectively describe and enforce limits. Within that clear framework, obedient children are free to be curious, to explore, to invent; in short, to be as independent as their maturity allows. Contrast this type of respect with the "respect" demanded by the authoritarian parent, who usually equates respect with fear. Children who fear their parents don't obey, they submit. On the other hand, children who are truly obedient are not fearful. They are self-confident and secure. They are even secure enough to indulge in a certain amount of rebellion. Children who fear their parents often become deceptive. They learn to lie in order to avoid consequences and slip through the net of restrictions their parents try to enforce. Children who are obedient are more likely to be honest and forthright, especially when they do wrong things, because they have been treated honestly and in accord with what they truly need.

Obedience, furthermore, is self-rewarding. To the degree children accept and function responsibly within the limits their parents define, those limits should steadily expand. Eventually, the children no longer need someone else to define limits for them. Obedience, then, paves the road to maturity. (PP)

July 5

Some thoughts on toys:

• The best toy is one the child creates. Take your child outside and show him how to build forts out of sticks, to dig moats with an old soup spoon, to make boats out of folded paper, to build walls out of stones, to fashion trees out of pinecones—the possibilities are infinite!

• The best commercial toys are flexible (they can be used in lots of different ways) and encourage imaginative play. Small, doll-like figures and other true-to-life miniatures are fine, as are simple building sets, clay, crayons, watercolors, finger paints, and so on.

• For the most part, steer clear of so-called educational toys. Generally speaking, they have little, if anything, in common with a child's developmental or educational needs. Their "problems" are largely irrelevant and tend to inhibit, rather than encourage, creative thinking.

• Instead of buying toys that "do"—toys that perform—give children a few, basic things they can manipulate. Let the children's imagination do the "doing."

• Don't limit children to toys traditionally considered appropriate to only one sex. If a boy wants to play with dolls, buy him dolls. If a girl wants to play baseball, buy her a bat and ball. The freer children are to explore the possibilities of living, the better choice-makers they will become.

• In the final analysis, less is more.

July 6

Today's typical mother organizes her children's after-school activities, chauffeurs them around town, helps them with their homework, does their science projects for them, and then spends much of the rest of her time worrying if she's doing enough.

The fact is, she's doing entirely too much. Today's children whine more and are more disrespectful than children of previous generations and throw tantrums long past the age when yesterday's kids were over them completely. These are symptoms of hand-and-foot disease, which is usually prompted by being waited on by an overly solicitous parent, usually female.

In the vernacular of today's youth, Mom, get a life. Stop serving your children and become a little more selfish. Stop revolving around and hovering over them, giving them attention and doing things for them. Instead, expect your children to revolve around *you*, give *you* attention, and do things for *you*. Finally, do more for yourself.

Stand in front of a mirror and practice saying the following to your children until you can say it convincingly, meaning with firm calm: "No, I won't _____." You don't need a mother right now, and I'm not going to be one. Furthermore, if you don't find something to do and leave me alone, I will, without laying a hand on you, make you think I'm the meanest mother in the world."

If she was anything like my mother, your mother said words to that effect to you when you were a child. And you never thought that meant she didn't love you, now did you? So go ahead and say it to your children, and then stand ready to convince them that you *mean* business, you meany! (TOH)

July 7

Don't ever assign two or three siblings to the same job. I know, you want them to learn to work together cooperatively, and no one could argue with the logic of having all of the children pick up the toys that all of them were playing with, but there are times in the rearing of children when one must sacrifice ideals and logic in order to expedite the practical and preserve one's sanity. This is definitely one of those times.

Several unrelated children would probably cooperate willingly on just about any task you assigned to them (the operative word being unrelated). But siblings are another matter entirely. Siblings are always looking for ways of one-upping one another, of gaining the advantage, of passing the proverbial buck. If you assign siblings to the same chore, then be prepared for them to complain that "he/she isn't doing his/her share."

You can live a longer, happier life by accepting the inevitable. Stop fighting the same battle every evening and be proactive. Instead of expecting all three children to work together on the same job, assign each child a separate task. One child can pick up toys. One can sweep the kitchen floor. And one can turn down everyone's beds and put mints on the pillows.

Using the "one chore, one child" approach will circumvent lots of problems, but not eliminate them entirely. Your children will bicker until they are no longer children. But there will, I assure you, be later opportunities for revenge. For example, when it comes time to fund college educations, you and your husband could point at one another and cry "Make him/her do it!" That'll teach 'em.   (FV)

July 8

The more interesting a person you are, the more variety there is in your life, the more attention your children will pay you. Children are fascinated by adults who have lots of interests. The are also fascinated by adult-adult relationships, intent upon figuring them out. Children are not, however, fascinated by adults who pay a lot of attention to them. They take adults of that sort for granted.   (DGP)

The notion that children who make certain letter reversals are seeing things backward became widespread in the 1970s. Despite the fact that it borders on the absurd, it persists. If these children truly saw things backward, they would forever be walking into walls, in which case a symptom of dyslexia would be a flat, chronically bruised face. Even if they *did* see letters backward, *they would still write them correctly.* Think about it. Say, for instance, that for a certain child, "d's" look like "b's." When this child went to write a "d," therefore, he would write it so that it would look, to him, like a "b," which is to say he would write a "d." In other words, if there existed children who saw letters backward, no one would ever know, and the "problem" would cause these children no difficulties whatsoever.

The truth is, lots of six-year-olds reverse certain letters. In fact, letter reversals are fairly common in children through age eight. In most of these cases, the visual difference between one letter and the other is subtle and difficult to remember. So a child innocently substitutes "d" for "b" and "p" for "q." A patient teaching approach will usually correct the problem within a relatively short period of time. The child makes a reversal or substitution, the teacher gently points it out, the child corrects it, and the proper habit slowly but surely develops. To say that letter reversal is a symptom of dyslexia is like saying that a cough is a symptom of pneumonia. A child can have a cough without pneumonia, and a child can reverse letters without being learning-disabled. In fact, only a small number of children who reverse letters are eventually found to have serious learning problems. Furthermore, just as it's possible to have pneumonia without a cough, the absence of letter reversals is no guarantee a child *doesn't* have a learning disability. (EHH)

July 10

Despite what proponents of antispanking laws would have you believe, the evidence is *not* on their side. Properly administered (the operative condition!), spankings do not cause children to lose trust in and become fearful of their parents. Properly administered spankings do not, as a matter of course, escalate in severity or cause children to become violent, either on the playground or in later life. The truth is, properly administered spankings can be, and have been, of inestimable value in the rearing of certain children.

The claims of the antispanking movement are absurdly simplistic. It takes more than spankings to make a bully, much less a criminal. It takes a lot more than an occasional swat or two on the butt to warp a child's mind. The bond of trust between parent and child will endure emotional upheavals far greater than spankings can produce. Unfortunately, simplistic arguments are often extremely seductive.

(SPNK)

When you feel that one of your children is telling a lie, simply say, "This sounds like a lie to me. When you're ready to tell the truth, let me know and we can continue this discussion." Put the ball in the child's court and walk away. Next, don't let lies distract you and bump you off track.

Punish the deed (but only if the deed truly deserves punishment), not the lie. Don't promise that things will go better if the child tells the truth. Don't threaten to make the punishment worse if the lie continues. Stay on track.

Lastly, provide the child the opportunity to become a more responsible member of the family. Stop spending so much energy trying to catch the lies and concentrate, instead, on helping the child adjust to performing chores around the home. I find, fairly consistently, that the more responsible these errant kids become within their families, the less they lie and steal.

Why? I don't know. Who cares?   (FV)

Perusing the "Child Care" section of any large bookstore, you will find books on how to rear the child with attention deficit disorder, the child with learning disabilities, the adopted child, the gifted child (always a best-seller), the strong-willed child, the difficult child, the only child, the middle child, the stepchild, the child born to older parents, and so on. Today's parent has been led to believe that in order to rear a child properly, you must first find out what *kind* of child you have. If you cannot figure it out on your own, you can pay a "helping" professional upward of one hundred dollars an hour to make the determination. Once you have discovered what category of child you are rearing, you go to the bookstore and buy every book available on the category in question, and—voila!—you now have your very own customized child-rearing kit which you then share with your child's teachers so that they will have sufficient appreciation of his "special needs."

Professionals have taken the "whole" of childhood and sliced it into ever-thinner sections, then held each section up to the light of psychological scrutiny and analysis. In the process of all of this dissecting, theorizing, and intellectualizing, professionals seem to have lost sight of the fact—and have caused American parents to lose sight of it as well—that *a child, regardless of prefix, is first and foremost a child.*

(FV)

July 13

The so-called "terrible twos," which last from eighteen to thirty-six months (give or take a few months on either side) are without question the most important time in the child's development, and the most important in the parent-child relationship, as well. It is during this critical eighteen-month period that parental authority is established; hopefully, that is. Keep in mind, however, that parental authority can only be constructed upon a firm foundation of trust laid during the first year and a half of life. Without that foundation, chaos in the parent/child relationship will not only be inevitable, but indefinite in its duration. The outcome will be either a child who runs the show forever (anarchy), or parents who rule (always tentatively) by intimidation and force.

At this stage, the child's parents' primary job, their utmost responsibility, becomes that of erecting a fortress of authority that is at first all-encompassing—an authority that encircles the child, providing not only direction but protection as well and, as a result, guaranteeing the child's welfare. The cornerstone of that fortress becomes the cornerstone of a new and far more stable sense of security, one based upon the child's belief that his parents are the most powerful people in the known world, capable of providing for and protecting him under any and all circumstances. In effect, the parent's task is that of firmly yet gently convincing the child that the impression he formed during his first eighteen months of life was in error; that he does not rule the world, *they do.* (TT)

July 14

The game of "Who Had the Worst Day?" begins around 5:30 in the afternoon, when Dad arrives home from work. Dad the Downtrodden shuffles up to the door, dragging his briefcase behind him. As he opens the door, he's met by a stampede of children—each of them wanting his attention.

Let's not forget Mom! She's standing in the background, viewing this chaos from the shadows. Mom's pupils are dilated, her nostrils are flared, and every vein in her neck is taut. She doesn't have to say anything, because every nuance of her body language screams, *"I've had it!"* If she says anything at all, it's something along the lines of, "Well, it's about *time* you got home from your eight-hour vacation, buddy! Now, it's time for *you* to find out what it's like to be a parent! From this moment on, they're all yours!"

And the game is on! Occasionally, the husband "wins." He persuades his wife to sympathize with what a bad day he's had, how rotten his boss is, how hard he works, blah, blah, blah.

Sometimes the wife "wins." Her hangdog husband takes the kids out for a ride to let her relax, and he picks up supper at a Chinese restaurant so she doesn't have to cook, and he might even—if Mom's real lucky—put the kids to bed that night.

In the final analysis, however, "Who Had the Worst Day?" is a game with no winners. It's a game people play because they've already lost something, and that something is a proper sense of family priorities. Somewhere, back down the line, they misplaced the fact that the marriage is the most important commitment in their lives.

It should come as no surprise to hear that the divorce rate among people forty-five and older has been accelerating faster than the divorce rate for any other age group. In the last forty years or so, we've done such a good job of training wives to be mothers and husbands to be breadwinners that by the time their children leave home, they've forgotten how to be partners. (6PP)

Here are several ways of making quality time for the marriage as well as helping children understand that Mom and Dad's relationship is Numero Uno. (Note: Single parents! These apply to you, too!)

• Don't allow children to interrupt your conversations. Make them wait their turn, preferably in another room. Say, "We'll let you know when we're finished talking."

• Create a weekly "Parents' Night Out" and don't let anything except acts of God interfere with the commitment. Every now and then, go off for a weekend without the kids. They need to realize that the marriage is a separate, autonomous entity within the family; that it has a life, and needs, of its own.

• Put children to bed early. Remember that your children's bedtime is for *your* benefit. In other words, determine how much "down" time you need in the evening during which you have no child-rearing responsibilities and set bedtimes accordingly. Instead of putting children to bed when *they're* ready, put them to bed when *you're* ready to hand up your roles as mom and dad and just be husband and wife.

• Once the kids are in bed, reduce distractions that interfere with communication and intimacy. Agree not to do either housework or office work after the kids' bedtime. In this regard, the worst possible, least creative thing you can do is get in the habit of centering your time together in the evenings around television.   (6PP)

July 16

Parents are a child's first representation of God, a first and final powerfully loving (equal emphasis, please) authority. As the child grows toward adulthood, this concept mellows and transfers to other authority figures—teachers, lawmakers, ministers. Ever so gradually, it matures into an understanding that the universe is shaped and moved by a spiritual source/force beyond human comprehension—a source that is both infinitely powerful and infinitely loving/forgiving. This is the challenge that confronts the toddler's parents: to provide that model.   (TT)

Thumbsucking defies convention, and this makes adults uncomfortable. As long as adults have "reasons" for things, they feel okay. So, they've invented some to explain why an occasional thumb is found where it shouldn't be. Take your pick:

The "Bad Nerves Theory" says that sumbthucking is a thign of inthecurity. To parents who buy this idea, a thumbsucking child is a constant reminder of what bad parents they are. They become especially distraught when their child sucks in public, thus broadcasting his or her pathetic condition to the world.

Another theory, attributed by some to a certain Zigmund Fraud, says that children suck their thumbs because during infancy they experienced some trauma associated with breast-feeding. One such trauma is having *never* been fed with a breast. These supposedly miserable kids grow up sucking on one substitute nipple after another— cigarettes, straws, siphon tubes, Life Savers, anything. As adults, they are the weirdos who prefer to drink their beer straight from the bottle.

Then there are the horror stories—Bedtime Tales for Thumbsuckers: "There once was a frog-prince who sucked his thumb. When he grew up, his teeth were crooked, his eyes were crossed, his ears stuck out and flapped in the wind, he caught a dread disease, his cheeks dimpled, and the princess would not marry him." The part about the dimples gets 'em every time.

I have my own theory. Because of thumbs, people can build the things mankind dreams of, like rocket ships and time machines. A child who sucks her thumb is saying, "I love my thumb. I love being human." Now isn't that nicer than bad nerves and a face like Alfred E. Newman? As far as I can tell, children suck their thumbs simply because it feels good. Thumbsucking is calming and relaxing to a child. It is a portable source of pleasure, always right on hand! The answer to why some children suck their thumbs and others don't is simply, "Because." It's no more significant than liking or not liking spinach.   (PP)

July 18

Today's parents need to cultivate the art of being mean, but *mean* isn't screaming and yelling. That's out of control. Mean isn't cruel, either. Truly *mean* parents are calm, consistent, and insistent. They do not tolerate misbehavior, although they know it's bound to occur. Knowing it's inevitable, they don't get angry when it happens.

Mean parents are assertive. They don't give second, third, and fourth chances. They insist that children do what they're told, the first time they're told. They don't count to ten or engage in other equally ridiculous games of chance. They don't make threats, they make promises. Meanest of all, they *keep* their promises.

Mean parents are consistent. They uphold the same standards from one day to the next. The ways they enforce those standards may vary from situation to situation, but the standards themselves do not.

Mean parents don't shoulder emotional responsibility for their children's misbehavior. When the child of truly mean parents misbehaves, the parents don't feel bad about it. Instead, they make sure the *child* feels bad about it.

It's very simple, really. Mean parents make rules and enforce them dispassionately, without any great to-do. Their children may not like the rules, but they respect them.   (NP)

July 19

The next time your child tells you that *all* of his friends can do something you won't let him do, or don't have to do something you make him do, or have something you won't let him have, just look him squarely in the eye and with a slight smile, say, "Well, then you're going to be the most special child in your entire peer group." At this point, your child is likely to storm off to his room, screaming words to the effect that he hates living in your house and can't wait to be gone (!), and won't talk to you for upward of several days. Lucky you! (DGP)

July 20

The job of parent is that of balancing love and authority such that one is lovingly authoritative as well as authoritatively loving. Parenting "experts" of the '60s and '70s said that parental authority damaged the self-esteem of children because it placed children in "one-down" positions relative to their parents. Balderdash! Poppycock! Frogfeathers! That opinion is a construction of misguided imagination. It is *not* a representation of reality. The reality is that a child's self-esteem is synonymous with security; that security is provided by parents who balance love and authority in their caring for the child; that a child's security/self-esteem is not disrupted by exercise of authority, but is disrupted when love and authority are not in balance; when, in other words, parents are either over-indulgent (love without authority) or disapprovingly tyrannical (authority without love).

(TT)

My wonderful, tolerant wife Willie, and I celebrated our twenty-eighth anniversary on this date in 1996. "What's your secret?" people ask. In addition to fidelity, learning to listen with respect, and giving one another "space" (pardon my lapse into trendiness), we came up with some counsel you won't find in any of the books on marriage that have proliferated in this age of easy divorce:

Accept the Big Reality. Namely, that staying married is the single most difficult challenge you will ever undertake. Both you and your spouse are highly imperfect beings, each no less so than the other. When two imperfect beings join together in an imperfect union, and their respective imperfections start to collide, imperfection begins to multiply. Accept your *equal* part in all this and you will be able to retain your sense of humor, which is an outstanding feature of every truly successful marriage.

Compromise as little as possible. Compromise is fine in certain situations, but compromise is often the weakest of three alternatives: (1) your stubborn way of doing things; (2) your spouse's equally stubborn ideas on the subject; and (3) the compromise, which is a point approximately midway in between. Like my great, great, great grandfather used to tell me, "The middle of a bridge is its weakest point."

Accept that neither of your personalities is ever going to change. To stay married, you must accept your differences and apply no value judgments to them, as in, "That's irrational." You must not only roll with one another's differences and the natural friction they create, but learn to celebrate them!

Be stubborn. Huh? That's right, as in, "I'm going to do everything I can to make this marriage work, no matter what!" Why are so many of today's marriages failing? In large part because the people in those marriages just aren't stubborn enough. Many of them have never had to work hard for anything, never had to persevere, never had to hang in there when the going got rougher than rough. As a result, when it comes time in their marriages to do any or all of the above, they just can't cut the mustard. (FV)

July 22

You can call your child "forgetful" if it makes you feel better. I'd probably call the same child *disobedient*. More often than not, "I forgot" is an evasive way of saying, "I didn't want to" or something equally noncompliant.

Consider the fact that "forgetting" is always so suspiciously selective. The same child who almost always "forgets" to feed the dog or come in when the streetlights go on never forgets things like the presence of ice cream in the freezer or the casual mention his parents made, several weeks ago, of a possible trip to the zoo. The typical child remembers things he wants to remember and "forgets" those things he would rather do without, like chores and inconvenient rules. (6PP)

July 23

When our son, Eric, turned fourteen, his curfew on non–school nights was ten o'clock. He told us that was early, and we agreed. We also told him we were tired of being "enforcers." How would he like to set his own curfew? His eyes got big as saucers, and we proceeded to explain.

The "deal," as we called it, was this: If he did not violate his present curfew for six months, his curfew would become 10:30. If during that six months, however, he came in even one minute late, the six months would begin anew. And no excuses would be accepted. Every six months thereafter, assuming no violations, his curfew would increase by thirty minutes. A violation would simply reset the six-month clock. When he had earned a midnight curfew and not violated it for six months, he would be able from that point to set his own curfew.

"You mean," he said, still not quite believing what he was hearing, "I'll be able to come in when I choose?"

"That's right, Eric," I replied, "but understand one thing. Even when you are setting your own curfew, your mother and I will want to know where you are and who you are with. Furthermore, if you say you are going to be in by two o'clock, then we expect you in at two o'clock, and not a minute later. If you violate the curfew you set for yourself, then we go back to midnight for six months. In other words, Eric, being eventually able to set your own curfew means freedom, but it also means commitment and responsibility and, most of all perhaps, trust."

I don't think we ever had to reset the six-month clock. Shortly after obtaining his driver's license and his own four wheels, he earned the dubious privilege of setting his own curfew. I say dubious because he was generally more conservative than his mother and I would have been. More than a few times, he set curfews for himself that were earlier by a long shot than I would have set for him. I never told him so, of course.

(FV)

There is absolutely no substance to the popular notion that children should come to kindergarten already equipped with certain basic academic skills, including letter and number recognition and the ability to write their names. Recent research tends to indicate that not only is it inappropriate to apply these sorts of expectations at the preschool level but also potentially damaging. A premature attempt to push these skills can create problems that would not have developed otherwise. There are, in fact, a number of experts who believe that we are creating a fair number of learning disabilities by pushing literacy at children too early and too hard. In this regard, it's interesting to note that in European school systems, where formal academic instruction doesn't generally begin until children are at least six, if not seven years old, the incidence of learning disabilities is virtually negligible, as is the incidence of illiteracy among seventeen-year-olds (the U.S. rate is one-in-five, and climbing). (EHH)

July 25

How can parents get children to begin taking care of their toys and other possessions? Simple. Stop giving them so much.

When I was five years old, I had a few basic toys: a set of Lincoln Logs, a set of Tinker Toys, a cap pistol, some army men, and an electric train. I had them until I was a teenager, when they disappeared from the house during one of my mother's cleaning frenzies. I took care of my toys because if one broke, another was not forthcoming. In fact, if I broke a toy, it would be regarded as proof I wasn't responsible, and it would be a long time, indeed, before another would take its place.

Today's child has no reason to take care of his toys. By age five, the typical American child has received 250 of them! That works out to a toy a week from birth on. Under the circumstances, anything parents say about the need to take care of one's possessions is meaningless. So, the child receives a toy, abuses the toy, breaks the toy, and sure enough, another is forthcoming.

Silver-platter syndrome, I call it. And mind you, it's not the child's fault. The syndrome is caused by good intentions, which, as I constantly remind parents, count for naught in child rearing. (NP)

Watched-pot syndrome (WPS) is one of the most vicious cycles in parent-child relationships. A parent gives an instruction and then, certain that compliance will not happen otherwise, stands over the "pot," inviting noncompliance (the self-fulfilling prophecy again). The child, having someone with whom to engage in a power struggle, struggles.

Not realizing that the very act of watching the pot prevents it from boiling, the parent begins referring to the child by such epithets as "strong-willed" and "stubborn," when the fact is that the child simply knows a golden opportunity when he sees one. One of the most common arenas for WPS is the dining room table after six o'clock in the evening on school nights, where one is likely to find mother and child locked in a struggle over homework. If one asks Mom, "Why are you sitting here, night after night, obviously allowing yourself to be driven crazy?" she will answer, "Because Deuteronomy won't do her homework on her own." The "forest" Mom can't see because she's so fanatically focused on one of its trees is that her very presence at the homework table prevents little Deut from getting down to business.

The obvious solution to any and all situations of this sort: Stop watching the pot. When you want a child to do something, give the instruction and walk away. Make like a tree and leave. Give the pot a chance to boil. If, after a reasonable amount of time, the child hasn't complied, then lower the boom. If the toys aren't picked up within five minutes, for example, send the child to his room for the remainder of the day (Yes, even if it's eight o'clock on Saturday morning) and put him to bed, lights out, immediately after supper. The idea is to impose a penalty that, while not painful, is nonetheless unforgettable.   (FV)

As metaphor, the biblical "rod" can justly be interpreted as a symbol of parental authority, just as in ancient days the scepter was the symbol of a ruler's authority and the staff the symbol of a priest's. The rod is also a traditional and ancient measure of length, and as such means that parents should define clear limits for their children. Being a strong, straight stick, the rod is also a metaphor for firmness and consistency in discipline. The same term is also used elsewhere in the Bible in an obviously figurative sense (e.g., Psalms 2:9: "Thou shalt break them with a rod of iron; Thou shalt shatter them like earthenware").

As regards Proverbs 23:13, ("Do not hold back discipline from the child; Although you beat him with the rod, he will not die"), one might ask, What kind of "rod" can a child be beaten with and yet stand absolutely no chance of dying? After all, if an *adult* slave might possibly die from having been beaten with a rod (see Exodus 21:20), then why not a small child, pray tell? One way, perhaps the only way, of reconciling this apparent contradiction is to assume that the rod of Proverbs is not a stick at all, but rather a metaphor, representing steadfast discipline in many forms. (SPNK)

July 28

The years since World War II have seen parents become increasingly confused concerning how to properly raise children. Much of this confusion was manufactured by experts who marketed to an unsuspecting public such absurd and altogether destructive notions as the "democratic family" and the "child-centered family." These experts took the realities of parenthood and replaced them with rhetoric. They took the common sense of raising a child and replaced it with nonsense. In the process, they undermined the confidence of nearly an entire generation of parents, who began to feel as if they had no authority other than that which their children would accept, which was little, if any. So, instead of expecting obedience, which the experts had told them they had no right to do, parents began *wishing* for it. This wishful thinking takes the form of pleading, bargaining, bribing, threatening, haggling, haranguing, and most of all, *arguing* with children. Unfortunately, children don't grant adult wishes.

(EHH)

July 29

In his inaugural address, President John Kennedy said, "Ask not what your country can do for you—ask what you can do for your country." In other words, a responsible citizen is one who looks more for opportunities to *contribute* to the system than for opportunities to take from it. No one would argue that good citizenship begins at home. Therefore, our child-rearing practices should reflect this same principle. We should teach children that the reward of membership in a family comes more from what they put into the family than from what they take out of it. When this principle is turned upside down, when children are allowed to take from the family in greater measure than their contribution justifies, their relationship to the family becomes parasitic. Inherent to this condition is a lack of motivation, perpetual self-centeredness, and the entirely false idea that something can be had for nothing, all of which are afflicting entirely too many of today's children. (6PP)

July 30

Without realizing it, parents who are highly anxious concerning drug and/or alcohol use may actually increase the chances their children will develop such problems. Under the circumstances, substance abuse becomes a way for the child to assert autonomy and secure center stage in the family.

I sense that what a lot of parents truly fear concerning drugs is the feeling of having failed. The fact is, impeccable child rearing is no guarantee the child in question won't use drugs. I can't say this loudly enough: *Parents are not responsible for everything their children do.* Our job is not to prevent our children from making mistakes, because we can't. Our job is to see to it that they *learn* from their mistakes. (BHG)

July 31

There are three fundamental things parents should do to build a solid foundation of learning skills during the preschool years:

• First, parents should provide safe, stimulating environments that encourage inquiry and exploration. If, from his earliest months, a child's inquiries into the world are rewarding (as opposed to frustrating), and if parents feed (as opposed to deprive) his appetite for discovery, he will want, when the appropriate time comes, to rummage as eagerly through books as he did through drawers and cabinets when he was younger.

• Second, parents should spend lots of time reading to children. And read with gusto! Breathe life into the story! Make the child's eyes grow wide with wonder at the power of the printed word!

• Third, parents should read to themselves. Children follow the examples set by their parents. If parents read, children will want to follow suit when the time is right. If, on the other hand, parents rely on the television as a primary source of entertainment and information, so will their children. (EHH)

Homework done in the kitchen or any other family area will quickly become a *family affair*. This virtually guarantees that homework will become a central, if not *the* central, issue in the family for most of the evening. Homework will command family attention, distract family members from other, more important responsibilities (such as being married), and drain energy from the family that might otherwise be available for more creative, productive pursuits (i.e., communication and intimacy). The child who is allowed to do homework at the kitchen table is being handed an opportunity to exercise a unique sort of control over the family. He sits in a position of potential power, at the center of a potential hurricane that he can set to swirling simply by acting incompetent. And once a child accidentally discovers what havoc he can cause and how much attention he can garner simply by acting incompetent, he will act incompetent more and more often. It is not, mind you, a manipulation. The child doesn't *want* to be incompetent, he doesn't want to pay this price. It's simply that he hasn't learned how to resist the temptation.

(EHH)

Here are a few suggestions for controlling a young child's behavior in shopping centers and other public places:

• In advance, tell the child the purpose of the outing, so he knows what to expect, and (perhaps even more important) what *not* to expect.

• Do not make promises of the "If you're good, we'll buy you a so-and-so" sort. Deals like this teach a child to expect compensation for appropriate behavior.

• You can save yourself a lot of grief if you do not teach your young'un to expect a goodie every time the family goes shopping. Not only will he never acquire the obnoxious habit of constantly pleading for toys, etc., during shopping trips, but he will be surprised and appreciative when you do present him with something special.

• Just before going into the shopping center or restaurant, remind your child of a few simple rules, such as, "Stay in your stroller, talk quietly, and touch things only with your eyes."

• When rules are broken, or need to be created on the spot, take your child immediately aside and either remind or inform.

• If your child starts screaming or acting out of control, take him quickly into a remote area of the store and sit with him until the tantrum subsides or control is reestablished. The quicker you stop the momentum of the child's misbehavior, the better.

• A spanking administered at the scene rarely accomplishes anything except louder screams and lots of disapproving looks. If you feel that a spanking is warranted, please take your child into a private place before administering it. No, public spankings are not necessarily abusive, but they definitely disturb the public peace.

• For extreme emergencies, I recommend that each parent carry a set of fake nose and glasses, so that if all else fails, they can beat a hasty retreat into anonymity.   (PP)

Many parents think that being consistent means administering the same discipline each and every time a child misbehaves in a certain manner. Not so. Consistency is more a matter of attitude than technique. In fact, it is unrealistic to suppose that you will always be able to deliver the same technique every time a child misbehaves in a certain way. But you can always deliver the same *attitude*. In other words, you can display your disapproval and do something as a demonstration that you are in control. The something you do doesn't have to be the same something from misbehavior to misbehavior. It just needs to be something that says, "I won't allow you to behave like that."

In dealing with a discipline problem, more important than *what* you do is the act of *doing*. For every specific problem there are myriad effective solutions. It doesn't matter which one you select—you can even invent a new one—because for any and all discipline problems the real solution has nothing to do with technique or method. It's called commitment. It's the sense of purpose, the determination, the resolve you invest in the method of your choice (or invention). Commitment is the backbone of discipline. (TT, PP)

That a parent reports a "wonderful" relationship with a child is the self-congratulatory, feel-good sort of thing that masquerades for terrific child rearing these days, but in truth, it's nothing short of silly. In the first place, parents who really and truly understand and act consistently upon my advice—which is derived from the tried-and-true child rearing of previous generations—are not likely to have "wonderful" relationships with their children until those children are well into their teens, at best. Until then, their relationships with their children are likely to be on-again, off-again, up-and-down sorts of affairs.

In all likelihood, there will be many days when their children will not like them, and a good number of days when the feeling will be mutual. But, you see, children aren't supposed to like their parents that much anyway. They are, let me remind you, supposed to *want to leave home.* And let me assure you, this has nothing to do with loving one's parents.

I didn't like my parents that much. I wouldn't, for example, have chosen them as friends. They annoyed me, inconvenienced me, and made me angry. I loved my annoying, frustrating parents, but I couldn't wait to leave home, which simply means they did a good job. They convinced me I could make a better life for myself than they were willing to make for me. And, by gosh, I did!

Today's parents, by all accounts, are not doing nearly as good a job of convincing their children likewise. When I was twenty, I was married and on my own. The average age of economic emancipation in my generation was, in fact, twenty. Today, that average age is approaching twenty-five. In my time, for a child to live at home well into his or her twenties was considered an indication of something very odd in the parent-child relationship. Today it is considered normal. (NP)

Today's mother has a proprietary view of herself as a parent. She demands "ownership" of the child-rearing process out of fear that if she lets the control slip through her fingers, everything will fall apart. In the final analysis, however, it's herself she is protecting, not her child.

As a consequence of Mother-Anxiety and Mother-Guilt—neither of which, I hope the reader clearly understands, has anything whatsoever to do with the biological state of being female—the average American mother is, in her own mind, a single parent. She must do it all because if she relinquishes control of the process for any length of time, her carefully constructed child-rearing "house of cards" will come tumbling down and her children will turn out all wrong and it will all be her fault. So, back off, Dad, cause Mom's in town!

The average American father is nothing more than a "parenting aide." Like a teacher's aide, Dad's job is to assist Mom when she needs assistance and step in for her when she needs a break. In either case, his involvement is peripheral, temporary, and carried out at Mom's direction only. Fathers all over America have told me that their wives want them to "get more involved" in the rearing of the kids, but when they get involved, they are often quickly told by their wives that they're doing it wrong. And not surprisingly, mothers all over America have told me that their husbands just can't be trusted to do it right. Unless they're supervised properly, that is.   (FV)

People ask, "How can someone tell if their family is child-centered or not?"

It's actually easy to determine. A family is child-centered if, when adults and children are together, the adults act primarily from within the roles of mother and father/buddy as opposed to the roles of husband and wife.

"Mom" and "Dad" are focused on children. That's child-centeredness. Husband and wife are focused primarily on one another or the responsibilities appertaining to that commitment. That's marriage-centeredness. Neither state can be exclusive, of course. There will be times in even the most marriage-centered of families when necessity or custom will dictate child-centeredness: when a child is sick, for example, or has a birthday, or is graduating from high school. And there are, and well should be, times when child-centeredness just happens rather naturally. Nonetheless, the roles of mother and father should never become "habits." When they are called for or just happen, they should be put on *over* the roles of husband and wife, not substituted for them.

Marriage-centeredness creates more security for children. Nothing makes a child more *insecure,* after all, than the feeling his parents are in a state of discord. Conversely, nothing makes a child feel more secure than the feeling his parents are in a state of accord, of unity. The *only* way, therefore, to properly meet a child's need for security is to put the marriage center stage. (FV)

Now that my children are grown and living on their own, I realize that nearly every time one of them accused me of "liking" the other one better, the accusation was right on target—sort of. For example, I liked my son, Eric, for his sensitivity, his willingness to take risks, and his easy ability to make friends. On the other hand, I liked Amy for her madcap sense of humor, her insight into human nature, her flights of creativity. Unfortunately, my children, being children, failed to see that although assigned differently, my affections were balanced. So, when I laughed at one of Amy's impressions, Eric accused me of thinking she was "funnier." Translate: I "liked" her better. And Amy was equally sensitive to any attention I gave her brother. After years of talking myself blue in the face, I finally realized these were imagined "wounds" that only time would heal.

The bottom line: You, like all parents, play favorites. Stop denying it! Accept, admit, relax. Stop trying to explain yourself. Above all else, stop taking your children so seriously. When they're much older, and have children of their own who cannot get enough "fairness," they'll forgive you. To paraphrase Orson Welles, "No whine will stop before its time." (FV)

At the very least, a four- or five-year-old child should be responsible for keeping his room and bathroom orderly. A six-year-old can be taught to vacuum, starting with his own room. By age seven or eight, the child should be responsible for daily upkeep of his room and bathroom as well as several chores around the home. Once a week a child that age should be required to do a major cleaning of his room and bathroom. This should include vacuuming, dusting, changing bath and bed linens, and cleaning the tub, lavatory, and commode.

A nine- to ten-year-old should contribute about forty-five minutes of "chore time" to the family on a daily basis and about two hours on Saturday. It helps to organize the daily routine into three fifteen-minute blocks. The first of these should take place first thing in the morning (e.g., straighten room and bathroom and feed the dog); the second, right after school (e.g., unload the dishwasher and put everything away); the third, after supper (e.g., clear the table and take out the garbage).

By the way, in this scheme of things, there's no such thing as "boy-work" and "girl-work." It's all "people-work." If you are "people," then you work.

By the age of eighteen, all children—male and female—should be familiar with and practiced at *every single aspect* of running a home. They should be able to wash and iron their own clothes, plan basic meals, run a vacuum cleaner, disinfect bathrooms, replace furnace filters, mow grass, weed garden areas, and so on. They should also be responsible for earning a portion of their spending money and budgeting it sensibly. This training not only helps prepare children for independence, it also helps develop in them an appreciation for the effort their parents put into maintaining a household, an effort they will otherwise take for granted.   (6PP)

I read the news today, oh boy: Yuppie parents, it seems, are now demonstrating their commitment to better parenting by enrolling their toddlers in exercise programs!

Aren't toddlers active enough as it is? I know mine were. By the time they were eighteen months old, they were climbing bookcases, escaping from their cribs, jumping on furniture, throwing food, and running away from us in stores, airports, and other crowded places.

Not only are baby exercise programs unnecessary, they're downright dangerous to the mental health of parents! I can see it now: As the baby exercise craze sweeps the nation, we begin hearing reports of nine-month-olds vaulting out of their playpens, twelve-month-olds escaping down crib-sheet ropes from their bedroom windows, and eighteen-month-olds running merrily through the streets of America with their parents in hot, panting pursuit; going slowly, but aerobically, insane. (TT)

Typically, children have a difficult time letting go of their foolishness and adjusting to realities. As a consequence, when their parents reflect realities in the decisions they make, children often react by screaming. They scream things like, "I hate you!" and "I wish you weren't my parents!" and "You're dumb and stupid and your feet stink!"

Unfortunately, many parents take this screaming seriously. Their overly serious reaction takes one of two forms:

(1) Some parents think their children's screams are an indication that the parent-child relationship is falling apart and that their children are going to grow up not to like them.

(2) Other parents think their children's screams constitute flagrant disrespect which must be squelched.

Both reactions are foolish, which just goes to show that foolishness is not exclusive to children. In the first place, it takes much, much more than parents making unpopular decisions for a child to grow up with bitter memories of childhood.

In the second place, this screaming is not how children come to disrespect their parents. I cannot stress it enough: This screaming is a by-product of the foolishness that is bound up in the heart of every child. It merits no credence whatsoever. Now, if the child is so caught up in foolishness that he cannot seem to stop screaming on his own within a reasonable time, he might need to be sent to his room until he regains control of himself. In fact, since most children get "on a roll" fairly easily, it's probably a good idea to banish them to their rooms if the screaming lasts any longer than five seconds. And if a child, in the course of screaming because reality is biting him all over his little psyche, lets loose with some "choice" words, then banishment, preceded perhaps by a swat or two to the "spank absorber," is certainly in order. But banishing a child to his room—with or without a spanking—and getting all bent out of shape are two different things. A child's screams do not merit getting bent out of shape, believe me. Remember, screaming is a natural reaction to being bitten by reality. After all, reality has very sharp teeth. (FV)

By getting involved in the bickering that is almost inevitable to sibling relationships, parents unwittingly teach children to act like losers. To prevent children from playing this dangerous game, parents must transfer responsibility for the problem to them.

Call a conference with the kids and say, "Guess what, kids? We've figured out a way for the two of you to fight all you want without driving us crazy! We call it 'Problem, Problem, Now You Guys Have the Problem.' From now on, every time you guys bother one or both of us with your squabbling, we're going to confine you to your respective rooms for thirty minutes. It won't matter who started the squabbling, who was being fair or unfair, who had 'it' first, or whatever. Regardless, you will both spend thirty minutes in your rooms.

"Now listen carefully, because the third time we have to send you to your rooms on any given day it won't be for thirty minutes; it will be for the rest of the day. You'll be allowed out only to use the bathroom and eat meals with the family. Any questions?"

Now, instead of fighting with one another for the purpose of getting you involved, the children must learn to cooperate in order to *keep* you from getting involved. Aren't you clever?   (6PP)

August 12

There's been lots of talk about the need for parents to become supportively *involved* in their children's education. As a result, parents are asking, "How should we get involved, and how can we best demonstrate our support of education?"

The best way to get involved, the best way to support the efforts of your children's teachers, is to put first things first. At home, concentrate on building strong foundations for learning and excellence by teaching the "Three R's" of Respect, Responsibility, and Resourcefulness. As I've said time after time, *teachers cannot do what parents are supposed to have already done at home.* Teachers can only capitalize on what parents have *already* accomplished and are continuing to reinforce.

A child's education is a two-handed process. On the one hand are those responsibilities that belong to the child's school. On the other are those responsibilities that belong to the child's parents. Only if the school and the parents join hands effectively will the child be able to accept those responsibilities that belong to *him.*   (6PP)

August 13

All arguments with children get started in one of two ways. Either (1) a parent makes a decision that the child doesn't like, and the child strains forward, grimaces, and in a voice that sounds like fingernails being dragged across a chalkboard, screeches, "Why?!!" or (2) a parent makes a decision that the child doesn't like and the child strains forward, grimaces, and in a voice that sounds like fingernails being dragged across a chalkboard, screeches, "Why not?!!"

Arguments start because parents make the mistake of thinking these are questions. They aren't questions at all! They're invitations to do battle, and by accepting the invitation, you step squarely into quicksand. And the harder you struggle to be understood, the faster and farther you will sink.

You *cannot* win an argument with a child. Winning an argument with someone means you change that person's way of thinking. As a result of the information or point of view you share, that person adopts a new and probably more mature point of view. But children can't understand an adult point of view. To compensate, they adopt an irrational position and hold on to it for dear life. So no matter how eloquent or how correct, parents cannot win because children can see only one point of view—their own. (6PP)

Properly conceived and delivered, parental discipline enables the gradual development of self-control or self-discipline. The crux of self-control is the ability to anticipate consequences and adjust one's behavior accordingly. It follows that children cannot develop self-control unless they're able to successfully predict the consequences of their actions. That becomes impossible when parents are inconsistent. Inconsistency, therefore, prevents the development of self-control. This all boils down to one point of fact: In order to successfully discipline children, parents must themselves be self-disciplined.

Self-discipline and self-confidence go hand in hand. They are, in effect, synonymous. As I've already said (but cannot overemphasize), the successful discipline of a child is not a matter of proper selection of consequences. It's a matter of communicating one's self-confidence to the child—of communicating that you know where you stand and where you want the child to stand as well. This means that consistency is not necessarily a matter of delivering the same consequence each and every time the child misbehaves in a certain way; it is more a matter of always communicating your resolute, yet loving disapproval of that misbehavior. In other words, when it comes to the discipline of a child, form is secondary to substance.   (FV)

In general, when a child is having a conflict with an adult authority figure, I think it's best for parents to give the benefit of doubt to the adult. It's important for children to see that adults support one another concerning disciplinary matters.

Veteran teachers consistently tell me that thirty-plus years ago, if a child created a problem in school, the child's parents could be counted upon to follow through at home. Adults supported one another's authority and, in the process, communicated a fairly uniform set of standards to children concerning their behavior and school performance.

These same teachers tell me that today's parent, upon hearing that a child was disciplined at school, is likely to challenge the teacher's judgment and defend—or at least rationalize—the child's actions. Not only does this permit children to divide and conquer, it also allows them to escape accountability for misbehavior.

Whenever either one of our children came to us with a complaint concerning a teacher, our first question was, "Is the teacher treating every child the way she is treating you?" The answer was always, "No, she's only picking on me!" We'd respond, "Then you must be doing *something* to attract her attention to you, and the something must be inappropriate. We expect you to solve the problem, and quickly, or we will get together with your teacher and help you solve it." That usually was the last we heard of it.

There are very few teachers out there who do not have the best interests of children at heart. When a teacher says a child misbehaved, there's a 99 percent likelihood the child misbehaved. And although it always could be said the teacher could have handled the situation "differently," the teacher probably handled it well.

(TOH)

One parent I know, when his fifteen-year-old son came home obviously high on marijuana, simply took him aside and said, "Son, I want you to know that you can't smoke pot or drink alcohol without my knowing about it. I don't intend to punish you for this, and I'm not going to start following you around, spying on you. If you want to do drugs badly enough, you'll do them. In fact, since you now know that you can't hide it from me, and I'm not going to try and stop you, you might as well just do them right here, at home. What do you say?"

The startled son stammered, "Dad, I'm not going to smoke marijuana here at home, in front of you and Mom!"

"Why not?" the father responded. "We're going to know about it, either way."

"Because, well, because, I'd be embarrassed. I'd feel foolish."

"Ah," the father said. "You'd feel foolish because it *is* foolish. In that regard, I just want to point out one simple fact: You are never, ever going to hear an adult express regret over *not* having done drugs as a teenager. Think about it."

That was all that father said, but it must have been enough, because the son never smoked marijuana again. Had the father overreacted, however, there's no telling what might have happened. As my grandmother used to say, "Blow a lot of air on a smoldering twig, and it just might become a forest fire."

In the final analysis, parents who have modeled good values and built good relationships with their children before the teen years have very little to worry about. Their children may experiment, but aren't likely to flagrantly violate the trust their parents have placed in them.

(TOH)

I'll be blunt. A child can either be a participant in the family or he can be a parasite. A parasite is an organism that attaches itself to another, usually larger, organism and extracts benefit from the relationship while contributing little, if anything, of value to it. It is a "something for nothing" arrangement. Likewise, "You can get something for nothing" is the powerful message sent to a child who is not a fully participating/responsible member of his or her family.

The idea that something can be had for nothing is a falsehood, but a child who has been brought up within the fantasy that's implicit to that falsehood is very likely to bring that fantasy to school. He is likely to believe that education, like everything else that's ever come his way, is something someone *gives* you. This, of course, isn't true. Education, like self-esteem, is something you *get*, something your work for. Someone may extend to you the opportunity, but whether you take advantage of the opportunity or not is strictly a matter of choice.

The question becomes: How do you want your child to choose?

(EHH)

August 18

Americans have not had to make significant sacrifice on behalf of our country since World War II. There have been no national emergencies that required a parking of plows and leaving of families. Because of wars and depressions, every generation that came of age before the postwar "baby boom" had to make such sacrifice on a wholesale level. But then, every one of those generations had been prepared, within their families, for such sacrifice. The foremost tenets of good citizenship—respect for legitimate authority and service above self—had been actively practiced in their families, not just paid lip service; therefore, when the time came for sacrifice, it was not an alien demand. It was, in fact, regarded as a duty, so those who had to be coerced into national service were few and far between. Having enjoyed the fruits of discipline and love in the home, and thus prepared to fully partake of the fruits of American freedom and opportunity, these were people who were prepared to do whatever it took to protect those traditions and liberties.

It has been more than fifty years since a national emergency on the scale of those that regularly occurred up to and including World War II. And during those same fifty years, American child rearing has "softened" to the point where if a national emergency were to occur, there is a good likelihood we would find ourselves without enough people who were willing to shoulder the load and stay the course, but plenty of people who were more than willing to compromise America right out of existence. The last half century has been, for North Americans, a historically unique time. Our luck isn't likely to last forever.

(NP)

There are *always* alternatives to spanking. The question, however, becomes: In any given situation, is the alternative as effective as a spanking would have been? After having assisted in the rearing of two children and nearly twenty-five years of working with families, I've reached the conclusion that there are times when a quick spank to the rear of a child is worth more than a thousand words. The spanking serves as a *catalyst*, a *spice* that enhances the child's "taste" of his or her parent's authority, the message, and the consequence. (SPNK)

Over the past few years, I've conducted two informal polls that shed light on the "Nothin'-to-Do Blues." In the first poll, I asked parents from foreign countries representing every populated continent (and subcontinent) on the planet, "Do children in your country frequently complain of being bored, of having nothing to do?" In every instance, the answer has been "no," accompanied by incredulity at the notion that such a complaint is even possible from a child. Frequent feelings of boredom, I've discovered, have nothing to do with being a child, but everything to do with being an *American* child.

In the second poll, I asked people who, like my parents, reared their children in the '40s and '50s, "Did we, as children, frequently complain of being bored, of having nothing to do?" The generic answer: "Oh, you children may have complained of that some, but certainly not often. Come to think of it, on those rare occasions when one of you had the audacity to complain of having nothing to do, we simply told you that if you couldn't find something to do, we'd find something for you." That nipped that particular complaint in the bud, now didn't it? Feeling bored, therefore, is only epidemic within the most recent generation of American children. Consider the implications of this as we make the transition to a global economy, one in which the rewards will accrue to those players who are the most resourceful.   (FV)

I find it supremely ironic when, on the one hand, a parent worries over whether her child will be able to resist peer pressure during his teen years, but, on the other hand, doesn't want this same child to do without anything his friends have. This is a prime example of one hand not knowing what the other is doing. (DGP)

Whereas one of the four Hebrew words for *rod* can, indeed, imply a large, threatening implement (i.e., Exodus 21:20), the word used in Proverbs is also used in Isaiah 28:27 to suggest a relatively flimsy instrument used to thresh caraway *so as not to damage it.* In this regard, it is interesting to note that threshing is the process of separating the useful part of the grain from its chaff. Applied to child rearing, this yields the metaphor of discipline as the prolonged process of separating useful behaviors from those that are of no use. Furthermore, in threshing one must take care not to use too much force, lest the useful grain be damaged. Taken as metaphor, this says that when spankings are excessive, either in number or in force, the outcome is likely to be counterproductive. (SPNK)

Sometime between 1950 and the present, there occurred a radical, if insidious, shift in our attitudes toward the raising of children. During that time, the language of child rearing changed to reflect this shift. Raising children became "parenting," a much more serious, high-tech word. Self-confidence became "self-esteem," a much more fragile, sensitive word. Along the way, we created a new profession—the "parenting expert." Prior to this, mind you, there were people among us who were *experts* at rearing children. We called them "Maw-Maw" and "Paw-Paw" and silly things like that. The new parenting experts have fancy degrees and fancy offices. They sit behind big desks and say things while stroking their chins. And with their mostly meddlesome "help," the upbringing of children became not just a bigger deal than it had ever been before, but a more *difficult* deal as well.   (EHH)

In the late '60s and early '70s, several books were written on the subject of self-esteem in children. These books became the child-rearing "bibles" of their day. To a person, the authors maintained that children developed self-esteem only if their parents showed proper respect for them. Parents demonstrated this respect by treating their children as equals. These authors maintained that the only psychologically healthy family was a "democratic" family. In a democratic family, they said, no one was more powerful than anyone else.

As nice as it sounds, the democratic family is, was, and always will be fiction. You can, if it makes you feel better, pretend to have "democracy" in your family, but pretense is as far as it will go. The illusion of democracy in a so-called "democratic" family is created and maintained with lots of words, lots of unnecessary (and usually counterproductive) discussions, lots of unnecessary explanations, and lots of asking the children for their opinions. On the surface, all this may sound very "democratic." But if you sift down through the rhetoric and get to the bottom of things, you will discover an incontrovertible truth: In the so-called democratic family, someone always has the final say. That simple fact strips away any and all illusions of democracy. Furthermore, the someone who has the final say better be an adult, or everyone in the family is in big trouble.   (6PP)

The most important thing two working parents can give their children is a strong marriage. I'm not saying quality time spent with your child isn't important; I'm saying it's *more* important that you spend quality time with one another. If five out of seven days a week you have only three hours in which to be a family, that's all the more reason for you to keep your family priorities in order during that time. To be sure, a child needs attention from parents, and the younger the child, the more attention is needed. But parents also need time together as husband and wife, and children need to see their parents spending this time together. A child cannot learn that her parents' marriage is the "keystone" relationship in the family if, whenever they're together as a family, they act almost exclusively from within the roles of mother and father.   (TT)

The language of television watching conceals its reality. People talk about watching television "together," but the two things—watching television and togetherness—are mutually exclusive. You always watch television alone, locked into your own audio-visual tunnel. Television is the single greatest threat to communication and intimacy within the family that has ever existed. You may as well be two hundred miles away from the person sitting next to you if you're both watching television. (DGP)

I am *completely opposed* to the practice of slapping a toddler on the back of his hand for touching something off limits. (But I have to admit, I cannot support my objection with evidence that this is any more damaging, demeaning, or whatever, than a traditional spanking. I just don't *like* the practice; and because I am the author of this book, it is my prerogative to object to something simply on the basis of not liking it.) This rule applies even if he is reaching for something hot. If parents have time to slap, they also have time to grab the child's hand and pull it away with a sharp "no!" At this point, and depending on the child's verbal skills, the parent should either distract or, having secured the child's attention, briefly explain why the child should keep his distance from the item in question.

(SPNK)

All too often, when a child misbehaves, parents unwittingly shoulder the consequences of the problem. They take on the emotional consequences of the problem by feeling angry, frustrated, worried, embarrassed, and/or guilty. They take on the practical, tangible consequences by absorbing the inconveniences caused by the child's misbehavior.

Responsibility for a problem is measured in terms of its consequences. When parents absorb the lion's share of the emotional and tangible consequences of the child's misbehavior, they unwittingly accept responsibility for that misbehavior. In effect, the problem now belongs to *them,* and *they* will therefore try to solve it. But the harder they try, the more frustrated they will become, because the only person who can solve it is its rightful owner, the child.

Situations of this sort call for an enactment of the "Agony Principle": *Parents should never agonize over anything a child does or fails to do if the child is perfectly capable of agonizing over it himself.* In other words, when a child misbehaves, the child should be assigned both the emotional and tangible consequences of that misbehavior. Not until and unless the "agony" of the problem rests squarely on the child's shoulders will the child be motivated to solve it. Simply put, when a child does something bad, *he* should feel bad about it, and *he* should be required to take whatever steps are necessary to correct it.

(6PP)

Middle childhood is generally somewhat of a "honeymoon" in the parent-child relationship, but it's not destined to last forever. As puberty begins its incessant drumbeat, the child begins transferring allegiance from parents to peer group. He puts his pre-adolescent colleagues at the center of his attention and begins looking to them for cues as to how to act. As the tables thus turn, his parents feel themselves to be losing control, something they've enjoyed for too long to give it up without a fight. All too often, the more a child attempts to pull away and establish a comfortable "place" for himself with peers, the more anxious his parents become concerning peer influence, and the more they become their own worst enemies—forcing the youngster to prove that *obedience is always a choice*. In other words, the less willing parents are to support a young teen's need for independence (within limits, of course), the more likely it is the youngster will exercise free will in self-defeating ways.

The fact is, most young teens want more freedom than they can responsibly handle. Equally true, however, is that many, if not most, parents of young teens are guilty of not giving their children enough freedom, enough opportunity to learn by trial-and-error how to make good personal and social choices. Almost inevitably, parents who see it as their job to prevent their youngsters from making errors are those whose children end up making the most, and worse, errors.

It's also true that parents who feel the most secure in their ability to control are those who have the easiest time giving up that control. Thus, the paradox is this: The more effectively parents establish their "government" during the early years, the more willing they will later be to let the child pull away and begin the stumble toward self-government. In short, the time to begin parenting a teenager is some ten years earlier. Get it right the first time, and it's less likely to go wrong later on. (NP)

When parents of old said "you're going to stew in your own juices over this" to their children, they also meant "and we're not going to get in the pot with you, so you can cook all you want." Subscribing to this dictum kept parents out of argument with their children.

I talk a lot with people who reared children before World War II. They consistently tell me that they didn't have arguments with their children. Furthermore, their children, for the most part, never even asked "Why?" and "Why not?" concerning parental decisions. They simply accepted whatever decisions were made, whether they liked them or not. This means one of two things: Either there is not, as I said before, any such thing as an "argumentative child"; or, the "argumentative" gene was introduced into our gene pool by evil aliens sometime around 1955 and has been spreading like a virulent bacteria ever since. (FV)

I have a two-part rule governing the giving of explanations (for decisions parents make) to children. It's called "The Save-Your-Breath Principle."

Part One: Until a child is mature enough to understand a certain explanation, no amount of words will successfully convey that understanding. In that case, it is in the child's best interest for the parent to say "Because I said so" or words to that same effect.

Part Two: When a child is old enough to understand the explanation, he's also old enough to figure it out on his own.

So save your breath.   (6PP)

A true story from the "lost manuscripts" of the Three Little Pigs:

As children, the three little pigs live side-by-side-by-side in three houses in the same neighborhood. It just so happens they were born on the same day, attend the same grade in the same school, and make pretty much the same grades. A lot of people, not knowing otherwise, think they are siblings. Their parents, in fact, all work for the same company, and their family incomes are equivalent. The three families attend the same church and even go on vacations together.

Ah, but that's where the similarities between the Three Little Pigs' lives ends, because the first Little Pig's parents insist that he cannot leave their backyard without adult supervision. The second Little Pig's parents let him out of their backyard without adult supervision, but not off the block. The third Little Pig's parents let him off the block, but not out of the neighborhood.

Everything else being fairly equal, there is only one way to explain the fact that each of the Little Pig's parents draw this particular "line" in three entirely different places: Each set of parents draws the line where their comfort ends and their anxiety begins. For each set of parents, that line is in a different place. It cannot be said that one line is better than either of the others or, by extension, that one set of parents is doing the best job. They are all, in fact, doing the job of setting limits, and they are all doing good jobs. Yet, they are setting limits in three different places. Each set of pig-parents draws the line where they want it to be, not where it *should* be (no one really knows where it should be), or where scientists say it ought to be, or where psychologists deem best for self-esteem enhancement. They don't draw the line where "experts" say it should be drawn. In each case, it's drawn where the parents say it should be drawn. Because they say so, that's why. (FV)

A parent who finds himself frequently saying, "How many times have I told you to do (or not to do) so-and-so?" needs to realize this simply means he has failed to convince the child that he meant business the very first time he so "told." This is clearly not a child problem. It is a *parent problem*, and the parent in question will be forever complaining of having to say the same things over and over again until he accepts that humbling fact. (DGP)

When the ideal of child rearing was to produce responsible citizens, parents were not likely to lose sight of the "forest"—their obligations to the community and the culture as a whole—for the "trees"—their obligations to their children. They were better able to keep the two considerations in balance, realizing that the only way to strengthen the community was to produce a child of strong character.

When the ideal of child rearing became that of producing, in the child, something called "good self-esteem," that balance was destroyed. In the course of spending so much time and attention on the theoretical needs of a certain tree, today's typical parent has lost sight of the forest. The problem is that when parents lost sight of the forest, the "trees" lost sight of it as well. They grow up oblivious to their own obligations to the community and the larger culture. This is a disaster in the making. There is a time bomb ticking in the heart of America. (NP)

September 4

A journalist once asked what I thought was the biggest mistake made by the average well-intentioned parent. As I was trying to formulate a cogent answer, I thought of my fifteen-month-old grandson, Jack Henry Rosemond, and there it was! Although I'm fairly certain he understands at least five out of every ten instructions given him, he complies with one out of ten, maybe. If he's told *not* to do something, he immediately does it, and he's beginning to throw tantrums when he doesn't get his way. Now, all this is typical of fifteen-month-olds, primarily because they have every reason to believe their parents were put on the planet to wait on them hand and foot. Putting one's child at the center of attention and "catering" is, in fact, a hallmark of parental responsibility and commitment during infancy and early toddlerhood. As a parent, you're *supposed* to do that. For two years. Then you're supposed to stop catering and take your rightful place at the center of *your child's* attention.

The problem is that many of today's parents *never* turn the "tide" of their children's lives. They do an absolutely wonderful job during the first two years; then, because they never shift gears, things begin to fall apart. Long past their children's toddlerhoods, one finds these parents still catering, still serving, still reinforcing their children's self-centeredness. They don't realize that the last sixteen years of one's active parenthood must be spent undoing what was done during the first two years. This undoing is key to the child's discipline, socialization, and emancipation.   (NP)

Benevolently dictatorial parents derive no pleasure out of bossing children around. They simply recognize that it's every child's right to be governed well, and every parent's responsibility to provide good government.

In a benevolent dictatorship, as children mature, they are honored with increasing responsibility and privilege. In a *malevolent* dictatorship, children have no honor.

Parents cannot effectively discipline (dictate) unless they are also sources of genuine love (benevolence). Put another way, a child will not seek to please someone who cannot be pleased.

Likewise, parents cannot genuinely love unless they are sources of effective discipline. Put another way, a child cannot form a solid bond with someone he can't pin down. (DGP)

September 6

A mom in Birmingham, Alabama, confirms that good old-fashioned discipline is not only still alive, but still works! She relates an incident with her eight-year-old son that began with her purchasing a shirt for a sibling which the eight-year-old felt was "better" than the shirt purchased for him. The next morning, still miffed, he refused to eat his breakfast, "forgot" to make his bed, and dawdled over getting dressed. He missed the bus.

The family lives one and a half miles from the school, and on that particular morning the temperature was 28 degrees. His parents informed him he was going to walk. (His mother walked with him to insure his safety.) At the half-mile mark, the youngster said, "I don't care. Actually, this is turning out to be fun." This, writes his mother, was before his shoelace came untied, ants crawled up his leg (looking, no doubt, for warmth), and the cold worked its way through his coat and gloves.

She writes: "By the time we arrived at school, his hands were cold and he was most unhappy. I escorted him to the rest room and suggested he warm his hands under running water. When he emerged, I reminded him it was his responsibility to make the bus every morning, and that the next time he missed it, he and I would walk every morning for five days."

The little fella has been quite punctual since then. "The puzzling thing," his mother writes, "has been the number of parents who tell me they admire our handling of the situation, but say they couldn't have done it themselves!" No, there aren't too many parents these days who have the courage to let a child experience the real-life consequences of irresponsibility, and to not give a hoot whether their discipline is looked upon favorably by their peers. Kudos to a mom in Birmingham for her grit and for sharing a story about love—the old-fashioned (and therefore the best!) kind!   (NP)

September 7

A journalist recently asked me what happened that caused this generation of American parents to become so permissive. The term, I immediately pointed out, is not an accurate reflection of what has happened within America's child-rearing culture. To correctly assert that today's parents are permissive means that they are willing to grant their children freedoms that were not generally allowed children in previous times. Permissiveness is a stance of leniency taken because one thinks it is proper.

In the course of delivering some two hundred presentations a year, I talk to parents all over the country, and I dare say the ones I encounter are typical in every sense of the term. I do not, however, get the impression that any significant number of them are permissive. The more accurate descriptor is unassertive. For the most part, today's parents are nice, well-intentioned folks, and that's the problem. They let their children walk all over them, not because they believe children should be allowed to do so, but because they do not feel they have the right to assertively disallow it.

No, today's parents are not permissive. They are milquetoast, afraid to just say no and stand by it. They know, in their hearts, they shouldn't give their children so much freedom and are truly afraid of the consequences of doing so. Unfortunately, they're even more afraid of the consequences of saying "no." In short, today's parents are wimps. The good news is, it's never too late to take charge. I know this because I'm a recovering wimp. (NP)

September 8

The story of Amy and her sixth-grade science project: One evening during the first half of that school year, Amy came to me in a panic. Her science project was due the next day, she announced, her hands flapping in front of her, and she hadn't started it and I had to take her to the store for the project materials and I had to help her. Exclamation point plus!!!

I thought about that for a moment. "Well, Amy," I said, "you're out of luck tonight, because I have forgotten how to drive a car."

"No you didn't!"

"Okay, you're right, Amos," I said, "I really didn't. But I'm really not going to drive you to the store, and I can assure you, neither is Mom. Sometime in the next few days, when it's convenient, one of us will take you to the store. I guess this means you're going to turn your science project in late."

"BUT I'LL GET A BAD GRADE!!!!!"

"I trust that you will, Amy," I said. "In fact, if your teacher *doesn't* give you a bad grade, I will be the first parent in the history of that school to demand that his own child's grade be lowered."

And Amy begged, and she wailed, and she acted like she was coming apart at the seams and her self-esteem was being flushed forever down the toilet of life, but I refused to budge (so did Willie). We took Amy to the store a couple of days later but gave her no help with her project. She turned it in late, and her teacher saved me a visit to the school by giving Amy a low grade. And Amy never, ever again waited until the last minute to do a project.

That's how you motivate children. You don't paddle their canoes. Grandma said so. (FV)

September 9

You have a youngster who throws tantrums in stores? I have a guaranteed-to-work solution for you! It's called "dry runs": Plan a trip to the store when you have no shopping to do (that's right, *no shopping*). On the pretense of having to make a purchase, undertake the excursion as you normally would, taking your child along. Before you enter the store, however, stop outside and calmly inform your child that should he create a disturbance, no matter how small, you will immediately take him home where he will spend the remainder of the day indoors with no privileges (television, a friend over) and go to bed early.

Now, instead of dreading a disturbance, you're actually *hoping* for one. When it happens—and it will, believe me—you simply say, "You've just told me that you want to go home, so let's go." Take his hand, lead him immediately out of the store, take him directly home, and do exactly what you said you were going to do. Do not, under any circumstances, give him a second chance or renegotiate the consequence, regardless of what he might promise or how much he might plead.

You will, I guar-an-tee, secure your child's attention. Instead of getting flustered when he misbehaves, you respond with calm, purposeful resolve. Having taken him by surprise, you can expect a dramatic reaction on his part. He will, in all likelihood, wail and tell you he doesn't want to be your child any longer and then wail some more. Just say, "I'd be upset, too, if I had to go home and spend the rest of the day inside."

Over the next few weeks, plan as many unnecessary excursions to the store as you can, taking the same approach each time. Within a month, your child should be a model shopper. In the meantime, you may have to sacrifice one or two necessary shopping trips as well. If that happens, just remember there's a price to be paid for everything. In this case, however, the payment plan is virtually painless.

(TT)

If there's one valuable lesson the proponents of democratic, child-centered families have taught us, it's that authority is not inherent to being a parent. Rather, authority must be claimed and then acted upon. Furthermore, following this self-confirmation, it must be constantly asserted lest it fade away. The authoritative parent must affirm, on a daily basis, that she or he is in command of her- or himself, the child, and the circumstances of the child's life. This daily renewal constitutes the core of the parent's commitment to provide for and protect the child under any and all circumstances. The affirmation of this commitment forms the essence of the child's sense of security. Intuitively, a child understands that a parent who will not claim and affirm his or her own authority is a parent who cannot be relied upon for anything and has no "right," therefore, to respect, as measured by deference and obedience. Without intention, *nouveau* parenting "experts" provided legions of proof to this very effect. Parents who followed their well-intentioned advice were persuaded not to claim their authority. It would have been just if the price to be paid had been borne only by themselves. Unfortunately, their children were the real losers. (NP)

Complaints about how difficult it is to raise children are unique to this generation of parents, who wear their moaning and groaning like a badge of courage. Implicit to all this griping is the idea that unless raising children isn't wearing you out, you must not be working hard enough at it. This is soap opera, pure and simple, starring hardworking parent in constant search of self-esteem for her child as her own slides steadily downhill from self-neglect.

In the real world, child rearing is simple; it takes more common sense than intellect, and its success is more a matter of self-confidence than sacrifice, of parents who are sufficiently self-respecting, as opposed to parents who spend all their time "self-esteeming" their tyrannical little darlings. Child rearing doesn't have to be, and should not be, tremendously time-consuming and emotionally expensive. It is a practical process that can tolerate lots of error and still turn out well. Children are resilient, not fragile. They are not—I repeat, *not*—little Humpty Dumptys perched precariously on the wall of life, needing parents circling under them with safety nets lest they lose their balance and take the One Great Final Fall. (FV)

I've had several conversations of late with Asian parents, all of whom are recently arrived to these shores. Without exception, they tell me they are appalled at the behavior of American children, and they fear the bad influence upon their own. In the course of these conversations, I've discovered that these parents bring an entirely different set of assumptions to the child-rearing process, as 180-degrees-removed from those of the average American parent as China is from the United States.

The first is that children should pay more attention to parents than parents pay to children. These parents understand that you cannot discipline a child who is not paying attention to you. They also understand that the more attention parents pay to children, the less children will pay to parents.

Second, no attempt is made to persuade children to cooperate. In fact, since cooperation implies a state of equality, these parents don't even seek cooperation. Instead, they expect obedience.

Third, they don't explain themselves to their children. Therefore, their children's inquiries are directed to what the world is made of and how it works, rather than the "why?" and "why not?" of their parents' rules and expectations. In fact, these parents are amazed at the amount of time American parents waste dealing with such trivia.

Lastly, these parents do not tolerate misbehavior. Therefore, they do not bribe their children, not do they threaten them. How enlightening to realize that both bribe and threat are self-fulfilling!

The truly sad aspect of all this, however, is the realization that for the most part America's children used to be as well-behaved as those Asian kids. The good news is, it's not too late to save ourselves.

(NP)

For years, the politically correct explanation for the epidemic rise of depression, suicide, violence, and drug and alcohol use among America's teens has been "poor self-esteem." Troubled teens are but "acting out" their low opinions of themselves, or so the conventional wisdom has gone. Responsibility for the problem was thus assigned either to the child's parents or to "society," the assumption being that if high-risk kids could be made to "feel good about themselves," these epidemics could be mitigated.

Interestingly enough, rates of teen depression, drug and alcohol use (a form of withdrawal), and violence began rising sharply around the same time the "self-esteem movement" began picking up steam. The movement's promoters decried "blaming," which amounted to holding anyone singularly responsible for any and all antisocial behavior. "Blaming" was held to be a form of psychological assault on the right of every individual to "good self-esteem." Furthermore, said the "self-esteemers," if one made a sufficient attempt at "understanding," the familial or social cause of the person's behavior would become obvious. The ascendancy of this psychobabble ripped the lid off Pandora's box, and it is no wonder that the demons released have done outstanding damage to America's children.

Judeo-Christian scripture holds that wrongdoing requires *penance* —an admission of personal responsibility and a corresponding feeling of guilt. In other words, if you do something bad, you *should* feel bad about it. Penance drives atonement—the attempt to redress the wrong. It's this simple: If a wrongdoer is not penitent, he will not voluntarily atone. But that's not all. Not only does penance lead to atonement, but atonement leads to *healing*. What this means is that the damage done to America's youth and the damage they are doing to themselves cannot be healed as long as good intentions and sentimental ideas continue to hold sway in child rearing.

Children's heads are soft. It takes hard heads to rear 'em right.

(NP)

I've figured out that a grandparent's job description reads somewhat as follows:

• You will give advice when you feel the inspiration to do so, and without apology, but you will act as if you don't really care whether the grandchild's parents follow your advice.

• You will look for as many opportunities as possible to tell the parents the grandchild will do things for you that he will not do, or has not yet done, for them. For example, if he will not go to sleep at their house without being rocked, then you are obligated to teach him how to go quietly to sleep without being rocked.

• You will also look for as many opportunities as possible to point out to the parents that the grandchild did something for you before he did it for them. This includes such things as crawling, pulling himself to a standing position, and walking. In this regard, it's extremely important that the child's first word be either "Gam-pa" or "Gamma."

• You will laugh at things the grandchild does that make the parents anxious, frustrated, or embarrassed. You will do this not to ridicule or undermine the parents, but to keep reminding them that they should not take themselves, or the child, so seriously.

• When the grandchild is with you, you will see to it that he is thrown "off schedule," and he is allowed to do and have access to numerous things his parents do not allow, but when you are in the parent's domain, you must always support them, whether you approve of their decisions or not.

• You will tell everyone how wonderful grandparenthood is, and you will encourage people to throw caution to the wind and have children while they are young, so that they might still be young when their children have children.

• Above all else, and as often as possible, you will remind the parents that your job is to always spoil the grandchild, while their job is to never spoil him, and you will act sorely offended whenever you catch them trying to do your job. (NP)

Q: *Our thirteen-year-old adopted daughter has started asking questions about her biological parents, questions to which, for the most part, we have no answers. She says she wants to know who they are and possibly begin a relationship with them. We have an adoption registry in our state, but don't know if this is the time for our daughter to begin the process of searching out her biological roots or not.*

A: A thirteen-year-old child is not capable of making mature, rational decisions concerning these issues, and contrary to what many people, including many professionals, believe, you cannot *reason* with a young teenager.

In all likelihood, your daughter is a typical thirteen-year-old. She's decided that the two of you are simply the most embarrassing, dumb, burdensome parents who ever lived. It's not at all unusual for adopted children of this hyper-confused age to begin fantasizing that everything in their lives would now be hunky-dory if only their biological parents had not parted with them. This is, of course, pure soap opera, but it tends to throw adoptive parents into a state of anxiety. The adopted child, in turn, works the parents' insecurities for all they're worth. The implied, if not stated, threat becomes: If you don't give me my way, I'm going to find my biological parents and go live with them.

Needless to say, this is not the time to help your daughter find and begin forging ties with her biological mother and father. You should answer those questions you can, and respond with "we don't know" to those you can't. Explain that her biological parents, wherever they are, have lives and perhaps even a family of families of their own. Tell your daughter that when she graduates from high school, she will be free to begin a search for her biological parents, and that, if she wishes, you will even be willing to help in any way you can. By then, she will be old enough to make reasonably well-thought-out decisions about the issues involved. (NP)

A Des Moines, Iowa, couple once asked me for "the key" to successful discipline of a two-year-old. They were no doubt looking for some magical technique that would solve all their problems. I answered, "Pay more attention to your marriage than you do your child. Effective discipline flows from the fundamental understanding that the marriage is the most important relationship in the family, occupies center stage, and functions as 'ringmaster' in the family circus." You see, contrary to what most people think, successful discipline (of any child, at any age) is not a matter of technique; rather, it's a matter of what I'll call "family philosophy."

When, in a two-parent family, the child becomes the center of attention, and the child's relationship with one or both parents consumes more energy than does the parents' relationship with one another (when, in other words, they are mother and father more than they are husband and wife), it becomes easy for the child to "divide and conquer." Parents can only act decisively if they act in unison.

In a single-parent family, it must be equally clear that the parent is neither friend nor sibling, and that his/her life does not revolve around the child. It must be established that the single parent has a life of his/her own, completely independent of child-rearing responsibilities. A parent cannot be indulgently devoted to a child and define limits effectively. Nor can a parent be in a position of "service" to a child and promote the steady growth of the child's autonomy.

(TT)

Parents should keep tabs on how a child intends to use his allowance and retain the right of refusing to let him spend it irresponsibly or in ways that are incompatible with the values of the family. Parents should take every available opportunity to teach their children how to be intelligent consumers—how to recognize quality, how to compare, how to shop for value, and so on.

I remember when our son, Eric, was about eight years old, he took his two-dollar allowance and bought two cheap plastic cars—the kind that hold together about thirty minutes once they're out of the package—that were part of a toy display in a grocery store. When we found out what he had done with his money, we made him take one of them back for a refund. Several days later, we casually inquired about the car he had kept. "It broke," he said, with a don't-say-I-told-you-so look. Lesson learned. (BHG)

Reward-based motivational plans carry a built-in time bomb I call the Saturation Principle. Sooner or later, any child will become *saturated* with any reward. Whereas the reward might have been initially enticing enough to leverage improved performance, when saturation occurs—when, in other words, the child has "had his fill" of the reward—the child's interest in the reward will decline along with his performance.

At this point, in order to pump the child's performance up again, the adult must make the child another offer, more interesting than the first. Under the circumstances, therefore, the adult is taking responsibility for maintaining the child's performance at adequate levels. As such, this cannot be helping the child appreciate the intrinsic value of improved behavior/performance.

Adults run the risk with reward-based systems of teaching children that misbehavior/underachievement is the ticket to getting special things and privileges. It doesn't take them long to realize—at an intuitive level—that adults aren't making well-behaved, highly motivated children these offers. Conclusion: Misbehavior pays. (FV)

Because of "expert" psychobabble to the effect, today's parents—those who want to do the best job possible—are petrified at the possibility they might do something that will upset their children's supposedly delicate psyches and create conditions of permanent emotional turmoil. As a consequence, all too many well-intentioned parents are afraid of doing anything that might make their children unhappy, however temporarily. The ironic, darkly humorous upshot of this is that today's parents are the first generation of Americans who were, as children, intimidated by adults and who are, as adults, intimidated by children. In thirty years, the parent-child relationship has turned upside down. The victims of this inversion include the American child, who never learns to respect authority and cannot, therefore, ever develop true self-respect; the American parent, who exists in a state of perpetual child-centered neurosis; the American family, which lacks both a stout helm and a competent helmsman; and finally, America, which wobbles on an increasingly weak foundation. This ever-worsening situation will not be corrected until American parents retrieve the gumption to tell both their children and the "experts" to sit down and hold their tongues.   (TOH)

September 20

When I was in high school—shortly before "the pill" and long before AIDS—the world was a place of clear-cut dichotomies. Things were either one way, or they were the other. Shades of gray did not exist. The most significant of these either/or propositions, from the perspective of a young, hormone-saturated male (like myself), was that of nerd/cool. There was no mistaking the two. Nerds (like myself) were in the chess club and on the debating team, drove their mothers' station wagons, wore glasses, and stayed home on weekends. The guys with "cool" excelled in physically punishing sports, such as wrestling or football, drove fast cars, consumed great quantities of beer and other alcoholic beverages, and "scored" with girls. Lots of girls, to hear them talk about it, which they generally did after consuming great quantities of beer and other alcoholic beverages. And thus the line was drawn separating the "men" from the boys.

We just didn't get it, did we? Not even the nerds understood that beneath this bravado (or the worship of it) lay an insecurity that fed on the depersonalization of women. Compounding the problem was the fact that many of our fathers either ignored our emerging sexuality altogether or, at best, made awkward attempts to fill us in on the physiology of sex.

Eager to terminate this torture, we assured our dads that they'd performed their duties well and hastened for the nearest exit. Needless to say, not all fathers approached this issue in such cursory fashion, but by the time many males of my generation started dating, they were the hormone-powered equivalent of unguided missiles.

(NP)

When my son, Eric—now twenty-seven and married to Nancy, the daughter-in-law of my dreams—began showing interest in girls, I reflected back upon the foibles and fiascoes of my adolescence and promised myself he would be better prepared for datinghood. Undertaking this as a project meant defining my goals, selecting my strategies, and formulating contingency plans.

What, I asked myself, did I want to accomplish with Eric? The answer was simple: Everything my father had not, including:

• An open, anxiety-free line of communication concerning anything having to do with not only sexuality, but male/female relationships in general.

• A respectful attitude toward both himself and members of the opposite gender (a lack of respect for oneself always manifests itself in a lack of respect for others, and *vice versa*).

• An understanding of the "politics" of dating, including an appreciation of and respect for the worries, wishes, and expectations—both explicit and implicit—typical of a teenage girl's parents.

I also had to accept that there is no science to this, no approach that will guarantee the desired outcome. Do your best, I told myself, and do not accept the blame for mistakes Eric may make. I knew that the success of my venture was less a matter of intellect than a matter of sensitivity and intuition. In order to be "in tune" with Eric, I not only had to make myself available, but had to spend time with him on a regular basis. My professional experience had taught me that teenage boys who lack relationships with healthy adult male role models often take to acting out very distorted ideas of what makes for a "real man." During Eric's teen years, we built models, played golf, and went to many a rock concert together. The relationship was hardly free of antagonism, but it never lacked for energy.   (NP)

September 22

Concerning "the talk," I decided that what Eric needed from me was not a rundown of "the facts of life," but the freedom to bring his questions and concerns to me. If his sexual education was going to be meaningful, he would have to feel in control of it. So, shortly after his thirteenth birthday, I took the initiative to issue an open-ended invitation. I think we were working on a model together when the time suddenly felt right to say what I had to say:

"Eric, you know, as you get older, you're going to become more and more interested in girls, and you're going to have questions. When you have a question or want to discuss something concerning women and men or sex, I'd like you to ask me or Mom. We'd rather you asked one of us than one of your friends because their answers might not be correct. And remember, there's no such thing as a dumb question." And back to the model we went.

Needless to say, I could sense his relief at not being subjected to a long-winded discourse on the birds and the bees. This tack seems to have worked, because he *did* come to us with questions on more than a few occasions. And Willie and I always took those opportunities not just to give answers, but to add a few editorial comments as well.

If I learned one thing through all this, it was that a young man's education in opposite-gender relationships cannot be accomplished by hit-and-run, as my father had attempted. Nor is it a matter of—in the words of Detective Joe Friday—"the facts, ma'am, just the facts." It's a creative process that requires an ongoing commitment not just to the male child in question, but to the very health of our culture. One must, in other words, never lose sight of the forest for the trees. I also discovered, much to my vicarious satisfaction, that sex and "cool" have absolutely nothing to do with one another. The sins of the fathers do *not* have to be borne by the sons. Hallelujah!   (NP)

September 23

Since I began writing my syndicated newspaper column in 1976, it has become increasingly clear to me that the psychological community often functions more like a political party or a religion than a science. For example, although it often pretends to matters of *fact*, psychology consists of nothing more than a set of highly speculative (and constantly changing) theories concerning human behavior. Believing in these theories requires faith, and psychology certainly has its share of true believers. These theories constitute psychology's ideology or canon, and as is the case concerning an organized political party or religion, they are the subject of constant intraprofessional debate. There is, however, an unwritten rule that no party to these debates may ever say that another party is dead *wrong*. One may express skepticism, or reserve judgment, or politely disagree, but one may not scoff. Consequently, conflict among members of the profession almost always takes place with extreme respect for *form*, and always within the context of a certain agreed-upon "party line." Psychologists may sneer at the ideas and methods of mainstream psychiatry, but they may not sneer at mainstream psychology. Not without penalty, that is.

I know this because I am a heretic within my profession. My views on child rearing and family life are "psychologically incorrect." They rock the boat, upset applecarts, and provoke often vitriolic response. The simple explanation is that I have been willing to publicly state my disdain for the child-rearing ideology propounded since the 1950s by mainstream psychology. Furthermore, I go so far as to propose that previous generations of American parents reared children generally well. As long as there are psychologists who believe they have better ideas concerning child rearing than were held by our forebears, there will be psychologists who think I am a menace and display, in their denouncements, their intolerance for ideas inconsistent with their own parochial philosophy. In that context, I accept that I am a heretic. I not only accept it, I am proud of it, and I will continue to be a heretic until psychology gets its head out of the clouds and its feet on the ground. In anticipation of that, I'm not holding my breath. (FV)

I threaten America's mental health industry because I attempt through my work to convince parents that whether they realize it or not, they are competent to solve 98 percent of child-rearing problems on their own, without professional help. Mental health professionals, on the other hand, have spent enormous energy trying to convince the American public they are indispensable to nearly every aspect of child rearing. I'm willing to concede that some mental health professionals can, in some cases, be helpful, but then so can a coworker, your barber, your grandmother, a neighbor, or your best friend. Unlike the case with doctors, dentists, and automobile mechanics, however, there is no evidence that mental health professionals have improved the overall quality of life in America. In short, if by some miracle, they all disappeared from the face of the planet, life would go on, and suffering would not increase significantly. Trust me on this. Remember, I am a psychologist. If I disappeared from the face of the earth, life would go on, although the mean "humor quotient" of the world would drop ever so slightly.   (FV)

Parents create rules and children test them. Testing is, after all, a child's only way of discovering whether, in fact, a rule truly exists. Telling a child, "This is a rule," isn't enough. Children are concrete thinkers. They must be *shown*.

When a child breaks a rule, parents have an obligation to impose some form of discipline. This gets the child's attention and says, "See, we were telling you the truth." Consistency, therefore, is a demonstration of reliability. The more a child feels he can *rely* on (believe in) his parents, the more secure the child will feel. If, however, the child breaks a stated rule and instead of enforcing, parents threaten or talk themselves blue in the face or get excited but don't do anything, the child is forced to test the rule again, and again, and again. Testing of this sort "spins a child's wheels." It wastes time and energy that the child could otherwise be spending in creative, constructive, growth-producing activities. Because consistency frees children from the burden of having to repeatedly test rules, it helps them become all they are capable of becoming. (6PP)

Having proven that children really don't need reasons, and that "because I said so" is the one, true reason, I must now tell you that I think it's right and proper, in most cases, to give a child at least one reason other than "because I said so" whenever the child so demands. That's right. Actually, it's kind of obnoxious to say nothing but "because I said so" every time a child demands a reason. You begin to sound like a broken record. So, give children reasons. But, please, understand one thing: *If a child doesn't like a limit you've set or an expectation you've described, the child is not going to like any reason you use in defense of your decision, either.*

Let's face it, you have never, after making a decision one of your children didn't like, been able to "reason" the child in question into saying, "Oh, now I get it, Mom! I see the light! I understand perfectly! This is amazing! A minute ago, I disagreed with you and thought you were the stupidest person on the face of the earth and that your feet stunk, and with just a few words you've been able to prove to me how foolish I was! Oh, thank you, Mom! You're the greatest, and I love the smell of your feet!"

That has never happened, and it will not ever happen as long as your child is a child. Why? Because *children cannot understand adults.* Period.

So, give a reason for any limit-setting decision you make, but don't expect the child to agree. When he doesn't, don't try to help him understand, because he can't, and the attempt will only result in an argument. Just say, "Oh, I know you don't agree with me. Why, if I were you, I wouldn't agree with me either." And turn around and walk away.   (FV)

I am convinced that the typical father of the '50s was not, as myth would have it, "distant," "unapproachable," or "cold." The typical father of the '50s was busy in his work and a devoted husband/family man. Compared to his wife, who was generally at home through the day, he might have seemed less accessible, but that was a consequence of his responsibilities, not an inability to relate warmly to his kids.

Nonetheless, it's amazing how this myth has worked its way into the contemporary psyche. A father recently remarked to me, "I don't want to be like my dad. He was too busy for his kids, and when he was home, he was remote."

I asked, "When did you come to this conclusion, that your dad was remote?"

"What do you mean?" he rejoined.

"I mean," I said, "did you come to this conclusion as a child or as an adult?"

"I came to the conclusion recently," he answered.

"Then your father's 'remoteness' didn't bother you when you were young?" I asked, rhetorically.

He thought for a moment. "No," he finally said, "I guess not."

"Then what's the problem?" I asked.

He thought again. "So what you're telling me is that my dad was an okay dad and that somehow I've become lately convinced he wasn't?"

"Right," I said. "I'll just bet he was a good provider, a good husband, a paragon of masculinity, and a respected member of his community."

"Yes, he was all those things," the man replied. "So, tell me, how is it that I came to the conclusion that he wasn't a good father?"

"I'll just bet," I answered, "you've been reading too much."

(NP)

September 28

Is today's "I've got nothin' to do!" kid trying to tell us something? You bet, and it's high time we all listened up. If this child could explain his boredom in adult terms, here's what parents would hear: "I know, Mom and Dad, that you bought me all this stuff to keep me happy, and in a sense you succeeded. Every time you bought me a toy, I was happy, for a while. But in the course of buying me all these toys, you convinced me, without ever intending to do so, that my ability to occupy and entertain myself is in direct proportion to the number of toys I can claim as my own.

"You should have been trying to convince me that my ability to occupy myself has nothing to do with the number of things I have out there (pointing around), but is simply a matter of how much I have up here (pointing to his head). Mom and Dad, with the best of intentions, you caused me to believe in a trip to the toy store when you should have been teaching me to believe in *me*. Now, Mom and Dad, having explained all that, I have one question, and it may be the most important one I ever ask you: When are you going to cut it out?" (FV)

Success in life is not primarily a matter of what grades you made in school. Interestingly enough, the same question is always asked at those training sessions I conduct for teachers. When it is, I ask the group a series of questions:

"How many of you on a regular basis find yourselves needing to use what you learned in high school algebra?" In an audience of, say, one hundred, maybe three hands will rise.

"Chemistry?" A few hands.

"American Literature?" Maybe ten hands.

"World History?" Five hands, maybe.

At this point, I change my tack. "How many of you have found that in order to be successful, you need to manage your time effectively almost every day of your lives?" Every member of the audience raises a hand.

"Keep your hand up if you have found that in order to be successful, you need to accept responsibility for things you'd really rather avoid doing." All the hands stay up.

"Keep your hand up if you have found that exercising initiative is critical to success." Every right arm in the place is getting numb at this point, so I tell 'em to put their hands down.

My point is that whether we realize it or not, most of the subject matter a child learns in school is not going to matter one way or another in his life. What's going to matter is what the child learned in the *process* of struggling to master the subject matter. And the operative word in the last sentence is "struggling." In other words, the more effort parents expend, the less children struggle, and the less they learn what they need to learn to make successes of their lives.

(FV)

Self-esteem became the buzzword of "parenting" in the '70s and has retained that coveted status ever since. For twenty years or more, the professional community has told American parents their first obligation is to promote and protect this nebulous psychological entity. That same professional community created the impression that self-esteem is something adults bestow upon children by giving them an abundance of attention and praise. The more of those things you give your kids, the "experts" said, the better they will feel about themselves and the better their self-esteem (read: the happier they) will be. But self-esteem is not something bestowed upon children. It is something children work toward and discover for themselves. It is not something given to children by doting parents. It is earned, as are all truly valuable things. It does not grow in direct proportion to the amount of effort parents put into praising and doing things for children, or giving them attention. It grows as children learn to do for themselves. The "self-esteem" that accrues as a result of lots of attention and praise isn't self-esteem at all; it's self-centeredness, which a child must grow *out* of in order to grow *up*.   (TT)

October 1

Chores help children develop responsibility, self-discipline, and other essential values. An allowance helps a child develop money-management skills. Parents should make sure the two lessons don't get confused.

Paying a child for doing a chore tends to create the illusion that if the child doesn't want the money, he isn't obligated to perform the chore. Payment also takes away from the values a child learns by doing chores. A chore that's paid for is no longer a contribution for the sake of contribution, but a contribution for the sake of money.

In the final analysis, children should do chores for one reason only—because they are told to do them by their parents, who are wise enough to realize the importance of them. Parents who use money to elicit cooperation from a child are unwittingly undermining their own authority. The child ends up learning a lot about how to manipulate people, but nothing about respect for authority, responsibility, and self-discipline. (PP)

October 2

Q: *Is it all right for parents to give a child the chance to earn extra money by doing special work beyond that which is normally expected of him?*

A: Certainly. Whereas parents should not pay a child for doing jobs that are part of the household routine—taking out the garbage, feeding the pet tarantula, and so on—it's perfectly okay for parents to contract with a child for work over and above the daily call of duty, but deals of this nature should be the exception rather than the rule. No one should lose sight of the fact that within the family, work is not done for money, but simply because it needs to be done.

In and of itself, having multiple caretakers—each with a different personality, different expectations, different limits, and different ways of disciplining—isn't confusing to a child. What's confusing is when a particular caretaker draws the line one place one minute, another the next. Take it from me. When I was very young, I spent a significant amount of time with each of the following: my maternal grandmother, my paternal grandmother, my mother, and Mae, the woman who supervised me while my mother was at work or at school. One of these women spoiled me, another had very little patience for me, another was permissive, and another was matter-of-factly stern, yet loving. I had no problem whatsoever with this "inconsistency." In no time at all, I figured out what each one of them would and would not tolerate, what I could and could not put over on them, and I adjusted my behavior accordingly. Children are, after all, intuitively brilliant, and I was by no means exceptional in that regard. (NP)

Hobbies benefit children in a number of important ways. As expressions of personal accomplishment, they help build feelings of personal competence. Hobbies are an educational medium, as well. A child who becomes interested in rocketry learns about propulsion and aerodynamics. Stamp collections contain mini-lessons in history and geography. Working on hobbies, children learn to set goals, make complex decisions, and solve all sorts of practical problems. Hobbies exercise imagination and creativity in addition to helping children focus their interests and talents. The list of benefits is virtually endless. In short, hobbies are catalysts for growth along almost every conceivable dimension. (BHG)

Parents of teens often confuse running *off* with running *away.* Very few teens actually run away from home with no intention of ever returning. Those who do have almost always been abused. A significant number of teens, on the other hand, experiment with running *off.* Angry at their parents, they seek temporary refuge at the home of a friend. They're betting, of course, that this will cause their parents to "cave in" concerning a certain issue. If the parents do cave in, then the child is almost certain to run off in response to future conflicts. More teens threaten to run off than actually do. The more seriously parents take these threats, the more likely teens are to follow through on them. A teen who threatens to run "away" should be told she's welcome to do so, but that things at home will not change as a result. The parents should also point out that running away from conflict only confirms that she is not mature enough for certain privileges. In all likelihood, she will do nothing more than sulk. And stay home. (NP)

Spankings have absolutely no place in a school, public or private. Unless they take place in the context of a trusting, loving relationship, spankings will not be effective. In most cases, the only two people who have this kind of a relationship with a child are his or her parents. They are, therefore, the only people who have any business laying an open hand to the child's rear end. Without intimacy, a spanking is nothing more than an act of hit and run.

A spanking properly administered by a parent is an act of authority, but a spanking administered by a teacher is an act of desperation. In and of itself, it says the teacher has failed to adequately establish control of the classroom.

Granted, discipline in schools is more of a problem today than it was thirty or forty years ago. But the paddle is not going to restore it. Discipline will be restored to the classroom when high standards for teachers are restored and, in so doing, dignity to the profession of teaching; when high academic standards are restored, thus enhancing the seriousness of the educational process in the eyes of students; and most important, when parents of misbehaving children get their priorities in order and instead of defending their children when they misbehave in school, get solidly behind teachers and hold their children strictly accountable for their classroom behavior.

(SPNK)

Modern psychologists often seem more interested in explaining the "psychodynamics" of a problem than in helping to solve it as quickly as possible. This tendency grows out of the theory—which I was taught as a graduate student—that dealing with outward behavior is a "Band-Aid" approach to problems. Eventually, or so the theory goes, the Band-Aid will fall off. Its proponents claim that the psychodynamic approach, which usually involves months, if not years, of what I call "psychological archeology" (digging into a person's past to uncover psychological relics), may take longer, but its results are more permanent. I have long been an outspoken critic of this orientation, especially when it's applied to children. In my estimation and experience (and there's plenty of clinical evidence to back the following heretical contention), psychodynamic approaches to children's behavior problems are, generally speaking, neither cost-effective nor time-effective and involve significant risk of making matters worse instead of better. (FV)

October 8

Few words in the parlance of "parenting" have been so generally misused and misunderstood as "strict." Not only has the term descended to the depths of disrepute, but its original meaning has been corrupted almost beyond recognition. Strict! It even sounds harsh, like the crack of a whip. Not too many years ago (before it became stylish to worship children and let them walk all over us), "strictness" in child rearing was considered a virtue. Way back when children were children and parents were clearly in charge, to be strict meant defining rules clearly and enforcing obedience to them. And what is wrong with that? Nothing at all.

Truly strict parents do their children a great service, in many ways:

• They communicate expectations clearly, leaving little room for misunderstanding.

• They are decisive. England may swing like a pendulum do (as the old song said), but strict parents definitely do not. Their children, therefore, know where their parents stand and where their parents want them to stand.

• They teach their children to expect no more from a situation than they are willing to put into it. Gradually, their children distill a set of tried-and-true methods for living productive, satisfying lives.

A strict upbringing, then, is indispensable to learning the tenets of good citizenship. (PP)

October 9

Today's parents tend to take children entirely too seriously. A generation or so ago, a ten-year-old who lied would have been punished, but the likelihood is no one would have thought the misdeed out of the ordinary. Almost certainly, no one would have entertained a psychological explanation. The explanation, in fact, was (and still is) scriptural: Foolishness is bound in the heart of a child (Proverbs 22:15). Not *some* children's hearts, mind you, but *all* of them. They're all foolish, every single one of 'em.

Today's parents also take *themselves* entirely too seriously. The two—taking oneself and one's children too seriously—go hand in hand, of course. Today's parents give themselves entirely too much credit, in fact. They tend to think everything their children do is a product of upbringing. That little delusion borders on being grandiose. The truth is—take it from someone whose children are adults and who's now a grandpappy—that under the very best of circumstances, parents have a lot less control over their children than they think they do.

Children are human, and humans are blessed/cursed with free will. The combination of foolishness in the heart and free will in the head is extremely volatile and makes for unpredictable, incomprehensible behavior. If a certain child makes a habit of foolish behavior, his parents certainly need to take stock of themselves. But occasional foolishness—even if it's slightly outrageous—on the part of a child says very little about the child's parents.　　(FV)

In a marriage-centered family, a lot is expected of children. More than anything, they are expected to stand on their own two feet. It is another general observation of mine that children from families that are obviously marriage-centered (and you can tell, if you know the difference, in a heartbeat) are more obedient, more self-reliant, more cooperative, more responsible, more independent, and are higher achievers.

In a child-centered family, parents expect a lot of themselves, and their children expect a lot of them. Child-centered parents always act as if their first order of business is to *do* for their kids. And the more they do, the more their children want them to do, demand they do, whine for them to do. And the more the parents do, the less obedient, cooperative, responsible, achieving, and self-reliant the children are. It's quite simple, really. The more parents do for kids, the less kids do for themselves and the less they do *for their families.* You want a child to be a "jewel in the crown" of your family? Don't do a lot for the child. (FV)

October 11

I am absolutely convinced that parent-care during the first three years of life is clearly in the best interest of a child. This is not the "politically correct" position, however, and it raises the hackles of no small number of women.

I encourage any female reader who feels her hackles rising to reread the first sentence of this passage. Note that I am *not* gender-specific. I am *not* directing my remarks at women. It matters not, in my estimation, whether the parent providing the care is male or female, or whether two parents manage their work schedules such that they split child-care responsibilities.

Nonetheless, I'm fully aware that this is a much more sensitive issue for women than men. As a result, women will feel that I'm stepping on their toes. In today's socio-babble, to step on the collective toes of women is "sexist." I've been called worse.

To say that parent-care during infancy and toddlerhood is better—*much, much better* in fact—than day care suggests that a woman who chooses to go back to work full-time after having a child is not making a good decision when in fact she may have no real choice in the matter; not if she wants to put food on the table, that is. To women in those straits, I say, "Make your day-care choice carefully."

In a 1995 poll, more than one in four working mothers said they didn't have to work outside their homes. They simply *wanted* to. I'll be honest: I have a problem with that.

I am as much for women achieving self-fulfillment as I am for men. I believe that the best parents are, in fact, self-fulfilled. True self-fulfillment, however, is a mature quality. It is not reckless, impulsive, or driven by self-centeredness (as in, "I *want* to; therefore, I *will*."). A truly self-fulfilled individual does not disregard the needs of others or do things at anyone else's expense. Self-fulfillment, in other words, is not equivalent to self-gratification. In fact, a defining feature of maturity is the ability to postpone self-gratification. If, therefore, in order to provide at-home care for a young child, a parent or parents must postpone self-gratification, then so be it. More than anything else, children need parents who are able to make mature, responsible decisions. (TT)

"But I can afford to give my child a lot," a parent recently rejoined. "And besides, like my parents wanted for me, I want my child to have more than I did as a child."

In the first place, being able to afford something is no excuse. In the second, what previous generations of parents wanted to give their children was not more *things* than they themselves had enjoyed as children, but more *opportunities*. They understood, furthermore, that you cannot open the door of opportunity for someone; you can only prepare them with the skills they will need to open it for themselves. *The point: The more parents do for a child, the less the child is ultimately capable of doing for himself.* (FV)

You want your toddler to grow up with all the smarts he was born with, don't you? In order to activate those smarts, and keep them activated, a child needs to be *active*. The more opportunity a toddler has to explore and experiment upon the environment, the smarter he will become. My Formula for a Smart Kid consists of what I refer to as the "Six E's of Excellence": *Expose* the child to *Environments* and *Experiences* that *Encourage Exploration* and *Experimentation*. In that context, folks, television simply fails to cut the proverbial mustard. Television produces an electronic environment that depresses exploration and experimentation. For proof of what I'm saying, simply take up station (no pun intended) and watch a child watch television. See the blank expression? See the listless hands? See the lack of any creative, constructive behavior? You're looking at a child wasting time, and time is all the human mind has with which to develop its gifts. (TT)

A generation or so ago, if a child misbehaved in school, the school disciplined the child, confident the child's parents would not only support their actions, but also amplify upon them at home. Misbehaving children were thus caused to "feel bad about themselves," and it was generally agreed that well they should. When Billy misbehaved, he was penalized in some way, shape, or form. Adults asked not, "Why is Billy misbehaving?" but "What should be done about Billy's misbehavior?"

That was before mental health professionals sold us on the idea that bad behavior required not correcting, but *understanding*. Bad behavior, they said, was the result of poor self-esteem, which was a result of grievous errors—whether intentional or otherwise—on the child's parents' (probably his mother's) part. Billy was suddenly and miraculously no longer personally accountable for anything he did. Any misbehavior on his part, especially if it became chronic, was merely a symptom of some underlying distress brought on by a stressful and/or inadequately nurturing home life. His parents were expecting too much, rewarding too little, using "inappropriate" (old-fashioned) discipline, not giving him enough attention, or making him feel responsible for their marital discord.

These days, therefore, when Billy misbehaves, his parents are on the community hot seat, not him. As a result, they have become rather defensive regarding any report of misbehavior on his part. When they hear such a report, their tendency is to defend him, rather than correct him. They often insist that he is incapable of the misbehavior in question. Furthermore, since Billy is not ever to feel bad about himself, any disciplinary action on the part of a teacher or other adult that causes him to feel shame or guilt is likely to be regarded by his parents as a quasi-criminal assault on his fragile psyche.

(FV)

You should do nothing about your teen's choice of friends when . . . your disapproval is based solely on stereotypes, personal tastes, or opinions you may have of a friend's parents. These aren't valid reasons for doing anything other than keeping your opinions to yourself.

You should express your feelings and keep a close eye on things when . . . there are vaguely outward signs of potential problems, but no signs of actual trouble. Under circumstances such as these, tell your teen how you feel: "I'm probably just an old worry-wart, but I have to tell you I'm not completely comfortable with the friendship you've formed with so-and-so." Explain the reason behind your discomfort and state your expectations: "I'm going to keep closer tabs on this friendship than I normally would. You can prevent me from intervening by acting responsibly and staying out of trouble."

You should set some limits on the relationship when . . . the friend has a habit of getting into trouble, but only in certain, select situations; or, your teenager and the friend get into some minor trouble together. These are "marginal cases." Situations such as these demand that you put some logical restrictions on the relationship. For instance, if the friend's driving record is poor, don't let your teen ride with him. If the friend has been arrested for shoplifting, don't let them go to stores together, unless an adult is present to supervise. If they skipped school, put them off limits to one another for a while. You may want to put the relationship "on notice": "For the time being, I'm only going to put some controls on the association. If problems occur, I may have to put a complete freeze on things. It's all up to you and your friend."

You should prohibit the association altogether if . . . the friend is a proven, habitual troublemaker, or your child and the friend make major mischief together.

These guidelines can help you decide your first response to friendships that make you uncomfortable. At first, adopt the most liberal position possible. If problems begin to develop, go to the next most appropriate step.　　　　　　　　　　　　　　　(BHG)

A fellow psychologist, incensed at my heresy, wrote me a letter in which he claimed that psychology had brought about numerous advances in child rearing. Oh, really? Since *nouveau* parenting became the constantly shifting norm, childhood depression and suicide have sharply increased, violence on the part of children toward children has increased, discipline problems in school have increased, violence on the part of children toward parents and teachers has increased, sexual activity among teens has increased along with the incidence of unwed teenage parents, the high school dropout rate has increased, and youth crime in general has increased. Advances? I don't think so.

The same psychologist recalled, "with sadness," the many children who fell between the educational cracks because their learning and behavior problems were not recognized by a system characterized by "ignorance and lack of sophistication." He is obviously unaware that achievement levels were never higher than in the '50s, when the literacy level of high school graduates also peaked. If today's educators are serving problem children better, wouldn't it be reasonable to expect improved achievement and literacy levels? Unless, of course, there are a lot more problem children today than there were forty years ago, in which case we come back to the same question: What advances?

This sort of propaganda, common among "helping" professionals, is misinformation, pure and simple. The truth is, humans are faulted; therefore, everything we do is faulted; therefore, our families are faulted (all of them!) and our child rearing is faulted. "Grandma's house" was no more or less fraught with fault than was her grandmother's or is her grandchild's. Psychology, for all of its legitimate value, has not made better parents of us. And it cannot hope to do so until it begins to show proper respect for Grandma.

(FV)

October 17

At best, a spanking is nothing more, nothing less, than a rela-tively dramatic form of nonverbal communication. It's one means of getting the attention of a child who needs to give that attention quickly; of terminating a behavior that is rapidly escalating out of control; of putting an exclamation point in front of a message the child needs to hear. A spontaneous (as in: without warning) spank to the child's rear end says "Stop!" and "Now hear this!" Having terminated the behavior in question—a tantrum, for instance—and having secured the child's attention, it is necessary that the parent follow through with a consequence of one sort of another. The spank is merely the prelude to the consequence. In the final analysis, the spank is, therefore, *inconsequential*. The follow-through is what's im-portant.   (SPNK)

October 18

The neofeminist movement has succeeded at convincing significant numbers of women (and men) that there is no incompatibility whatsoever between career pursuit and child rearing. Reading a recent interview with a married professional woman who has two children, ages three and seven months, I came across the following statement: "I took eight weeks' maternity leave with my first child, six with my second. I could have taken longer, but in my profession, that's not looked upon favorably."

Excuse me? You have children and you put them in day care as quickly as you can (six weeks!) because you might be put on the "mommy track" if you don't? What are children, anyway? Hobbies? This woman was actually presented as a role model—living proof that it matters not whether children are taken care of during the day by parents or total strangers. What matters is that women do it at all!

The "Superwoman" of that interview represents a society that's had the wool pulled over its eyes. She embodies the myth that there are no consequences to a child of having parents who try to have their cake and eat it, too. In part because personal sacrifice has come to be viewed as just shy of degrading, we have become a nation of families in various states of fragmentation; families in which priorities have been inverted, everyone's in a perpetual state of hurry, and psychological resources are stretched to the limit. And families that don't fit this description—those that abide by tradition—are regarded almost suspiciously.   (TT)

October 19

Separation always involves a certain amount of anxiety. It is often frightening for a child and, assuming his parents are sensitive and caring people, it will be discomforting for them as well. The problem of separation, of moving from dependency toward a state of confident self-sufficiency is, in fact, the primary problem of growing up.

In his best-selling book *The Road Less Traveled*, psychiatrist Scott Peck says that many people never learn to accept the inherent pain of living. When confronted with a problem, they either attempt an impatient, knee-jerk solution or try to ignore it altogether. Parents who beat their children because they cry at bedtime fall into the first category. Parents who let their children sleep with them fall into the second. Both sets of parents have missed the point.

Sleeping in his or her own bed helps establish that the child is an independent, autonomous individual, with a clearly separate identity. In addition, parents sleeping together and separate from the child enhances the child's view of the marriage as not only a separate entity within the family but also the most important relationship within the family. A child who sleeps with his or her parents is in danger of not achieving this understanding, of feeling wrongly that the marriage is a "threesome." It's important that a child understand that his parents' marriage is exclusive and, therefore, does not include him. This distinction positions the marriage at center stage in the family, at the focal point of attention. Coming to grips with the fact that the husband/wife relationship is paramount in the family helps the young child divest of self-centeredness, acquire a sense of independence, and move securely toward eventual emancipation. Therefore, what may look like a very nurturing arrangement—the "family bed"—actually extends dependency and interferes significantly with emotional growth. Don't do it!

(TT)

October 20

You cannot maintain a child at the center of your attention and expect, at the same time, that the child will pay sufficient attention to you. If your child doesn't pay sufficient attention to you, discipline will forever be a problem, as will respect for legitimate authority figures. If your child isn't able to divest of the self-centeredness you catered to during his first two years, then he can be neither successfully socialized or emancipated (even if he leaves home "on schedule").

The well-intentioned mistake of treating a child as if he is forever a toddler is likely to result in an adult who still thinks he deserves to have his bread buttered on both sides, his cake and eat it, too, and to get something for nothing. This describes, of course, someone who is an adult in years only, but will probably never attain emotional or spiritual adulthood. Obviously, this bodes ill for the individual, but multiplied by a factor of thousands, it bodes ill for our culture. In fact, it spells the essential end of the values and character traits that have traditionally defined the American spirit: resourcefulness, a "never say die" attitude toward adversity, good neighborliness, a willingness to sacrifice self for the common good, a willingness to help those less fortunate, and a vital work ethic.

As my wife and I discovered—belatedly, but not too late—if you stop trying to be liked by your children while they are children, they will appreciate you that much more when they are adults. Prove it to yourselves. (NP)

When Eric, the older of our two children, turned sixteen, he asked for more freedom. Specifically, he wanted use of a car.

Willie and I had seen what often happened when teens were given freedom without responsibility. We'd seen kids abuse cars, incur speeding ticket after speeding ticket, and cause damage to themselves and others. We heard tales of grades plummeting, of arrests for driving while under the influence, of reputations ruined. Common to most of these tragedies was a teen who'd been given something for nothing.

Determined to prevent similar problems, we told Eric that if he wanted to drive, he had to not only buy his own gas, but also pay the difference in the insurance premium. Since his allowance was earmarked for clothes and recreation, that meant he had to get a job, which raised another set of potential problems. We stipulated that, initially at least, he could not work more than fifteen hours a week. We also gave him a two-month "grace period," during which we picked up his insurance tab while he looked for a part-time job. After that, no work, no drive.

Less than a month later, he was stocking shelves in a drugstore. Working for minimum wage meant that after he kicked in his share of the insurance, he had slightly less than half his paycheck left to do with as he pretty well pleased. Adults should be so lucky!

Then we added another domino to the equation. We told Eric he could keep his job only if he managed to keep his grades up. By linking grades, a job, and driving privileges, we created circumstances that approximated adult realities. In doing so, we gave Eric opportunity to begin learning the ins and outs of self-sufficiency. And he rose to the occasion. He learned to manage both his time and his money. His grades actually improved during his last two years of high school. At twenty-seven he still has a clean driving record.   (NP)

Nearly every day, the American schoolkid comes home with a note from his teacher that starts, "Dear Parents . . ." and goes on to give his or her "parents" that day's "involvement assignment." I put "parents" in quotes because every teacher knows full well that except in cases where the only parent in the home is male, the "parents" in question will be mothers. In effect, these notes are pop-tests for mothers. Those who willingly accept these assignments pass the tests and are, therefore, Good Mothers. Those who don't accept these assignments, or who do so half-heartedly, are "irresponsible." Because their reputations are on the line, most mothers take these assignments on without question. They've got something to prove, a test to pass.

Even mothers who know there's something wrong with expecting parents to help kids with homework go right ahead and accept these assignments. As one mother recently confessed, "My parents didn't do this stuff for me, and I don't think I should have to do it for my child, but if everyone else is doing it, and I'm not, then I'm afraid my child will fall behind. I'm also, quite frankly, afraid of what the teacher will think of me if she finds out."

What amazes me is that of all the supposedly smart educators in this country, none seems to have figured out that when children were expected to do their own homework and their own science projects and their own research for term papers and the like, two things were the case: First, more children did their homework and turned it in on time. Second, overall achievement levels were much, much higher. In short, when children were expected to be independently responsible for such things, they did a lot better in school! But that's not what counts, these days. These days, what counts is an educational philosophy that sounds good. Whether it works or not is irrelevant. Not secondary, mind you, but irrelevant.   (FV)

For twenty-plus years, the public education establishment has been terrified that taxpayers will wake up to the fact that as per-capita educational expenditures have tripled (in constant 1994 dollars), academic achievement has declined. The National Education Association (NEA) would have the taxpayer believe teachers are grossly underpaid and public education is starving for money. The truth:

• Considering they work nine months a year (including a two-week vacation in December), six or seven hours a day (including lunch and preparation time), teachers are very well compensated relative to other four-year college grads.

• A disproportionate amount of the educational dollar goes into paying administrative and administrative-support salaries and benefits. As demonstrated by the success of private and parochial schools, which conserve on administration, thus returning a greater share of their dollar to the classroom, most public school administrative positions are completely superfluous to educational quality. Public schools don't need more money; they need to trim their fat. (FV)

By the time a child is two, and sometimes earlier, the child has seen that his parents defer to the authority of his pediatrician (or the family physician) and has concluded—albeit at an intuitive level—that the doctor is someone whose commands cannot be questioned, much less challenged. In short, young children hold their doctors in awe, and this is true regardless of whether or not there is fear associated with them.

Telling this age child that a rule or instruction has been handed down from "the doctor," therefore, reduces the likelihood of resistance. Parents who have used this technique consistently tell me that their children almost magically cooperate in such things as going to bed, picking up toys at a certain time of the day, and staying out of off-limits areas when the rule, etc., is prefaced with, "The doctor says . . ."

I've discussed this with a number of pediatricians. They've all agreed it's a harmless way of avoiding potential power struggles, and several have pointed out that since they would undoubtedly be in favor of the rules and limits in question, parents who employ this method can hardly be accused of lying to their children.

I first tested this technique on my daughter, Amy, who is now a well-adjusted twenty-three-year-old. She readily accepted these sorts of "explanations" and did not, when she was old enough to realize that the rules actually came from Mommy and Daddy, lose trust in us, become depressed, begin resenting or fearing her pediatrician, or have any other baleful reaction. I've since passed the technique on to hundreds of parents (thousands if you count readers of my column) and their feedback has been universally positive. They report consistent success and their children, once they're old enough to realize the rules come from their parents, do not appear to suffer any "lying hangover" or exhibit "backlash."   (NP)

"My eight-year-old son *is* ADD," said the woman from Dubuque, referring to the ubiquitous attention deficit disorder.

Oh, my. This woman thinks her son *is*, in his entirety, in every fiber of his being, in every aspect of who he is and can ever hope to become, ADD. He is nothing more and nothing less than ADD. He is no longer simply a child. He has become a category, a subset, of child. He *is* a prefix. He *is* ADD. I am not questioning the diagnosis. I might have suggested it myself. But I would have told the woman this: "Do not be misled by this diagnosis, this condition we're going to call attention deficit disorder. It constitutes perhaps 10 percent of your son's overall makeup. The other 90 percent of him is just like every other eight-year-old child in the world. If you forget that, you do so at his, and your, peril."

That is obviously not what this mother was told. Whatever the diagnosing professional said, she came away with the impression that her son *is* ADD. Consequently, this diagnosis does not help her see her son more clearly or understand him better. It is a distorting lens through which she views him and all that he does. As a result of holding this lens up in front of her, she sees her son *less* clearly. She does not understand that he is first and foremost a child, more *like* other children than different. Much more. And because she now thinks she's rearing a child who is more *different* than alike, her child rearing is way off the mark. It's "aimed" at the 10 percent rather than the 90. This is nothing but sad. (NP)

Without a doubt, the best education in America today is being provided in Catholic schools. In the typical Catholic school, students receive a traditional education that is much like what public education was like in the 1950s, when student achievement was at an all-time high. Academic and behavioral expectations are high, grades are not artificially inflated, and classrooms are adequately disciplined.

The performance of students in Catholic elementary and high schools on standardized achievement tests consistently exceeds the performance of public school students, even when student characteristics and family background are controlled. Catholic school students spend more time on homework than their public school counterparts. The dropout rate in Catholic high schools is less than one-fourth the rate of public schools and absenteeism is perceived as a far less serious problem.

Catholic schools have even fewer administrators per student than private schools; therefore, an even greater percentage of their educational dollar goes into the classroom, where it belongs.

Elitism, a nagging aspect of most private schools, is not a factor in Catholic schools. One of Catholic education's missions is to provide quality education to children from all religious backgrounds, even non-Christian. In addition, Catholic schools traditionally have enrolled significant numbers of minority students as well as students from economically disadvantaged backgrounds. As a consequence of this "open door" policy, many Catholic school students are in classrooms that look more like the real world than do many public school classrooms.   (NP)

Q: *Our seventeen-year-old daughter has started to date a boy whose reputation is not good. Without going into details, we fear that his influence may undermine some of the values we have tried to instill in her. What should we do?*

A: It's what you *shouldn't do* that's important. You shouldn't prohibit the relationship, for example, on the basis of his reputation. You shouldn't criticize him to your daughter. You must make every effort to "keep your cool" concerning this whole issue. I would advise that you sit down with your daughter and tell her everything you've heard about this young man. Tell her that any parent in your situation would be concerned, even if the stories aren't all true. Then, affirm that you trust her and are confident that she will always use good judgment in the relationship. Make the young man welcome in your home. Roll out the red carpet, in fact. Invite him over for dinner. Consider including him in family activities. The more your daughter feels you accept the relationship, the more likely she is to act in accordance with the trust you place in her. Under the circumstances, the relationship will also run its course more quickly. But, then again, who knows? Your daughter just might cause this young man to turn over a new leaf. (NP)

October 28

Q: *My sixth-grade daughter is having what I'd term a "personality conflict" with one of her teachers. I haven't heard the teacher's side of the story yet, but from what my daughter tells me, the teacher is being a bit rough on her. Before I rush in protectively, do you have any advice?*

A: My general feeling about these matters is that you would do well to give the benefit of doubt to the teacher. Even with my own two children, I found that complaints of being treated unjustly by teachers were usually unjustified. Sometimes, I disagreed with a teacher's *way* of handling a problem, but I was never able to fault the teacher's feeling that there was a problem. I'm a firm believer in adults sticking together when it comes to children, and put this into practice with my own. One time, my son complained that one of his eighth-grade teachers didn't "like" him. He told me he didn't expect a good grade from her. I asked if she seemed to dislike everyone in the class.

"Oh, no," Eric replied, "just me and one or two other kids."

"Then you and one or two other kids must be doing something that she has every reason not to like," I said. "So I am telling you that I expect you to solve this problem and make a decent grade in her class. If you don't, there will be consequences."

Not another word was spoken about this supposedly unfair teacher. Eric must have solved the problem, because when report cards came out, he'd made a good grade in her class. Interestingly enough, she noted that he'd made "much improvement" since the beginning of the term.

Schedule a meeting with your child's teacher. Listen to what she has to say, accept it, and offer your support. There are very few teachers out there who don't have the best interests of children at heart, and you'll know immediately when you meet one.   (NP)

For the past thirty years, the American family has been "changing," or so the media informs us. The subliminal impression thus created is that some natural, inexorable evolutionary process is behind the steady increase in single-parent and two-income families; further, that the only problem arising from this is the failure of society and government to make sufficiently rapid and effective adjustments to the new set of circumstances.

Here's the truth: For more than a generation, the American family has been in a steady state of decline precipitated by social experiments and forces that are fundamentally at odds with a general state of family health.

Here's another undeniable truth: The American family worked better when there was a parent in the home during the day. In past generations, that parent was almost always female, but gender is irrelevant to the purpose of our discussion. That all-but-constant adult presence provided for greater family stability, smoother internal transitions, more effective overall time management, better supervision and care of children, and more efficient delegation of responsibilities, not to mention a lower level of stress. The comfortable division of labor between homemaker and breadwinner was more conductive to a sense of partnership and, therefore, tended to support marriage-centeredness. For all these reasons, the American family of previous generations was a more psychologically secure place in which to live. This despite the assertion of a significant number of "helping professionals" that most of us were raised in "dysfunctional" families lorded over by parents who were abusive in one way or another.

(TT)

October 30

When it comes to a spanking, in hesitation, all is lost. Furthermore, if you wait until you're at the "end of your rope" before you spank, you are only teaching your child how to pull your rope. Most parents make the mistake of giving one warning after another in the face of a child's misbehavior, accumulating more and more frustration in the process. Finally, unable to contain their frustration any longer, they explode. And unload. Instead of *whack!* or *whack whack!* it's *whack whack whack whack whack whack whack whack whack whack whack!* In the aftermath of this cataclysm, the parent feels guilty and the child feels resentful. Meanwhile, absolutely nothing has been accomplished. Furthermore, a history of that sort is destined to repeat itself. (SPNK)

Trying to explain away a young person's fears usually doesn't work. Three-year-olds are unable to understand that words exist for things that don't. Saying to a three-year-old, "There's no such thing as *"monsters"* amounts to a contradiction in terms, one the child finds impossible to reconcile.

Reason and imagination, furthermore, exist on separate, non-intersecting wavelengths. The attempt to explain a fear away, therefore, will only confuse a child of this age and increase his sense of isolation and vulnerability. The result is a child who is more afraid than ever because he's now convinced his parents don't understand him and are powerless to help.

The most effective approach to take with a child is to first acknowledge the fear: "We know the dark can be scary when you're little." Then identify with her: "When we were 3 years old, we were afraid of dark places, too." Finally, reassure her of your continuing ability to protect her: "We'll be in the living room, and we'll be taking care of you from there. Nothing can happen to you as long as we're here." Stay close enough to make the child feel protected, but not so close that your presence validates her fearfulness.

If one of you has theatrical talent, you can go into the child's room and "do battle" with the monster in her closet, finally ejecting it from your home forever. This approach is especially effective because it appeals to imagination, the very thing that created the monster in the first place.   (6PP)

November 1

It is significant to note that the "villain" in nearly all of Freud's psychological soap operas was Mother. Freud's mothers were the archetype of dysfunctionality. They traumatized their male children by being implicitly seductive; their female children by insisting upon excessive attention to cleanliness and refusing to adequately explain why girls lack penises. My own mother's reaction to this psychobabble was typical. Suddenly, after rearing me in the bliss of ignorance for twelve years or so, she became afflicted with anxiety. Needing to better understand the dos and don'ts of child rearing according to Fraud, she went straight to the source, reading and rereading nearly all of his arcane writings. I remember her telling me, when I was in my early adolescence, that she and I mustn't become too close lest I be unable to eventually disentangle myself from her apron strings. Thus permanently enmeshed, I would be incapacitated when it came to forming healthy relationships with women, in which case I might become a homosexual! Little did my mother realize that her well-intentioned warning was the single most traumatic event of my childhood. She couldn't have timed it any worse. I just got over it last week.

(FV)

306

The fact is, some toddlers bite and others don't, just like some such their thumbs and others don't. Why? No one knows. Let me assure you that no connection between parenting style and biting has ever been established. Nor is biting at this age indicative of psychological problems.

The more of a big deal one makes of a child's biting, the worse it is likely to become. Spanking, biting the biter, jumping up and down while imploring the heavens to lift this burden from your shoulders, and similar histrionics will probably prove to be a waste of time and energy. Time will cure the problem. In the meantime, parents can (a) try their best to prevent their little ones from biting and (b) respond effectively when they do. If you see signals that a child is working himself up to a bite (i.e., distress), move in and either remove him from the playing field for a time or distract him. When his teeth find their target, try the following suggestions:

• Remain calm. Take a deep breath. Think pleasant thoughts.

• As quickly as possible, separate teeth from flesh and remove the biter from the scene.

• Take him to a private area and admonish him, but briefly, as in, "No biting!" Tell him to remain where he is until you come back to get him.

• At this point, console the bitee, but take care not to make a big deal of the injury. If the bite has broken the skin, administer a topical antibiotic and call a pediatrician for further instructions. Actually, any nurse in his/her office will be able to answer your questions.

• Retrieve the biter and return him to the group.

• Be vigilant, but don't let on that you're on the alert for another incident. Yawn a lot.

• Remember that Rome wasn't built in a day.   (TOH)

Shame on educators for telling parents to get "involved" in their children's homework! Of all people, they ought to know parental participation in homework is counterproductive. About the only thing such involvement accomplishes is better grades. At this point, the average parent would ask, "So what's wrong with better grades?" and I would answer, "Nothing, except that when parents are the reason for those better grades, then in the final analysis, the child in question is losing far more than he or she is gaining."

The most valuable learning takes place by trial and error. To the degree someone learning a task is prevented from making an error, that same someone is prevented from learning. When parents become involved in homework, it is almost inevitable that they will begin to take their children's grades personally. The more personally they take them, the more they will act to prevent their children from making errors. Inadvertently, then, they short-circuit the learning process.

A child who is expected to do his or her own homework, in his or her own homework place (as opposed to a family area like the dinner table), may not always make A's and certainly will not always take to school homework assignments that are error-free. That child will, however, learn more effectively from his or her mistakes than would otherwise be the case. Furthermore, that child will steadily acquire what I term "Homework's Seven Hidden Values": Responsibility, autonomy, perseverance, time management, initiative, self-reliance, and resourcefulness. Those values are necessary to a successful life, and we do children no favors by sacrificing them on the altar of good grades. (TOH)

The problem with television and children is more one of process than content. In the final analysis, the nonact of watching is more disadvantageous to a child's development than the programs he or she is allowed to watch. Granted, programs that are saturated with gratuitous sex and violence are not healthy for children, but then I happen to feel they're not healthy for adults, either. During the formative years—birth through six—a child's competency skills develop through exercise. The more a child uses imagination, language, and various problem-solving skills, the more those abilities strengthen. When one considers that the average American child has watched close to five thousand hours of television before entering first grade— five thousand hours of doing nothing but staring at a rapidly flickering electronic image—the damage television can do to a child's overall development becomes evident. For this reason, I recommend that a child not watch more than an occasional program until he or she has learned to read well. At this point—which is usually reached around grades three or four—allowing the child a weekly television quota of five hours (but no more!) is reasonable and should pose no problems. To maximize the value of those five hours, the child should be watching programs that portray the world in realistic fashion. Documentaries, geographical specials, and even some historical movies fit this description. The evening news, however, does not.

(NP)

The unwritten understanding between parent and child should be, "When I, your parent, want your attention, you have no option other than to pay attention to me. However, when you want attention from me, *I* will decide whether it is prudent and necessary to give that attention to you." In other words, the parent has a choice, the child does not. Unfortunately, in many families, this fundamental dictum has been turned upside down and inside out. Many parents act as if they are obligated to pay attention to their children *whenever* their children want attention, and especially if they demand it. Today's parents seem to believe that if they deny their children attention, they will make them insecure. This belief was handed down from on high by a number of so-called "parenting experts" who wrote books about child rearing, and it has since become solidly entrenched in our culture. The myth is that children need a lot of attention, that the more attention you pay a child, the more you inflate his sense of self-esteem. The truth is that infants need a lot of attention, but that past the third birthday, a child's *need* for attention declines dramatically while his/her need for *supervision* increases. Self-esteem has little to do with how much attention a child receives from his parents and everything to do with how much his parents encourage self-sufficiency and respect for others. (EHH)

Discussion requires the participation of two people who are as willing to listen as they are wanting to be heard. Children want to be *heard*, but they rarely want to *listen*. As a parent explains, a child waits for an opportunity to interrupt.

This is why I believe in the power of "because I said so." As a child, I couldn't stand to hear these four words. They made me mad! So mad, in fact, that I promised myself I would never say them to my children. When I became a parent, I kept this promise for several years. Then, having brought myself to the brink of disaster, I woke up to reality and belatedly (but not too late) broke my ill-fated promise. "Because I said so" became part of my parenting vocabulary.

Some people say that children have a right to know the reasons behind the decisions we make. I agree, but with certain amendments; to wit: (1) They have a right to know in terms they can understand. (2) They have a right to know *only* if they are willing to listen. Finally, if the truth is "because I said so" (which it usually, in fact, is), they have a right to know that, too.   (6PP)

The best time to inform a child he or she was adopted is between ages four and five. This is when children begin to realize that life has a definite beginning and a definite end. As a result, they begin asking questions about such things as where babies come from. This age child is not only curious concerning these matters, but also intellectually capable of understanding the answers, as long as they are simple and to the point.

As to the best approach, honesty and straightforwardness constitute the best policy. Make sure the child understands the basic facts of conception, pregnancy, and birth, and that he knows what "adoption" means. In that regard, a mini-course in sex education may be necessary. Just remember to keep things simple. Give the child examples of other people—including other children, if possible—he knows or knows about who were adopted. Answer the child's questions as clearly and succinctly as possible. Above all else, let the child know that *you* are his or her *real* parents. (BHG)

The phrase "guilt trip" carries a lot of negative connotations. The idea that guilt, all guilt, is bad came out of the "Do Your Own Thing" philosophy of the '60s and '70s. At its extremes, guilt is certainly maladaptive. At one extreme are found people who are incapable of feeling guilt, no matter how badly they behave. These charming people are called "sociopaths." They do what they please without regard for anyone else and feel no remorse, regardless of what hurt they cause others. At the other end of the guilt spectrum are neurotics, people who are constantly haunted by the idea that they're doing something wrong, even when they aren't.

In the middle are perfectly healthy folks who feel guilt when it's appropriate to do so. In moderation of this sort, guilt is a very adaptive emotion. Without it, civilization couldn't exist; anarchy would reign. Guilt is a message from inside that says we misbehaved and shouldn't act that way again.

Our job as parents is to socialize our children. You can't teach a child how to act without also teaching him how to think and even how to feel, including when and how to feel guilt. Children won't know to feel guilty unless adults first teach them that guilt is appropriate to certain situations. That's how a child's conscience develops. Once you've taught a child the basics, you can then trust him to come to feelings of guilt on his own, when such feelings are appropriate. But with even the most well-socialized child, there will probably be times when parents will need to drive the point home. They will need, in other words, to put the child on a "guilt trip." This is done for the child's own good, and the good of the rest of us as well.

(6PP)

Discipline is the process of creating a disciple—one who will voluntarily (the operative word) follow your lead. To secure the attention of a child, you must *distinguish* yourself, meaning that you must stand at a slight distance from your child. You must also establish yourself as an interesting person with a well-rounded life of your own.

(Fact: A child will not take sufficient interest in a parent whose life revolves around the child.)

Your primary relationship must not, therefore, be with your child, but with your peers, and if you are married, your spouse.

(Fact: Children are fascinated by adult relationships. They take for granted, however, adults who act fascinated with them.)

Once you have secured your child's attention, the process of turning him or her into a disciple becomes a relatively easy matter.

(Fact: Most discipline problems arise because parents either give their children too much attention or too little. In either case, the children in question fail to learn to pay attention to parents and, therefore, to adults in general.)

One natural consequence of having successfully secured your child's attention is that your child will respect your wisdom and seek your guidance. This all but eliminates communication problems.

There is a distinct difference between a child making a behavioral mistake *(Fact: All children will make mistakes)* and a child choosing misbehavior when he knows better. If the child isn't aware of the mistake, pointing it out and making it clear that repeat performances will not be looked upon favorably is generally sufficient.

Too often, parents punish when correction could, and should, have been accomplished with far less drama—a look, a word, a brief expression of disappointment. There are times, for sure, in the rearing of just about every child when drama is necessary, but if you lay the cornerstones properly those times will not predominate.

(NP)

There's a time for being consistent and a time for being inconsistent. Yes, children need routine. It simplifies their lives, promotes security, and provides a stable framework within which freedom is possible. Yes, every child needs parents who agree on the rules and boundaries that guide the child's growing. But no, parents do *not* have to agree on how those rules are enforced. To the degree two parents feel they must agree on the "how" of enforcing the rules, they will have conflict. It is unrealistic to expect that two fundamentally different people, who came into their marriage with different ideas about children, can possibly agree on a single set of tools with which to regulate a child's behavior. What counts in maintaining harmony in the family is that Mom and Dad agree on the importance of the First, Most Important, Rule: Do What We Tell You to Do, and are both quick to act when Junior gets out of line.

Let's say Junior disobeys Mom on Tuesday and she spanks him and makes him sit in a chair for thirty minutes. And let's say Junior disobeys Dad on Wednesday and he sends Junior to his room for the remainder of the day. In that case, Mom and Dad are acting consistently, even though differently, to enforce the rule.   (PP)

A spanking is fairly worthless without a suitable follow-through. In other words, a spanking alone is not disciplinary in the sense that it does not *teach* a child anything. The teaching, the discipline, comes *after* the spanking. The follow-through should be delivered immediately and decisively, meaning calmly yet in no uncertain terms. It must be perfectly clear to the child that you are disapproving of his behavior, if not angry—*using* your temper as opposed to losing it. In some cases, a few words of reprimand may be sufficient to put the child back on track. If you feel that a more demonstrative follow-through is necessary—and you should by all means go with your intuitions—then:

- Take away an important privilege, such as going outside, for the remainder of the day.
- Require that the child apologize to the offended party.
- Banish the child to his room for an extended period of time.
- Send the child to bed early.
- Require that the child write the same sentence (e.g., "In the future, I will not scream when my parents tell me to do something.") twenty-five or more times.
- Confine the child to an isolated, boring area of the home for ten to thirty minutes.
- Combine two or more of the above as you see fit.

You don't have to be consistent in your choice of follow-through, but you must, by all means, be consistent about following through. (SPNK)

Let's face it, most of the decisions parents make are arbitrary. They are matters of personal preference, not universal absolutes. Why, for example, must your child go to bed at eight o'clock when the neighbor's child, a year younger, is allowed to stay up until nine o'clock? Any and all attempts at explaining this inconsistency come down to simply this: "That's the way I want it." Why don't you allow your child to ride his bike past the corner, when his best friend can ride three blocks to the convenience store? Again, any and all explanations boil down to, "That's just the way I want it." In other words, "Because I said so."

If those four words stick in your throat, try "Because this decision belongs to me" or "Because I'm the parent and making decisions of this sort is my responsibility." If you feel you simply must give some manner of "correct" explanation, save your breath by trimming it to twenty-five words or less. Remember, however, that regardless of how carefully you phrase your answer, the child is not going to agree. In fact, you just might want to preface your answer with, "Okay, I'll pretend you're really asking me a question, and I'll give you an answer. But I don't expect you to agree. On the other hand, don't expect me to change my mind." When the inevitable happens, say "That's all right. As I said, I didn't expect you to agree. I'm also not changing my mind." (6PP)

One of the things parenthood has taught me is that you don't necessarily do children any favors by trying to make them happy. Sometimes, in order to promote a child's progress toward self-sufficiency, parents must do highly unpopular things. Unfortunately, many of today's parents are reluctant to do anything that might result in their children becoming even temporarily unhappy. There are three factors at work here:

1. The mistaken belief that unhappiness threatens a child's self-esteem.

2. The fear on the part of parents that if they upset their children, their children will feel unloved or—horror of horrors—won't *like* them.

3. The fear on the part of parents that their peers will disapprove of their child-rearing methods.

Fearing these things, parents get into lock-step with the crowd and dedicate themselves to the popular cause of keeping their children happy, no matter what the cost. In the process, they unwittingly deprive their children of essential opportunities to develop self-sufficiency, and therefore *true* self-esteem. What these parents fail to realize is that it's often necessary to temporarily threaten a child's happiness in order to promote the lasting reward of truly good self-esteem. (EHH)

With few exceptions (which I chalk up to luck), parents tell me that try as hard as they can, they can't seem to get *nouveau* "parenting" to work. They do what the books and talk-show psychologists tell them to do: They praise their kids a lot, they try to talk through parent-child conflicts, they help their kids with their homework, they use "time-out" instead of spanking, they don't ever say, "Because I said so." They practice all the prescribed dos and eschew the proscribed don'ts; nonetheless, they can't get it to work.

"Helping" professionals have an explanation for this state of affairs. Where there is a parent who cannot get their advice to work, they are apt to say, there is a "dysfunctional" family. The parent in question is "resistant", "defensive," "sabotaging," "enmeshed," or "codependent." In other words, professional advice is immaculate; the problem is that some people don't have it together enough to pull it off, to make it work. This, folks, amounts to a classic double-bind or, in popular parlance, a "catch-22": If you ask a "helping" professional for advice, and he gives you advice that doesn't help, then *you* are sick and so, in all likelihood, is your entire family. And since the splintered baton of dysfunctionality is handed down from generation to generation, so, too, were your parents and grandparents and so on back through history to the most notorious sabotaging codependents of all time: Adam and Eve!

Well, I'm a psychologist and I'm a parent and I'm here to tell you that the failure of *nouveau* child rearing is due not to sick parents who rule over dysfunctional families (although there are certainly some out there), but to counterproductive, impractical, and just downright dumb professional advice.   (FV)

At the University of Minnesota, researchers have discovered that in some mysterious way, political beliefs are influenced by genes. Identical twins (who are genetically indistinguishable) are far more likely to hold similar political beliefs than fraternal twins, even when the identical twins are reared apart and compared with fraternal twins reared in the same household.

It is not, therefore, outlandish to posit that if genes influence political ideology, they might also influence—and in similar directions—parenting ideology. Political conservatives—whom Daniel Seligman defines as people who respect established authority and hold traditional values—may, in fact, tend to be more "old-fashioned" in their child rearing than political liberals. Liberals, on the other hand, may be more "democratic."

Think about it. Conflicts over child rearing account for a significant amount of marital discord. If a relationship between political orientation and parenting style is someday established, potential spouses might be able to spare themselves a lot of eventual grief by simply asking one another, "For whom did you vote in the last election?" before deciding to get married and have children.   (NP)

November 16

Stifling, confining, demeaning, degrading, and humiliating: That's what the prescriptions of *nouveau* parenting have been for this generation of women. The '90s woman may have access to more economic, political, and professional opportunity than did the woman of the '50s, but the '90s woman will not be *truly* liberated until she can look her children square in their eyes and with strength of purpose tell them to *leave her alone*.

I said as much to an audience in Charlotte, North Carolina, a few years back. An older woman approached me afterward and said, "Now I understand why my daughter, who's thirty-five, single, and raising my only grandchild, will stand up to men in the workplace, but goes home in the evening and lets her five-year-old son push her around."

That little anecdote reeks with irony. Not only is the mother in the story a walking contradiction, but unbeknownst to her, she is inculcating into her son the one thing she has worked most of her adult life to overcome: *the perception that women are weak, and that their natural state is that of service to men.* After all, if this five-year-old male child is allowed to push his mother around now, how will he ever learn to treat women with dignity and respect?   (FV)

November 17

Raising a child on one's own is surely *different* from raising a child within a two-parent family, but it is only as *difficult* as the single parent thinks it is. For every argument supporting the belief that raising children is a Herculean task for one person, there is another, more optimistic interpretation of the evidence. Someone might point out, for instance, that single parents deserve sympathy because they are on the front lines *all* of the time, with no one to fall back on for emotional support. But it can just as easily be said that single parenthood is relatively uncomplicated. One single parent curses her isolation, saying, "I have to make *all* the decisions." Another rejoices at her independence, saying, "I get to make *all* the decisions." As with any other enterprise, there are, upon comparison, advantages and disadvantages. Select the perspective of your choice. Whose point of view is right? Everybody's! If you believe that raising children on your own is an insurmountable hardship, it will be just that. If, on the other hand, you convince yourself that raising children independently is one of the greatest opportunities for creative living you've ever had, then you will use that positive force to create opportunity after opportunity for yourself and your children. Whatever we believe of ourselves we generally manage to prove right.   (PP)

November 18

When Eric was born, Willie and I, like many young parents, tended to be almost neurotically territorial, especially around our own parents. We were excessively sensitive to their "interference," and any suggestion from them, no matter how constructive, was regarded as criticism.

It galled me, for instance, that Willie's parents would stuff Eric's mouth with sweets, his arms with toys, and his pockets with money. The more these things galled me, of course, the more they did them. It took us years to realize that grandparents do no harm by "spoiling." In fact, I'm now firmly convinced that it is as proper for grandparents to spoil their grandchildren as it is *improper* for parents to spoil those same children. One of the greatest pleasures of the grandparent generation is that of making children happy, and no one has a right to interfere in that pursuit. Those who are betwixt and between the innocence of childhood and the wisdom of old age, caught in the complexities and oft-grandiose seriousness of adulthood, would do well, when it comes to grandparents and grandchildren, to butt out and let things be.

So, shortly after our first grandchild, John McHenry Rosemond (or Jack Henry, as he is affectionately known) was born, Willie and I sat down with Eric and Nancy and said, "Concerning this child, there is one simple rule that we must all respect: It is our job (referring to Willie and myself) to *always* spoil Jack Henry. It is your job to *never* spoil him. If you don't try to do our job, then we won't have to try and do yours."

So far, that's worked out wonderfully for all concerned, especially Jack! (NP)

When either the child or the problem seems especially resistant to correction, I generally recommend an approach my parents occasionally used with me. They called it "lowering the boom." It's very, very psychologically incorrect, so don't expect to hear many other members of my profession applauding me on this one (as if they ever do).

The "boom" refers to a consequence that, while not harsh and certainly not hurtful, is sufficient to cause the child significant, albeit harmless, discomfort. In order for the "boom" to be effective, parents should not lower it often. It should be reserved for problems that are either extremely grave, or chronic, or both. Instead of inconveniencing a misbehaving child in some *minor* way by assigning him to time-out for five minutes or by taking a privilege away for a short time, his parents impose a major inconvenience *all at once.* They lower the boom and keep it bearing down on the child for a significant period of time. Because the feeling of the lowered boom is boldly and permanently engraved into the child's memory banks, the problem is unlikely to persist.   (FV)

Public spankings are humiliating to a child, and the self-conscious feelings that ensue are likely to drive further misbehavior. Furthermore, in a public situation the child is too aware of the presence of other people to focus sufficiently on the parent and, therefore, the message. Lastly, publicly administered spankings are downright inconsiderate of other people, who have no desire whatsoever to watch other parents spank their kids. If a child begins to misbehave in a public setting, and the parent feels that a spanking is warranted to set the child back on track, the parent should remove the child to a private area before applying open hand to *derriére*. In short, a public spanking is *rude*. If I had my way, parents who spanked in public would be cited not for child abuse, but for disturbing the public peace. (SPNK)

You can begin administering "vitamin N" (No!) to your child in the following ways:

• Turn his world right-side-up by giving him all of what he truly needs, but no more than 20 percent of what he simply wants. I call this the "Principle of Benign Deprivation." If you think 20 percent sounds too conservative, consider that an adult who manages to obtain 20 percent of what he wants is either very wealthy or doesn't want much.

• Don't do for him what he's capable of doing for himself, even if he says he "can't." Remember that you, the parent, know what's best.

• Don't make a policy of rescuing him from failure and/or disappointment.

• Remember that just because a child doesn't like something doesn't mean it shouldn't happen or exist. Confront your child with things unpleasant. Not life-threatening, mind you. Unpleasant!

• Don't worry about treating him fairly. Remember that to a child, "fair" means "me first!"

• Remember that simply because you enjoy a good standard of living doesn't mean you're obligated to share it in full measure with your child. Give him something to strive for when he becomes an adult. He'll thank you for it. But not any time soon.   (6PP)

November 22

Ask yourself, "What do we call a woman who has children and works outside the home?" The answer, of course, is "working mother." Let that sink in a minute.

Now, ask yourself, "What do we call a man who has children and works outside the home?" We don't call him a "working father," now do we? We call him a "guy with a job"—a plumber, a doctor, a mechanic, or whatever.

You see, the phrase "working mother" isn't innocuous at all. It's part and parcel of the straitjacket we've built (and quite innocently so) for this generation of women. Reading between the lines, it says, "If you're a woman with children, your primary obligation is forever and always to them. Any choice (i.e., a job) you make in your life that takes you away from your children on a regular basis for any significant length of time is a choice you've made *at your children's expense*. Therefore, when you return to your children, you have something to make up for: namely, your absence from their lives for the last four to nine hours."

In order to expiate the guilt that comes from deciding to do something for herself, something independent of her roles as wife and mother, when the "working mother" gets home from her job, she proceeds to beat herself into what I call a "quality-time frenzy" in the name of making up to her children what she thinks she has so selfishly deprived them of during the time she was at work.   (EHH)

The child-rearing language of previous generations didn't exactly sound good, replete as it was with such aphorisms as "Children should be seen and not heard," "I'm going to give you as much rope as you need to hang yourself," "Money doesn't grow on trees," "You made your bed, now you're going to lie in it," "You're going to have to stew in your own juices over this," and the most hated of them all: "Because I said so." Each one of these terse sayings embodied an idea inherent to a common (as in commonly held) sense of child rearing, and taken together, they summed up the parenting philosophy of our forebears. Baby-boomers like myself grew up hearing one or more of these things on almost a daily basis. As a result, we came to associate them with times when our parents were teaching us "lessons," which we were learning "the hard way." It was, therefore, relatively easy for "helping" professionals to convince us, as adults, that the child-rearing philosophy and methodology represented by these sayings was bogus, if not downright harmful, if not downright abusive.

And convince the majority of us they did. As a consequence, American parents have by and large distanced themselves from this bare-bones wisdom, seduced as most of us were by the idea that the emperor really *was* wearing new and wonderful clothes. Today's parents "parent" according to what sounds good, but it's becoming increasingly clear that what sounds good hasn't worked. Today's all-too-typical child is demanding, disobedient, uncooperative, disrespectful, and irresponsible. Today's all-too-typical parent is frustrated, anxious, and guilt-ridden, and the American family is in a state of crisis unrivaled in history. (FV)

The old-fashioned notion that *children should be seen and not heard* profited children in two important ways:

• *It greatly enhanced their social education.* Note that the first half of the aphorism clearly says that children could be *seen*. If a child entered a room where adults were holding a conversation, he was not told rudely to leave (albeit he might have been told *politely* to leave if the adults were talking about something that was not for consumption by little pitchers with big ears). He was simply expected to take a seat at the periphery of the conversation and listen, pay attention. No one was going to pretend—for the sake of "making him feel good about himself"—that he was socially, intellectually, or emotionally mature enough to participate in an adult conversation. However, if he listened, he would learn! So, the idea that children should be seen and not heard did not, by any means, reflect a hostile, antichild attitude. It was, in fact, prochild! It reflected a realistic appraisal of the state of childhood as well as the potential contained within that state. It put children "in their proper place," which is the best of all possible places for them.

• *It enhanced their respect for adults.* By creating boundaries of this sort between themselves and children, adults *distinguished* themselves. They created a separate culture that excluded children, for the most part. Children, therefore, aspired to membership in adult culture. That aspiration caused them to look up to adults. Adulthood was "where it was at" for kids. By attracting the respect of children, adults provided children the opportunity to eventually acquire self-respect. Any way one looks at it, *children should be seen and not heard* was of tremendous benefit to its subjects.   (FV)

The health of public education has been deteriorating for some thirty years. The viruses include tenure policies that make it almost impossible to get rid of mediocre teachers; bureaucracies that are administratively top-heavy; school boards consisting of wannabe politicians; an increasing emphasis on social-engineering experiments at the expense of academics; the institutionalized pampering of undisciplined students; and a pseudo-educational rhetoric created from the whole cloth of "self-esteem," the last of which has resulted in what I term "educational welfare," a peculiar form of entitlement that has watered down standards and transformed grades into a joke.

Now, the facts:

• Since 1965, per-capita expenditures by public schools have risen more than 200 percent (in 1993 dollars) while student achievement has declined. As exemplified by Minnesota, which is twenty-fifth in per-capita spending, yet close to the top in student achievement, there is little, if any, correlation between the two. Conclusion: Public schools don't need more money, they need to become more efficient.

• American public school students score well behind those from other industrialized countries in science and math, yet think their knowledge in these areas is more than adequate. Conclusion: Public schools seem to be doing a better job of making children "feel good about themselves" than of imparting real, marketable skills.

• An intelligent student with a solid grounding in good family values is likely to achieve as well in public as in private school. Conclusion: Public schools seem to be failing average students (the majority) more than any others.

We could go a long way toward rehabilitating public education by (a) abolishing the Department of Education and returning control of education to states, and (b) implementing school choice (vouchers), thus bringing to bear market forces and accountability.

(TOH)

During the formative years, a child's brain is "programmed" by the character of his/her environment. Researchers have discovered that adverse environmental circumstances actually "undernourish" certain areas of the brain, resulting in disabilities of one sort or another. Some of these disabilities are obvious (e.g., pronounced communication disorders), while some show themselves only under certain circumstances (e.g., a lack of musical ability). Researchers have also found that certain areas of the brains of many individuals diagnosed with attention deficit disorder (ADD) are structurally and/or chemically abnormal. These two sets of findings raise the possibility that ADD can be the result of adverse environmental experiences.

At this point, we encounter the sticky wicket. The notion that parents who are poor, uncaring, or burdened with mental problems often create undernourishing environments for their children is taken for granted. But a disproportionate number of middle- and upper-middle-class children are diagnosed with ADD. The idea that caring, responsible middle-class parents might be creating unfavorable environments for their children (even unwittingly) is highly threatening, so much so that even to suggest it causes paroxysms among such parents and their professional allies.

Television is the one thing privileged and underprivileged children have in common. The average American preschool child watches more than five thousand hours of television—more than one-fourth of his waking time. We can assume that this is having significant impact on brain development. There's a distinct possibility that the "flicker" (constant change of picture) typical of television programs might well be disabling the attention spans of significant numbers of American children within all social classes.

This hypothesis raises the possibility that in certain cases—perhaps most!— ADD can be reversed if television is eliminated from the child's environment before the damage "sets." The brain's capacity to repair itself is well documented. I saw this very reversal happen with my son, and I've heard of it happening numerous times since.

(TOH)

Parents are always wanting to have child-rearing matters precisely quantified. How much is too much? they ask, wanting to know precisely how many toys a child of, say, six should have, how many minutes of one-on-one attention a child of three needs from his or her parents on a daily basis, when to give help with homework and when not to, and how many times in a week, and for what length of time, etc. What these parents don't understand is that knowing where to draw the line isn't a matter of quantities; rather, it's a matter of common sense. Willie and I eventually decided that by simply asking ourselves, "Where, in this situation, would *our parents* have drawn the line?" we would, more often than not, end up drawing the line in a proper place for the child in question. Our parents raised us according to common sense, not books. And as all parents will, they made mistakes, but their successes outweighed their mistakes; and in the final analysis, their successes, not their mistakes, defined their child rearing. (FV)

"**H**elping" professionals see a mother and a father who are unable to communicate, much less be consistent, concerning a child's problems and conclude that the marriage (and by extension, the family) is "dysfunctional." They propose that the child's misbehavior is either an unconscious means of forcing his parents to resolve their dysfunctionality or a means of drawing the "heat" away from their relationship and toward himself, thus preventing them from having a complete marital meltdown. I've long thought this explanation was, more often than not, malarkey. It usually seems obvious that the child's problems are not the *result* of marital dysfunction; rather, they are the catalyst for those problems. The marriage is not the problem; rather, the problem is probably, usually, Mom's sense of inadequacy as a parent, which she hides as well as possible.

But Mom is not to blame, by any means. She has simply fallen victim to forty-odd years of psychological babbling to the effect that behind every problem child there is a Bad Mother. In the late '50s and '60s, she was overly attentive. Then, around 1970, she became insufficiently attentive. Most odd, eh? Dad wants to put the onus of the child's misbehavior and/or underachievement in school on the child, but Mom can't allow that to happen because she, and only she, knows who's *really* to blame. So when Dad tries to discipline, Mom jumps in, screaming, "No! Don't do that!" because she's convinced the child "can't help it!" and that Dad's discipline will only make matters worse. No, the blame doesn't belong to Mom. It belongs to a generation of "not-so-helping" professionals who have fitted today's female for the straitjacket of Mother-Guilt.   (TOH)

The more often a child is spanked, the less dramatic any given spanking will be. Fact is, children who are spanked a lot eventually become "immune" to being spanked. They develop a "so what?" attitude toward spankings. So how much is too much? The answer depends on the age of the child. With a toddler, more than once a week is probably too much. With a four- or five-year-old, once a month is a good benchmark. With a child six and older, you reach the point of diminishing returns at one spanking every three months or so. And, by the way, by the time a child is nine or ten, spankings should cease entirely. If you don't have a child's respect and attention by then, no amount of slapping the child's rear end is going to matter.

(SPNK)

There is nothing new about mothers working outside of their homes. My mother did. So did a number of my childhood buddies' mothers. What's new is guilt over doing so and—consequently—large numbers of women flogging themselves into frenzies of "I've got to make it up to my children" every evening and on weekends.

Take, for example, my mother. For the first seven years of my life, she was a single parent. Then she remarried. In neither situation did she come home from her job feeling she owed me something. Quite the contrary. She came home feeling—are you ready for this?—*I owed her something!* What a concept! Specifically, I owed her for putting a roof over my head, food in my stomach, clothes on my back, and shoes on my feet. For her sacrifice, Mom felt she deserved respect, obedience, and peace and quiet. And she got it. She expected me to keep myself busy and do my own homework. And I did.

Thus did I grow up with the feeling that I was obligated to my mother. By contrast, overwhelming numbers of today's kids are growing up thinking their mothers are obligated to them. Because the mother-child relationship has turned upside-down, inside-out, and backward in the course of forty years, today's child is at great risk of becoming a petulant, demanding, ungrateful brat. Unfortunately, the more petulant and demanding he becomes, the more likely it is his mother will feel she's not doing enough for him. And around and around they go, this codependent union of mother and child.

What America needs is yet another women's liberation movement. This time, however, women should burn not their bras, but their minivans. (TOH)

December 1

It's important that the worlds of adults and children be distinct and often exclusive. In other words, adults should be involved primarily with other adults, *not* with children; and children, likewise, should be involved primarily with other children, *not* adults. The more adults become involved with children, the more children want to be involved with adults, and the less able adults are to *distinguish* themselves. Adults who fail to distinguish themselves reap what they sow—their children fail to pay attention to them and learn to manipulate them instead of coming to respect them. Unfortunately, if a farmer fails to properly tend a plant, the plant suffers far more than does the farmer. (NP)

December 2

One of the myths circulating about "because I said so" says it stifles curiosity and prevents children from learning to question authority. There is, let me assure you, no evidence whatsoever that might lend even a shred of credence to this ludicrous contention. I am reasonably certain that George Washington, Thomas Jefferson, Martin Luther King, Mahatma Ghandi, Rosa Parks, Marie Curie, Booker T. Washington, Louis Pasteur, Chuck Yeager, and Albert Einstein were all reared by parents who insisted they obey for no other reason than "because I said so." Yet they were all extremely curious, and they all questioned established authority (and/or challenged previously established limits of one sort or another). There exists, furthermore, a body of evidence which strongly suggests that curiosity and risk-taking (both involved in questioning established authority) are inborn, rather than learned. It would appear that if a child is genetically predisposed toward such activity, it will emerge irrespective (relatively speaking) of the child's early learning. The question then becomes, will the child's natural tendencies toward curiosity and risk-taking be well-disciplined (as was obviously the case with the individuals cited above) or not? In the latter instance, those same traits may drive highly dangerous, even self-destructive, "rebel without a cause" behavior. Early learning, which is primarily a matter of upbringing, would *definitely* influence this outcome. I would contend that highly curious children require the discipline inherent to "because I said so" as much, if not slightly more, than children who might not be so inclined. (FV)

During a stint as a guest on a nationally syndicated radio talk show, the host remarked that he didn't hear me talking much about the "joy" of parenthood. He asked if I had, indeed, enjoyed being a parent.

No, I replied. I hadn't *enjoyed* being a parent—not overall, at least. Looking back, there were certainly immensely enjoyable times, but they were the exception, not the rule. The rule was by no means unpleasant or unhappy, but it wasn't enjoyable, either. I looked at parenthood as a responsibility, not a playground where I was supposed to have a good time. God gave Willie and me two packages of such responsibility and charged us with doing a good job, not having fun. Nonetheless, we had our share of fun, and it may well be that fun was more plentiful and more real in our family than in many because we weren't trying to manufacture it.

It's too bad that today's parents have been led to believe that parenthood should, if one is successful at it, be an almost constant state of joy. Parenthood is not a romantic endeavor. Nor is it glorious. If one is successful at it, the payoff comes when one's children are independent adults. Parents who think child rearing should be joyful are setting themselves up for a big disappointment. Instead of feeling successful at it, they're more likely to feel a lot of frustration, anger, anxiety, and guilt. In that regard, it's just like any other job. If you have unrealistic expectations concerning your employment, you're probably going to wind up hating it. If, on the other hand, your expectations are realistic, you'll be better able to retain a sense of humor when things aren't going so well. Believe me, you'll laugh a lot more if you're *not* expecting parenthood to be a lot of fun.

(NP)

Common sense will tell you that, in general, a child is better off living with both of his or her parents than with one. But *in general* is the operative phrase in that statement. Common sense will also tell you that a child is better off in a relatively peaceful, low-stress household than in one that's punctuated with constant strife. If a marriage doesn't work, or if one never took place to begin with, that's less than fortunate, but it's not necessarily cause for concern about the child or children involved. As my mother proved, a single parent is as capable as any two parents of raising healthy, happy children. A single parent can't be a mother and a father too (and shouldn't even try to manage that juggling act), but a single parent can be a whole, fulfilled person, with more than enough vitality to share with his or her children. The job is never too big for one person, if the person is big enough for the job. (PP)

December 5

Whole language was one of many *nouveau* reforms to sweep through public education in the 1980s. Also known as "literature-based" instruction, its advocates maintain that the most natural way for children to learn to read and write is through the trial and error of simply doing so. After all, they reason, children learn to talk without ever being taught formal rules of speech, so the same should apply to learning to read, etc. Phonics instruction is unnecessary "drudgery" say some WL apologists, even going so far as to claim that it is a negative experience that causes children to hate reading. Keep in mind that when phonics reigned supreme in the teaching of reading, far fewer children had reading problems than is the case today. In this context, the claims of WL advocates are just another example of how rhetoric often fails to mirror reality.

But don't take my word for it. In July 1995, forty professors of linguistics and psycholinguistics from Harvard, Massachusetts Institute of Technology, Northeastern University, University of Massachusetts, Brandeis, and Boston University sent a letter to the Massachusetts Commissioner of Education strongly criticizing the state's plan to mandate WL as the standard for reading instruction.

The professors said that WL is a "scientifically unfounded" view of reading instruction. They accused WL of treating "the alphabetic nature of our writing system as little more than an accident, when in fact it is the most important property of written English." Whole language, they said, is based on an "erroneous view of how human language works, a view that runs counter to most of the major scientific results of more than one hundred years of linguistics and psycholinguistics."

So, with all due respect to well-intentioned educators who have climbed on the WL bandwagon, I think it's safe to say WL's days are numbered. (NP)

Many parents, it would seem, dislike it when their children throw tantrums, but refuse to do what must be done to stop them. Quite a few parents are intimidated, even downright frightened, by tantrums, whether the two-year-old sort of rolling on the floor while screaming and frothing at the mouth or the sixteen-year-old sort of stomping around and slamming doors while spewing forth a steady stream of verbal abuse. So they give in.

When asked, "Why do you give in to this foolishness?" they answer, "Because it's easier."

That's true, it *is* easier, but only in the short run. Giving in solves the immediate problem. It turns off the tantrum. Unfortunately, the more often parents give in to a child's tantrums, the worse the child's tantrums will become. Every time parents give in to a tantrum, they virtually guarantee the occurrence of at least fifty more.   (6PP)

December 7

When a child misbehaves, some consequence is due; punishment, however, is but one of the available options. Other options include a stern (albeit calm) reprimand, an open discussion of why the behavior took place and how it can be prevented in the future, or even a simple acknowledgment of the misdeed along with an equally simple statement of disapproval, as in "I know you got in trouble at school today, and all I have to say is I'm not pleased."

Your choice is determined by a number of variables, including the child's age, the nature of the misbehavior in question and whether or not it's chronic, the child's emotional status, and whether it tends to take place in public or only in the home. It is not necessarily true that consequences must escalate as the "severity" of the "crime" increases. It is sometimes, in fact, more strategic to take a low-key approach with a serious infraction. Likewise, it might be best to impose a heavy penalty for a problem that's relatively minor, but occurs fairly often. (FV)

Following a speaking engagement in Albuquerque, New Mexico, in 1994, one of my hosts sent me a clipping from the local newspaper advertising one of the "latest things" in parenting programs. To identify the program by name would be gratuitous; suffice to say what attracted my attention was the ad's "hook," which read, "Children Are Flowers, Not Weeds."

To say that children are flowers, not weeds, sure does sound good, doesn't it? The problem is it's completely meaningless, and the analogy is all wrong.

Children are *not* flowers. They aren't weeds either. The truth is, children are *wild things* that must be constantly pruned lest they become completely unmanageable. They are self-centered, foolish, undersocialized, undercivilized little people who, if left to their own devices, are capable of incredible selfishness and cruelty, some more than others. The author of this flowery snippet of saccharine sentiment ought to be made to do penance by hand-copying William Golding's *Lord of the Flies*.

It's not that children aren't lovable, but patronization and love are entirely different things. "Children are flowers" is patronizing, and therefore disrespectful. One is capable of loving children honestly and respectfully only if one faces facts:

Fact: Children are fraught with fault.

Fact: Their fault is inherent. It is the result of being human; of being born with free will in the head and foolishness in the heart.

Fact: It is precisely because they all share in humanity's faults— and through no fault of their own—that children require unconditional love, and lots of it.

A realistic, unsentimental appraisal of children is essential not only to truly loving and respecting them, but also to properly disciplining them. If, as a parent, you do not see your children with clarity, their mischievous ways are likely to throw you off balance, and you cannot discipline effectively if you have lost your center of gravity.

(FV)

This generation of parents has done a wonderful job of sharing their standard of living with their children, but a miserable job of endowing those same children with the skills they'll need to achieve that standard on their own. As a result, too many children are growing up believing it's someone else's responsibility to take care of their needs and wants. Never having learned to accept responsibility for their own well-being, they are likely to go through life expecting other people to make them happy and blaming anything and everything that goes wrong on some*one* or some*thing* else. Unfortunately, as we all know, a person who fails to take full responsibility for his or her own happiness will never be fully happy. The paradox is this: The more parents try to make their children happy, the more they guarantee that their children will someday be miserable.   (6PP)

By and large, today's parents feel they are obligated to explain themselves to their children. Furthermore, they seem to believe that their explanations must be acceptable to their children.

Consequently, their explanations take on a persuasive, pleading, even apologetic character. Implicit in this is the absolutely absurd idea that parents don't have a right to enforce a decision unless (a) it can be supported by reasons other than personal preference, (b) the children understand the reasons, and (c) the children agree with them.

Now, hear me clearly: *I'm not saying that parents should never give reasons to children.* I'm saying parents should make no attempt to *reason* with children, and the difference is night and day. Reasoning is the futile attempt to persuade a child that your point of view is valid. Face it, our children will understand an adult point of view when they are adults, and no sooner. No amount of words will instill an appreciation for an adult point of view into the mind of a child.

If you want to explain yourself, then by all means do so. But don't expect your child to agree. When he doesn't, simply say, "I'm not asking you to agree. I wouldn't agree with me, either, if I was your age. You have my permission to disagree, but you don't have permission to disobey."

In other words, the child does what he is told not because you succeed at providing an explanation that smoothes his ruffled feathers, but simply because he's been told. So, you see, even in the act of giving reasons, the bottom line is still "because I said so."   (TT)

Parents who spank a lot generally do so because they believe spankings are in and of themselves *corrective*—that the pain of a spanking will persuade the child to never misbehave in that particular fashion again. The evidence to the contrary is overwhelming. Children who are spanked a lot do *not* stop misbehaving. They misbehave not only more and more, but also more and more cleverly. In other words, they learn how to get away with misbehavior. Eventually, getting away with misbehavior becomes a game and they begin setting bigger and bigger goals for themselves. What can I get away with next? becomes the dominant challenge in their lives. Meanwhile, their parents spank more and more, with less and less effect. Finally, the parents give up, saying, "I can't do a thing with him." And they're absolutely right! Now, unfortunately, it's society's turn, and society has never done as good a job as parents could have done in the first place. When it comes to spanking, less is definitely more.

(SPNK)

December 12

The "single-parent trap" is more likely to snare single mothers than single fathers. For a number of reasons, mothers are more likely than fathers to neglect their own needs in the course of meeting their children's. Mothers also have more difficulty making the distinction between what their children truly *need* and what they simply *want*. When single mothers have primary custody of their children, which is most often the case, they often feel they need to overcompensate for the absence of a father in the home. In the process, they fall into the trap of overindulging/overprotecting their children, and wind up stretching their emotional resources to the breaking point.

Look at it this way: You can't supply anyone else's "warehouse" unless your own is fully stocked. But instead of taking care of themselves well enough to keep their own warehouses full, single mothers often feel compelled to forgo *their* needs in favor of their children's. Eventually and inevitably, the single mother's ability to go on giving collapses, and she vents her frustration at her children. Then guilt sets in. At this point, our single mother feels compelled to do something special for her children in order to make up for having lost her temper at them.

And it's back to business as usual.   (6PP)

December 13

With a child who misbehaves only occasionally, sitting in the bathroom or an out-of-the-way chair for a few minutes serves as a generally effective reminder of the rules and the parent's authority. However, the difficult, disobedient child is likely to "immunize" to time-out rather quickly. Time-out may, at first, upend such a child, resulting in temporary improvement. In short order, however, it usually becomes no big deal. The child becomes willing to pay the relatively insignificant price of a few minutes in a chair in order to continue dominating the center of attention in the family.

In and of itself, time-out is a fairly weak response to misbehavior. The more pronounced the misbehavior, the weaker it is, by comparison. Highly oppositional children require powerful (not painful, *powerful*) consequences. Nothing less will keep their attention. Professionals are often reluctant to recommend powerful consequences because they cause children distress, thus (supposedly) lowering self-esteem. Ah, but unless the child's misbehavior results in more distress for the child than for the parent, the child has no reason to change his behavior. (FV)

December 14

Grandparents can relax the rules a bit without undermining parents' authority or the values they're trying to teach their children. By trial and error, my wife and I discovered that the best policy concerning grandparents is "when in Rome, do as the Romans do, and when the Romans come to you, do as the Romans do." In other words, don't interfere in how grandparents choose to dote on grandchildren. There's just no point in letting conflicts over trivia like this spoil family get-togethers, especially when the family doesn't get together that often. (FV)

By and large, today's parent seems to think that letting a child fall flat on his face when the fall could have been prevented is not only irresponsible, but downright cruel. Because this says, in effect, that the parent, not the child, is responsible for the child's mistakes, parents who feel thusly spend inordinate effort trying to prevent their children from making mistakes.

I call this sort of obsessive hovering "Parenting by Helicopter," the upshot of which is that many of today's children never learn to accept responsibility for their behavior. Why? Because their parents are doing a fine job of accepting that responsibility for them. But responsibility isn't the only thing at stake. So is *learning* itself.

Almost all learning is accomplished through trial and error. If error is prevented, so is learning. By making mistakes, one learns what works and what doesn't. Eventually, after some initial failure, the learner fine-tunes his or her skills and masters the task at hand. Standing back and letting that failure occur, in a supportive but non-interfering way, gives a child room to develop initiative, resourcefulness, and effective problem-solving skills. It also lets the child come to grips with the frustration inherent to the learning of any skill—social, academic, emotional, and so on. That's how children learn to persevere, and perseverance—as we all know from experience—is the main ingredient in *every* success story.

It all boils down to this: If you want your children to learn how to successfully stand on their own two feet, you must be willing to occasionally let them fall flat on their faces. (6PP)

December 16

Despite rhetoric to the contrary, the American family *worked* as well as could reasonably be expected when husbands were bread-winners and wives stayed home with the children. (It goes without saying that I'm speaking in general terms here.) Once upon a time, this was regarded as nothing more than a logical and necessary division of responsibilities. Unfortunately, over time, this tradition gave rise to female stereotypes that were, to some degree, debasing. We began to confuse what women had and had not done with what they were and were not *capable* of doing. This confusion pumped adrenaline into the neofeminist movement and provided ideal opportunity for the movement to broaden its power base by convincing American women they were members of a victim class. According to the new feminist manifesto, a woman was not complete, and therefore not liberated, if she relegated herself to the role of housewife. Thus began the cultural devaluing of the traditional female role of full-time wife and mother. As women were seduced and intimidated by this insidiously antifamily agenda into putting their children into day care and entering the job force, the American family went into a precipitous state of decline. In the official language, the American family has simply been "changing" over the last thirty years. This is nothing but a euphemistic way of saying that for at least three decades, the American family has been in a steady state of decline, getting progressively weaker and weaker. And as the family goes, so goes the culture. In the final analysis, America is only as strong as its families are healthy. Restoring our domestic health, therefore, has less to do with raising or lowering taxes to create or eliminate this or that government program, and more to do with a reaffirmation of the traditional family values that were the backbone of this country since its inception. (TT)

In order to demonstrate their commitment to their children and their determination to perform as perfectly as possible at parenting, today's female is likely, upon becoming a mother, to give up most, if not all, of the interests, diversions, hobbies, etc., that once occupied her spare time and brought her pleasure. This self-sacrifice is part and parcel of what I'm referring to when I point out that American female parents, by and large, "can't stop being mothers." If they stop serving their children for any significant length of time, they feel guilty and must do some additional form of self-sacrifice as penance for their sins.

Men, on the other hand, do not generally give up fishing, golf, hunting, etc., when they become fathers. And I'm by no means suggesting they should. Rather, I suggest to women that the next time their husbands go fishing, *they should get a sitter for the kids and go along!* (NP)

It didn't take me long to figure out that one of a grandparent's jobs is to always pretend there is very little a child can do that's bothersome. Young parents tend to worry a lot about minutiae and overreact to things children have been doing since time immemorial. Grandparents do young parents (and grandchildren) great service by being the counterpoint to all this anxiousness. That's why grandparents have a reputation for saying things like, "He's just a boy" and "Oh my goodness, yes, I remember you doing the same thing when you were that age and you've turned out just fine, now haven't you?" Human tranquilizers, that's what grandparents must stand ready to be.

When parents become upended, it's the job of grandparents to set them upright again. Grandparents know that parents, whether they realize it or not, are capable of dealing successfully with anything a child is capable of doing. Those who've "been there and done that" know there is nothing to fear concerning children and their behavior except fear itself.

People ask, "How are you going to keep from giving advice?" I'm not. Grandparents are supposed to advise, even manipulate. The trick is to manipulate parents into making correct decisions without realizing they've been manipulated. Whether it's a matter of money, discipline, education, or recreation, the best grandparents exert their wise, all-knowing influence by "remote control," never letting on that the parents are merely following subtle commands.

For example, a wise grandparent never says, "Well, I think this is the way to do this or that." Instead, the grandparent tells a funny story concerning a similar issue from their own parenthood experience. The parents laugh and do exactly what the grandparent means for them to do, never realizing they are merely puppets of vastly superior beings.   (NP)

December 19

There are several caution flags I raise with parents of only children:

First, because all the parents' "eggs," so to speak, are in one basket, the only child tends to receive more attention and more things than he would if he were in a family of two or more children. Overindulgence leads to behaviors typically associated with the "spoiled" child—making unreasonable demands, acting "starved" for attention, throwing tantrums, disrespect, and disobedience.

Second, as a result of being included in so many adult activities, the child begins to perceive the marriage as a *threesome*, centered around him. This family dynamic makes it difficult, if not impossible, for the child to outgrow his infantile self-centeredness. Also, to the degree a child is treated and regards himself as an equal, parents will have a difficult time establishing themselves as authority figures. Furthermore, because the boundary between the child and the marriage is blurred, the child may fail to develop a clear sense of his own identity.

In the course of the bickering that often characterizes sibling relationships, siblings help each other learn how to share and resolve conflict. Only children sometimes have problems in both of these areas. With other children, they may tend to be possessive of their belongings and want everything to go their way. These potential problems are made worse by the fact that, by virtue of being included in so many adult activities, the only child is often better socialized to adults than to peers. Consequently, the only child is often perceived by peers as having a superior, "know-it-all" attitude.

A little foresight can prevent these problems from ever developing:

• Center the family around the marriage, not the child.

• Limit the child's inclusion in adult activities.

• Enroll the child in day care no later than age three.

• Avoid indulging the child with either too much attention or too many things. (6PP)

December 20

Child rearing—or *parenting*, as it's now called—has been transformed into a pseudo-intellectual "science," something people think they must strain their brains at in order to do properly. But parenting is anything but an intellectual endeavor. In fact, the more you strain your brain at it, the more likely you are to find yourself lost among the trees, oblivious to the forest.

Good parenting does not emanate primarily from the head; it comes from the heart and the gut. It is not a matter of long, hard thought, but a matter of how intuitively sensitive you are to *your* needs as well as the needs of your child, and a matter of how firmly grounded you are in the soil of common sense. Parents who think too much tend to say things like, "Raising a child is the hardest thing I've ever done." I understand. I used to think that way myself. Then I stopped thinking so much about it, stopped obsessing over all the little details, stopped worrying about whether one wrong decision was going to ruin my children for life, and started paying at least as much attention to my own needs and the needs of my marriage as I did to my kids. That's when raising children became relatively easy and enjoyable. (6PP)

Parents who fail to establish their *command* act as if they don't know where to stand and don't know, furthermore, where they want their children to stand. Because limits and expectations are uncertain, here-today-gone-tomorrow propositions, their children are forced to constantly test. For these children, testing (misbehavior) amounts to a vain attempt to pin their parents down, to get them to stand in one place, to be constant.

Unfortunately, it is inevitable that a parent who isn't clear on where she should stand is also unable to see that her child's constant testing is a symptom of her own indecisiveness. She blames the child, describing him as "strong-willed," "stubborn," "mean," "difficult," or the like. She might even say the child has "attention deficit disorder" or an "oppositional disorder." Because she does not see the forest for the trees, her child's testing frustrates her "to no end." It induces an overload of stress into the relationship, and that stress interferes with her ability to communicate the love she genuinely feels for her child.

She complains, "It seems like I'm always yelling, but I don't know how to stop."

She doesn't realize that her yelling is a function of her failure to stand in one place. If she ever decides to stand in one place and let her child's testing run its course (which it will in relatively short order), she will stop yelling. But as long as she dances around, her child will test, she will be frustrated, and she will yell.

The bottom line is this: If you want to create circumstances within which you will be able to effectively demonstrate to your child your love for him, then you had better stand in one place. Parent, discipline thyself!   (FV)

December 22

The Bible tells us that "Foolishness is bound up in the heart of a child" (Proverbs 22:15). It takes children the majority of eighteen years to release from their heart an amount of foolishness sufficient to become constructive members of society. In the meantime, their opinions and feelings do not count for much.

Don't get me wrong, please! It's not that adults shouldn't listen to children, because we should. We should listen with tolerance for their foolishness and an ear to whatever opportunities we might have to gently pry it loose from their hearts. It's not that adults should treat children as if they aren't important, because children are very important. Their opinions and feelings aren't that important, but they themselves are very important, indeed. They are the future. As such, it is vital that adults not give them the impression that their foolish opinions and foolish feelings are the stuff of importance, lest they not let that foolishness go and instead carry it with them into their adult lives. And it's not that *none* of their opinions and feelings are relatively unimportant; just most of them. Every once in a while, a child comes forth with a truly valid opinion or feeling, and those, dear reader, must be carefully cultivated. It's all part of separating wheat from chaff. (FV)

I was never able to reason with my children—both intelligent, sane individuals—when they were teens. By this I don't mean that I was unable to explain certain things to them, however. When, for example, my son was boggled by a relatively complex algebra problem at age fourteen, I was able to clear up his confusion. But when, one year later, he wanted a motorcycle, forget it.

"No need to waste your time talking about it, kid," I replied, "because you will never get a motorcycle from us."

His shoulders went back, his chin jutted forward, and he leaned forward so as to give the faux-question more emphasis: "Why not?!!!"

"Because," I said, "motorcycles are dangerous and you are not old enough to appreciate the danger; nor will you be for many years to come."

He loosened up a bit, and said, in his most placable tone, "No, Dad, I knew you were going to say that, and I know motorcycles are dangerous, Dad, and I promise, I'll be careful."

"Eric," I said, "if I were in your shoes, I'd say the same thing." And without further ado I turned around and walked away.

Now, I'd like for someone who thinks teenagers can be reasoned with to please tell me what I could have said to Eric on that occasion that would have caused him to agree with me that, no, he shouldn't have a motorcycle under any circumstances, as in, "Well, Dad, now that you put it that way, I see the error of my thinking on this matter, and I concur 100 percent. I'm sorry I even brought it up."

Naw. You can't reason with a teenager. You can either say "yes" or "no", just like with any other age child. When Eric is forty and his first is fifteen and asks for something outrageous, then he'll understand why I did what I did way back when. But then, you can reason with a forty-year-old. Most of the time.   (NP)

December 24

I recently heard a social worker who specializes in adoption tell an audience that from infancy onward, adoptive parents should frequently insert the word "adopted" and "adoption" into bedtime stories as well as make up songs and nursery rhymes about the subject.

Talking about adoption nearly every day is as completely unnecessary as reminding a child every day that you are his or her birth parent. Making a mountain out of the adoption molehill also enlarges the possibility of what I term "The Adoption Myth"—the mistaken belief that any and all subsequent problems in the parent/child relationship are related in some way to the adoption.

Several years ago, I saw a family in which a young teenage girl was having conflict with her adoptive parents. Although the problems were universally typical of teens and parents, the parents were convinced they were the result of "unresolved anger" concerning the adoption along with "feelings of abandonment." They wanted me to talk to the girl and help her "work through her feelings."

Although fairly certain the girl was not in need of personal counseling, I did have one talk with her. I discovered that while she wasn't angry at having been adopted, she was "sick and tired" of her parents' constant references to it.

"They want to talk about it all the time," she said, "like it's something weird, you know? Adopted, adopted, adopted! I'm so sick of hearing it, I could scream!"

Her parents later told me they were only following the advice given them by the social workers at the adoption agency.

"You're lucky," I told them.

"How's that?" they asked.

"Because," I said, "despite the fact that you were encouraged to blow the adoption out of proportion, and did so with the best of intentions, your daughter still managed to keep straight in her own mind that adoption is really no big deal at all."   (NP)

A number of journalists have asked (1) whether I think children should be told that a jolly old elf named Santa Claus is the giver of all/some of their Christmas gifts, and (2) how and at what age parents should tell a child there is no Santa Claus.

1. I don't think it matters one way or another whether children are told there's a Santa Claus; however, given that most Christian children are being told that Santa brings toys to little boys and girls on Christmas morning, I'd suggest that parents who eschew this myth at least inform their children of its prevalence. In my view, the Santa myth is harmless, whimsical, and can serve the purpose of letting parents off the hook when one or more of the more expensive items on a child's "wish list" don't show up under the tree on Christmas morning. For those reasons, especially the third, my wife and I caused our children to believe in Santa.

2. Contrary to what most journalists apparently assume, the mere fact that parents cause a child to believe in Santa does not require them to inform him someday that Santa doesn't really take corporeal form. One reason I feel this way is because I happen to still believe that Santa exists. To me, the ageless elf is the spirit of Christmas. Please don't get me wrong: Jesus is the *meaning* of Christmas; nonetheless, Santa is its spirit. He is a symbol of unconditional love and selfless charity.

When our kids finally complained that some cynical playmate had told them Santa didn't exist, we simply replied, "Well, that's unfortunate for your playmate, because if you don't believe in Santa, he stops coming to your house on Christmas morning." We said this with a wink, and our children seemed to understand intuitively that this was a ruse with a redeeming purpose. Willie and I trust they will pass this valuable myth on to our grandchildren.   (NP)

December 26

Here's irrefutable, incontrovertible, indubitable proof that children don't need reasons: If children, as pseudo-intellectuals insist, truly *needed* reasons for the decisions adults make, they would express this need *every single time an adult made a decision*. But they don't. Children only ask—demand, actually—to know the reason or reasons behind an adult decision *when they don't like the decision*. They never, ever ask/demand a reason when an adult decision is to their liking.

If, for example, a parent tells a thirteen-year-old child that yes, she may go with older teenagers the parent doesn't know to a satanic heavy-metal concert in a town fifty miles away and spend the night at the home of a friend of one of the teens whom the parent doesn't know, the child is not going to roll her eyes, stomp her feet, and in a demanding tone, ask, "Why?!!"

Right? Of course I'm right. The child is only going to demand an explanation if the parent says, "You must be kidding. The answer is 'no.'"

Since children don't express this supposed "need" across the entire spectrum of adult decisions, but only concerning a certain class of decisions, we're obviously not talking about a need. Needs are not that selective. No, children don't *need* reasons; the truth is, they *want* them. They want them because they've learned that adults who are foolish enough to try and explain themselves to children can be lured into argument. And an adult who can be lured into an argument is an adult who can be defeated. Maybe. And children are gamblers when it comes to such matters. If a child manages to lure a foolish parent into ten arguments and only "wins"—gets his way—one out of the ten times, the child is certain to keep on trying to lure the parent into arguments.   (FV)

Rewards prevent children from accepting responsibility for their behavior. Instead of helping a child learn that inappropriate behavior has undesirable consequences (which is the way things work in the real world), rewards can result in the child developing a manipulative, "What's in it for me?" attitude toward appropriate behavior. In other words, instead of learning that good behavior is rewarding in and of itself, the child learns to use the promise of good behavior as a bargaining tool to get new toys, privileges, and other "goodies."

Not long ago I explained the risks of using rewards to a gathering of parents in Miami, Florida. Afterward, a mother approached me and thanked me for my remarks. She said, "I've used rewards a lot because I was under the impression that they helped promote good self-esteem. Now I understand why every time I take my child anywhere, he asks, "If I'm good, will you buy me a new toy?"

An occasional spontaneous reward, used as an acknowledgment of achievement or progress in a certain area, is fine. Rewards that have *not* been contracted for are more sincere and, therefore, more effective at promoting both good behavior and good self-esteem. Children should, of course, be praised for their accomplishments, but even praise is most effective when it's low-key and occasional.

(6PP)

My mother believed that children belonged outside, weather permitting, and she defined "weather permitting" very liberally. On those occasions when I happened to slip up and get "underfoot," she'd reprimand me, but not harshly. She'd say, "John Rosemond! You are underfoot! You know how I feel about that! Now, you can see that I'm very busy. You're just going to have to find something of your own to do!" And with that, she would usually usher me out of doors, and I'd find myself on the sidewalk in front of our apartment with five or six other kids who'd also been kicked out of their houses by their mothers, and we would play. In a sense, we were "exiles," but the thought that our mothers didn't love us never even occurred to us. We didn't feel all lousy inside for hours after this banishment. We didn't even give it a second thought. We just played. We had fun!

Sometimes, your mother put you outside and told you that if you came home, for any reason, before the next meal, you'd have to stay indoors as her helper the rest of the day. Some of the mothers in my neighborhood would put their children outside and lock the doors!

Now, I'm not advocating locking children outside. I think that's a bit extreme, in fact. Risky, even. I'm saying that when it came to their relationships with their children, most of the women of my mother's generation were *truly* liberated women. They erected what we today term "boundaries" between themselves and their kids, and they were in complete control of when their children were allowed through these boundaries. They were not, by any means, at their children's beck and call. It was, in fact, the other way around. If you heard your mother calling, *you* skeedaddled.   (FV)

Largely because of television, today's child is clearly more "sophisticated" than was the typical child of forty years past. One need not *learn* to watch television, and because its content is presented visually, even a preschool child is able to comprehend—albeit at a naive level—adult situations. For example, whereas a young child reading a passage in an adult novel might not understand that two people are making love, what's going on becomes obvious to the child when that same scene is played out on a television screen. In this manner (and the issue does not begin and end with sexual matters), the innocence of children is no longer being sheltered. Exposed to the very things our grandparents believed should be hidden from them, children are, indeed, becoming more "sophisticated."

I compare this situation to that of a plant that's been hothoused and, as a result, has well-developed foliage but an inadequate root system. Likewise, the hothoused child appears, on the surface, to be mature, knowledgeable, even charmingly wise beyond his years. Outward appearances, however, conceal a value system that is still underdeveloped.

Values are prerequisite to being able to process knowledge effectively. Put another way, knowledge without values is a dangerous thing. To cite but one concrete example: It is one thing to know how to participate in sexual intercourse; it is quite another to understand that to do so is wrong unless certain conditions are met. By watching television, today's child is able to learn how to engage in sex prior to developing a value system that will properly govern sexual behavior.

It takes most of childhood for a solid set of values to develop. It takes watching one television program for a child to become "educated" concerning all manner of adult behaviors, receive the impression that the ends often justify the means, or learn that marriage is arbitrary to the social contract. (NP)

Q: *Our son is fifteen, and we're coming to the sober realization that we've done it all wrong. We've given him too much and demanded too little, complained about his misbehavior instead of doing something about it, and defended him when he got in trouble at school instead of supporting his teachers. As a result, he's a mess. Is it too late?*

A: First off, you haven't done it all wrong. It's quite obvious you care, or you wouldn't even be giving your son's problems a second thought, much less evaluating your own contributions to them.

I sense your biggest mistake may have been that you doubted yourselves and consistently gave your son the benefit of the doubt. When he screamed because you wouldn't give him something, you questioned your judgment and gave in. When someone else complained about him, you wanted to believe it wasn't true, so you became his apologists.

The mere fact that you ask the question means it's not too late. But understand one thing: At this point, you may have more success rehabilitating yourselves than you do at rehabilitating your son. Nevertheless, I encourage you to go for it. If nothing else, you'll be able to live with yourselves more easily.

Stop giving in to his demands. Let him scream, rant, rave, and become otherwise apoplectic over your own rehabilitation. Start expecting him to cooperate in household chores (for free) and behave himself in a mannerly fashion within the family, even if it's only a mask. Insist that he behave himself in school and work to his potential. And tell him that you are going to chart this course, and stay this course, whether he rehabilitates himself or not. But, tell him, if he does not rehabilitate himself, it will be a freezing day in the lower regions before he gets the use of a car when he turns sixteen, much less one of his own. In short, introduce him to the real world where one must be responsible in order to have privilege, work hard in order to keep a job, and be respectful of others as well as willing to go beyond the call of mere duty (the sign of self-respect).

And if your son never corrects his mistakes, at least you'll be able to say, with pride, that you corrected your own. (FV)

December 31

You are going to make mistakes, and plenty of 'em. You are going to lose your patience, overreact, underreact, and fail to react until far too late. You are not a perfect being; therefore, you will never be a perfect parent. You won't even get close. Bad news, eh?

Ah, but the good news is that children are extremely resilient, much more so than their parents, usually. It follows that children generally recover from their parents' mistakes far more quickly than their parents recover from the anxiety and guilt of making them. Have you ever noticed how forgiving little children are? They seem to realize that their parents' mistakes are nothing more than a consequence of being human, slightly amplified by the tendency to take children much too seriously, and that their parents have great difficulty forgiving themselves. So, just when you can't feel any worse about some parenting "crime" you committed, your little one crawls up on your lap and snuggles in for a hug, as if to say, "There, there, now everything's still all right in my life, so take it easy on yourself, okay?"

And the further good news is that if you've taken the time to read this book, you're not the type of parent who's going to make the same mistakes over and over again. You're going to learn from them, and as time passes, you're going to become a better and better parent. You'll never be perfect, but you'll always be the only mother or father your child will ever want. So take that as a vote of confidence and do your best, because your best is always and forever going to be good enough.

Enjoy!

(TT)

366

About the Author

John Rosemond is a family psychologist whose syndicated newspaper column appears in more than one hundred newspapers around the country. Since 1985, John has written a monthly "parenting" feature for *Better Homes and Gardens* magazine. The book you're holding in your hands is one of seven he's written for Andrews and McMeel. Those previous titles include *John Rosemond's Six-Point Plan for Raising Happy, Healthy Children,* which is currently in its twentieth printing.

John directs The Center for Affirmative Parenting, which provides print, audio, and video resources for parents, schools, and professionals who work with families. By the way, John does not like the word "parenting" and will only use it if the correct term, "child rearing," sounds awkward, as in The Center for Affirmative Child Rearing. Giving some two-hundred-plus presentations a year, John is one of America's busiest and most popular public speakers, known for making his audiences laugh a lot.

John's six-page Internet site is one of the most popular parenting sites on the World Wide Web, visited weekly by thousands of people wanting to keep up with John's public speaking schedule, his commonsense advice, and his latest books, audios, and videos. Check it out at http://www.rosemond.com/parenting. In August 1996, the premier edition of John's bimonthly sixteen-page newsletter, *Affirmative Parenting,* was mailed to more than five thousand subscribers. It, too, is chock-full of John's commonsensical advice and insightful, thought-provoking commentary concerning children and families (for additional information, call 1-800-525-2778).

John and his wife of twenty-eight years, Willie, have two children:

Eric is twenty-seven, married to Nancy (the daughter-in-law of John and Willie's dreams), and a commercial pilot.

Amy is twenty-four, single, and the director of corporate sales for a very ritzy jewelry store.

On January 1, 1995, John and Willie became grandparents to John McHenry Rosemond, or "Jack Henry," Nancy and Eric's first child. Jack Henry is, of course, gifted. John is sure of this.

For more information concerning John's monthly newsletter, books, tapes, or speaking schedule:

• Write The Center for Affirmative Parenting, P.O. Box 4124 (or 1391-A East Garrison Blvd.), Gastonia, NC 28054.

• Send e-mail to jrosemond@aol.com or access John's Internet site (above).

• Call The Center for Affirmative Parenting at (704) 864-1012 between the hours of 9:00 A.M. and 2:00 P.M. (ET), Monday through Friday.

• For newsletter information/subscriptions only, call Affirmative Parenting at 1-800-525-2778.